The World of Dogs
Golden Retriever

Sue Pounds-Longhurst

Contents

Front cover: Mossburn Moon River (Dick of Tugwood x Mossburn McIsla). Bred by the author; owned by Richard and Lorraine Cave. Photo by Richard Cave.

Back cover: Puppies from an early Mossburn litter.

Title page: Mossburn Mulady (Ch Ritzilyn Cockney Robin x Ch Tokeida Temptress of Mossburn). Owned and bred by the author. Photo by the author.

Contents page: Pastel by Margo Claremont of Mossburn Sarah and Mossburn Sandpiper (bred by the author's parents from their first litter in 1967).

DEDICATION

To my late parents, Myrtle and Bernard Pounds, for establishing the Mossburn kennel, allowing me to participate fully in the family hobby of showing and working Goldens from the beginning and giving me Scotangus of Mossburn on my 22nd birthday who became my, and the kennel's, first full Champion three years later.

My husband Mike, who knew when he met me that, Goldens being the first love in my life, he would have to play second fiddle.

The Golden Retriever for giving me such a wonderful purpose in life and for seeing me through the good and bad times.

ACKNOWLEDGMENTS

For typing my manuscript: Barbara Mills.
For whelping box drawing: Peter Mills.
All photographs are solely by the author except for help and contributions kindly provided by the following:
John Sauvage BA Bvet Med Cert SAC MRCVS, Ralph Robinson, Dr Sue Guthrie BA Bvet Med MRCVS, Dawn and Tony Stevens, Joan Gill, Dr F G Startup BSc DVOphthal, MRCVS DipECVO, Mervyn Philpott, Ruth Turner, Richard and Lorraine Cave, Paul Keevil of Framed Philatelics, The Golden Retriever Club, Ian and Mandy Pett, Acorn House Residential Home, Chatham, Kent, Utility Gundog Society (Kent/East Sussex Branch), Margaret Poile, Eastern Counties GRC, Jenny Newton, Pat Rains, Albert Titterington, Louisa Nally, David Dalton, Diane Pearce, Gill Clark, Mary Wood, Phil Dentten, Jeremy O'Keeffe LRPS, Samantha Wilkinson, Jennifer and Gordon Hay, Mike Pounds-Longhurst, Myrtle and Bernard Pounds, Peter and Wendy Carey, Ray Hardie, NGRA UGRC SGRS, Joan Tudor, Ray and Sonia Scholes, Miss Harding, Mr Price-Harding, Mr and Mrs G Hay, Miss Rosemary Lages, Diana Ewings, Alistair Scott, John Lennon, Daphne Philpott, Brian and Carol Wilkinson, Bart van Maren, Mrs I MacKenzie, Rosemary Wilcock, Lyn Kipps, Ann Woodcock, Mr J Brownlie, Ron Hare, Jane Hunt, Brenda Lowe, Everett Massey, Lucy Ross, Val Harvey, David Dalton and Pauline Wilson.

For information and help:
The Kennel Club for permission to reproduce extracts from The Kennel Club Year Book 1999/2000, Breed Registrations, Litter Analysis, Crufts Entries and use of their records and archives for research. Barbara and Peter Mills, John Sauvage BA Bvet Med Cert SAC MRCVS, Kim Ellis, Heather Morss, The Kennel Club librarians, Liz Pope, all other Kennel Clubs around the World, Dawn and Tony Stevens, Robert Smith, Ruth Turner, Golden Retriever UK Clubs and their Secretaries, Alistair Scott, John Lennon, Joan Gill, Marian Dawson, Cynthia and Michael Twist, Alan Neill, Harald Becker, Brian Curd, Joan Lavender MBE, Carol Gilbert, Peter Carey, Graham Cox, Margaret Woods, Sue Ashley and Nina Collot d'Escury from The Smokey Klinic, Emsworth, Hants for reading and checking the Homeopathy chapter.

INTRODUCTION

The Author

I have had the honour of growing up and living with the lovely breed of Golden Retrievers for over 36 years, during which time I have made up two full Champions, bred and owned a CC winner, jointly owned a RCC winner, bred a RCC winner, and owned three Kennel Club Junior Warrant winners, two of which I bred.

I first exhibited a dog at Crufts in 1966 aged 11 years (pre-qualifier days and Junior handling classes) and was awarded a 'Special Prize' card by the late Mr F Warner-Hill for my handling efforts. This was wonderful encouragement from so eminent a judge. Two years later I won my first Championship show First Prize under the late Dr Ester Rickards at Windsor Championship Show which gave me even greater incentive to continue the family hobby.

Between 1969 and 1975, academic studies had to take priority and, between 1979 and 1989, my parents' and grandmother's illnesses and deaths restricted active participation in the dog scene.

When time has permitted, however, I have trained and competed successfully with my Goldens in working tests and trained them for their Show Gundog Working Certificates (SGWC) and picking up. I have also helped others train for test work and SGWCs. In 1995 my husband and I also completed a six month Agility course with two of our Goldens.

During the 1990s, with the support of Mike, I have achieved greater success with the kennel than in the previous three decades, both in the show and working scene.

I began judging the breed over 20 years ago, and since 1988 have judged at Championship shows on numerous occasions both in the United Kingdom, Europe and Canada. I have served on the committees of the Golden Retriever Club, the Southern Golden Retriever Society, my local branch of the Utility Gundog Society and the European Golden Retriever Association. I have stewarded at all levels, including Crufts, and at working tests and field trials.

Although I enjoy almost every aspect of the dog scene, my least favourite is breeding from my bitches as I feel there is always more that can go wrong than can go right!

Outside the dog scene, I worked as a local Government Officer for nearly 20 years at various levels, including managerial. Since 1992 I have spent more time with my Goldens and marginally expanded the kennel. Recently, other competitive hobbies include clay pigeon shooting and photography.

The Kennel

The first family pet was a Golden purchased in 1963 from Mr Chris Potts (Jucridor), a local breeder known to my father through his place of work.

In 1964, whilst attending a gymkhana, I persuaded my parents to enter Simon (Elegant of Jucridor) in the exemption show being run at the same event. Despite the lack of ring training, he won some awards. With advice from the breeder, he was entered later that year for a limited show and won three more awards under Mrs Lou Melville (Crouchers) and there the kennel story really begins.

My parents applied for an affix and were granted 'Mossburn' in 1965; I was granted a joint interest a few years later.

The first few years of the family's attempts to develop the kennel were dotted with disasters. For instance, one puppy caught distemper; although she was nursed back to good health, subsequently it was learned that she was infertile. Another bitch failed her eye examination. Other disappointments followed in later years.

The kennel's foundation bitch, Mossburn Joriemour Nicola (Sh Ch Anbria Tantalus x Joriemour Anbria Liana), was purchased in 1965 from Mrs Marjorie Clark (Joriemour) and is still behind one of the two breeding lines being maintained.

Nicola produced two lovely litters by Ch Camrose Tallyrand of Anbria, which was a grandfather/grand-daughter mating. The best known of her progeny was Mossburn Sandpiper (b. 17.8.1968), a KC Junior Warrant winner. In the 1970s, the latter produced two CC winners, one of which was my own Ch Scotangus of Mossburn who gained his title in 1979. The other was Westonholm Casino Royale, holder of two CCs and four RCCs, owned by Mr and Mrs A Parnell (Stanbreed).

For a few years during the 1970s, the kennel also became involved with a new breed, imported into the United Kingdom from West Germany – Large Munsterlanders. My parents were instrumental in helping with the formation of the Large Munsterlander Club and the production of the Breed Standard. My mother went on later to award CCs in the breed. For a while, my father also had an English Springer Spaniel from working stock for his shooting days.

In the late 1970s, my mother and Mrs J Tudor (Camrose) were instrumental in establishing the Southern Golden Retriever Society and my mother was Secretary for several years.

As mentioned earlier, family problems in the 1980s saw the kennel take a less active role in the dog scene and only one Mossburn litter was bred in 10 years. As circumstances prevented a puppy being kept from this litter, the kennel line was almost lost. By two strokes of good fortune, I was able to restock the kennel in the late 1980s with two Scotangus grand-daughters.

In 1990, I decided to strengthen the kennel stock with a second breeding line that would work as well as show and, in 1991, acquired Tokeida Temptress of Mossburn (Sh Ch Tokeida Starstealer x Tokeida Outlaws Floozy) from Mrs Sheila Nowell (Tokeida). Temptress became my second full Champion in 1996.

The kennel has mainly been small with no more than eight dogs kept at one time although, for a brief period in the 1970s, the numbers went up to 10. Breeding from the bitches has mainly been done only to furnish the kennel with the next generation and it may come as a surprise to learn that over the years there have only been 15 Mossburn Golden litters and one Large Munsterlander litter. Over the years the kennel has had 26 Goldens – 10 dogs (six of which were used at stud) and 16 bitches. Priority has been given to showing but the working aspect has never been lost sight of in the breeding and training. Three Goldens have been successful at working tests, eight have achieved their SGWC and a number have picked up with either my father or myself.

Currently there are seven Goldens in the kennel, all of which live indoors as companions to Mike and myself. Together they have achieved one Championship title, 7 Challenge Certificates, 5 Reserve Challenge Certificates, four KC Stud Book Numbers, three KC Junior Warrants, five SGWCs and seven working test awards. In 1996, Champion Tokeida Temptress of Mossburn was the highest placed Golden bitch in the Gundog Group at Championship Shows and Mantlemas Scelina of Mossburn was the Top Veteran in the breed. Temptress was a Pedigree Chum Veteran Stakes Finalist in 1998 and was also Top Veteran in the breed in 1998 and 1999. Mossburn McIsla was the breed's Top Veteran in 2000.

The Book

My aim has been to make the book an up-to-date, practical reference guide with plenty of tips, suggestions and photographs to help new and existing Golden owners enjoy their dogs to the full, wherever they live and for whatever purpose they own a dog.

As the history of the breed has been well researched and written about in many other breed specialist books, I have presented this information in a different format, hoping that it will appeal to those most interested in this aspect. It offers the scope for expansion and up-dates.

This book is very much a personal statement based on my experiences, and how things have worked best for me, but this is not to say that these are the only ideas and methods which can be used. Many aspects of dog ownership are a matter of individual judgement and opinion. In the end, I want to show what it is like to live with a Golden and to share my pleasure in the breed I know and love so well.

Sue Pounds-Longhurst

CHAPTER ONE

Why A Golden Retriever?

First Considerations

There are a number of things you should think about before you get any dog, never mind a Golden Retriever.

- Do you want a dog as a pet or for a particular activity?
- Are your current circumstances and future plans suitable for having a dog for 12 or more years?
- Is the Golden Retriever the right breed for you and is your situation right for the breed?
- Can you can afford the running costs of dog ownership as well as the initial outlay?
- Do you want a dog or a bitch?
- Are you prepared to buy from a reputable specialist breeder, not from an agent, dealer, puppy farmer or commercial breeder, and not to buy on impulse?
- Is your new pet to be a second dog?

    This chapter should assist you in answering these questions.

What You Should Know About Owning a Dog

Golden Retriever ownership has increased enormously over the last 30 years, due to the breed's lovely sound temperament. Before you decide whether the Golden Retriever is the right breed for you whether as a pet, for showing or working, you must not lose sight of the fact that Golden Retrievers are *dogs*, although many owners would have you think otherwise. You should therefore be aware that:

- Dogs prefer to live within a pack structure.
- The 'pack' can be made up of humans, dogs and other animals.
- The 'pack' provides a pack leader, support (moral and physical), protection, supervision, guidance, and decision making to its membership.

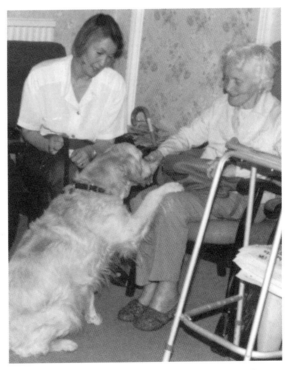

Ellie (Mossburn Make Believe), a registered PAT dog, makes regular visits to a residential home.

- The notions of 'pack' behaviour and submission to the pack leader are inherited by puppies at birth and reinforced by their dam.
- A dog's owner should be the pack leader in all circumstances. This does not mean you over-dominate, but lead in a fun, loving partnership.
- A contented dog is one that has been given a set of rules and a routine so he knows what is unacceptable behaviour.
- Some dogs may assume leadership in some particular situations amongst other animals, especially a group of dogs, but they should never be permitted to think they are greater in rank than any human members of the pack (adults or children).
- Dogs (male and female) will make periodic attempts to improve their ranking in the pack no matter whether the pack is solely human, canine or a combination. For example, at home the dog may try to push through a door before you or pull on his lead when out for a walk after he has been lead trained.
- The canine pack leader rarely resorts to physical conflict unless a pack member continually usurps their position. Control and discipline of the pack is mainly achieved through eye contact, body language and, occasionally, some verbal warning.

What You Should Know About a Dog's Behaviour Traits

Anyone who has owned a dog will already be familiar with most of these, but if you have never owned a dog you may find some traits unacceptable or unwelcome.

Usually if a dog is to integrate into any form of life with humans, an acceptable compromise needs to be, and can be, reached through careful training by the pack leader and/or hierarchy. It would, however, be totally unreasonable to expect all instinctive behaviour patterns to be totally rooted out.

Unless I have commented to the contrary, I have known Goldens to have or show signs of all the behaviour traits listed below.

- Barking (the most familiar trait) – to seek attention, alert, protect, defend and so on.
- Chewing objects, especially whilst teething (usually between the age of 3–6 months for Goldens) and to lessen boredom and hunger.
- Possessiveness over food and objects of desire.
- Collecting articles carrying the scent of his human pack members (I call it 'squirrelling').
- Taking accessible food (not to be regarded as stealing: it is part of their survival instinct).
- Rolling in and/or eating unpleasant smelling matter (for example, fox's faeces).
- Dams will clean and eat their puppies' faeces from birth until weaning is completed. Puppies may mimic this if care is not taken. See coprophagy in Chapter 6.
- Digging to unearth vermin (for example, moles), or to bury objects of desire.
- Flushing, chasing and catching birds, cats, rodents, deer and so on.
- Jumping up to greet known humans, to get as near as possible to their hands and faces. Goldens will also greet most unfamiliar humans, such is their outgoing and sometimes slightly exuberant nature.
- Licking humans and other dogs' muzzles as a sign of love and /or submission.
- Sniffing to gain information because smell is their most powerful sense.
- Urine marking, mainly done by males (to show dominance) and some dominant females. Urine marking and remarking by males may also be done to attempt to define territory.

- Males may try to escape to locate a bitch on heat. (I have never experienced this with males, but have known bitches who escaped to go exploring – not for sex.)
- Females mainly come into season for the first time between the ages of 6 and 24 months and, after this, the seasons recur at intervals anything from 6 to 15 months, but I have known exceptions at both ends of the time scale.
- Bitches that are kept together frequently enter into mock-mating play, both in and out of season. I have also seen out-of-season bitches do this to males.
- A bitch reaching the height of fertility in season may try to escape to invite a dog to mate her. I have never experienced this with Goldens but, when keeping dogs and bitches on the same premises, have known a bitch call for a mate.
- Dams may regurgitate food to wean their puppies.
- Dogs can be sick due to pleasure as well as illness and may eat their vomit. Usually, this does no harm.
- Most dogs wish to please their owners and offer love, loyalty and companionship.

If you feel you can understand the pack situation, can enforce being the pack leader and can cope with all these behaviour points, you will get much more pleasure from dog ownership and training will be easier.

Your next decision is to assess whether the Golden Retriever is the right breed for you and your circumstances and whether to acquire an adult or puppy. Most people opt for the latter as very few adults are available and there may be a long wait to find a suitable one. Now it is time to do your homework. Observe the breed at breeders' homes, at shows, and so on.

What You Should Know About the Golden Retriever Breed

Golden Retrievers were developed initially as a breed in the second half of the nineteenth century, for retrieving work on shooting estates. This remained their main function for nearly a century.

Increasingly, during the twentieth century, and particularly since the end of the Second World War, as the fashion of owning dogs as pets and showing them as a recreational activity grew, so did the popularity of the breed. This was due to the dog's lovely temperament, being kindly, friendly and confident. Also, despite being a working gundog breed, the Golden adores human companionship so he adapted very well to the roles of pet and show dog.

The Golden Retriever

- Is regarded as a large breed of dog. Adult males at the withers are 56–61cm (22–24in) and their approximate weight is 32–41kg (70–90lb). Adult females are 51–56cm (20–22in) at the withers and their approximate weight is 27–34kg (60–75lb). You should bear this information in mind for car size (when transporting the dog), sleeping accommodation, bedding, feeding, exercise, garden size and heights of fences and gates.
- Has a long coat with a dense water-resisting undercoat. Males generally moult at least once a year, occasionally twice. Females moult at least once a year, sometimes more often depending on their season cycle. Some Goldens living in centrally heated homes may moult continually. The coat will need regular grooming and periodic trimming to keep it clean, tidy and in good condition. The coat oils naturally disperse dried dirt on the coat into a fine dust, creating more housework. This is more noticeable if you own two or more

Goldens. Goldens that have been spayed or neutered will have a different coat texture which will require more grooming to prevent the finer hair from knotting.

- Has nails which should be clipped periodically for the dog's comfort.
- Has feathering on legs, tail and belly.
- Has a long tail that can scatter and break articles on low tables, shelves and even objects on the floor.
- Adores human companionship and is not suitable to spend a solitary existence in a kennel or run or in a home where he will be left unattended for long periods of time. Flats also are totally unsuitable.
- Retrieves articles, both human and dog toys and bones.
- Has a soft mouth for retrieving shot game and articles.
- Has a life expectancy of 12 or more years, with correct feeding, exercise and general care.
- Fits in well with most domestic situations.
- Is intelligent, active, lively, biddable, a fast learner with a will to please and therefore easily trainable, but is slow to mature under the age of 2 years and initially requires some patience.
- Adults require a reasonable amount of exercise but a growing puppy needs less.
- Can 'smile' by opening his mouth to show the teeth, one sided and occasionally all round, as a friendly greeting grin. This is often misunderstood as aggressive behaviour and results in the dog being chastised and becoming totally confused. To determine the behaviour, assess it with other body language.
- Is adaptable. Apart from being pets, show dogs and gundog workers, Goldens have been used competitively for Obedience, Working Trials, Field Trials, Working Tests, Agility and Flyball. They have also been used as dogs for the blind, deaf and physically handicapped as well as support dogs for ill people, drug sniffing, rescue and PAT dogs. Some have also made it into advertising, including television commercials, programmes and films.
- Has a love for water, clean or dirty!
- Is not totally free from hereditary defects. At present in the United Kingdom there are KC/BVA schemes for checking hip dysplasia, elbow dysplasia and the following eye conditions – cataract, CPRA (Centralised Progressive Retinal Atrophy), GPRA (Generalised Progressive Retinal Atrophy and MRD (Multifocal Retinal Dysplasia). (See Chapters 6 and 11 for more details.)
- Can be affected by other illnesses, conditions and diseases as are other breeds and cross-breed dogs.
- In countries with a high number of Goldens, the dogs are tested for other conditions when the number of clinical cases found is significant. For instance, in America and Canada, SAS (sub-aortic stenosis, a heart condition) and canine brucellosis, a bacterial infection not found in the United Kingdom. In Germany even temperament testing is carried out on the breed.
- Like all dogs, Goldens will require a large outside play space which is escape-proof and easily accessible from the home for toilet training.

On a less serious note, you may also wish to consider whether the colour of a Golden's coat is compatible with your home furnishings and wardrobe!

Do ensure that everyone in the family wants the dog, as the commitment is so long term. Do not buy any dog as a surprise for any reason, as it is unfair to take a dog into an unwelcoming environment, particularly where only one party wants the dog. Goldens are sensitive to atmosphere and may show stress reactions in such circumstances.

If after considering all these points you believe the Golden Retriever is the right breed for you, and you are ready to commit to him for 12 years or more, one last consideration is when will be the right time to buy your dog. The first 6–12 months of a puppy's life are very time-consuming for the owner as it will be in this period that most of the socialising and training is carried out and bonding and the development of a rapport with your young Golden needs to be undertaken. However, spare a thought for whether you will have the time to look after your Golden once the ageing process begins, when he is 8–13 years old. He may require as much help and attention during this time of his life as he did when he was a puppy.

Dogs are not a commodity to be disposed of once they start to fail. They are not cars.

Costs of Buying and Owning a Dog

This issue should also be closely examined before the final decision is made. I have covered the major items below.

Purchase Price

The price of a 7–8 week-old puppy has steadily increased in the United Kingdom from 15 guineas (£15.15s/£15.75) in the mid-1960s to £450 or more and will no doubt continue to rise. Whilst prices vary abroad, and I know Golden puppies in NW Europe are sold for much more, I believe the trend will continue to increase rather than decrease, unless the supply outstrips the demand. The purchase price may seem to be a large sum but, compared to all the other costs of owning a dog for 12 or more years, proportionately it is quite small.

The purchase price of a puppy lessens once he is over 4–6 months of age. Puppies of these ages are usually difficult to acquire unless they are being discarded by a breeder because they will not make the grade for showing, working or breeding. However, they still make lovely companions. Occasionally, an adult dog may become available but, unless he has much to offer as a breed specimen for showing, he is unlikely to be sold for the value of a puppy.

Some prospective owners can provide wonderful pet homes for Goldens and cope with the running costs of dog ownership, but find it impossible to pay the large purchase price or cope with the training and liveliness of a puppy. If you find yourself in either of these predicaments you may like to consider rehoming or rescuing a Golden. If so, contact your nearest breed clubs and ask for details of their rescue schemes.

You may have to go on a breed club rescue waiting list to be vetted. Then, if your circumstances are deemed suitable, you will be transferred to another list to await a suitable Golden to be matched to your requirements and circumstances. Usually there is no charge for the service or price to be paid for the Golden you may be rehoming, but you will be expected to give a reasonable donation to help the rescue services to continue their work. A rescue dog's papers are not normally handed to the new owner so it would not be possible to compete in Kennel Club events or register any progeny from a rescued Golden.

Other canine welfare sources are the National Canine Defence League (NCDL), RSPCA, Blue Cross, Battersea Dogs' Home and Wood Green Animal Shelter.

Registration with Your Country's Kennel Club

This is usually included in the purchase price and done by the breeder, but you may find it is an additional cost. It is essential that your Golden has registration papers if you wish to compete in any events organised under the jurisdiction of a kennel club, such as dog shows, gundog working tests and field trials.

In the United Kingdom, the current cost at the time of publication is £10.00 per puppy in a litter up to the age of 12 months old.

Kennel Club Transfer of Ownership

Again, it is essential to pay for transfer of ownership if you wish to take part in competitive events under the auspices of your country's kennel club.

Insurance

Some puppies are insured by the breeder when they are sold, usually for six weeks from the day of purchase. It is then up to the new owners to make their own arrangements. A wide range of comprehensive policies and plans are available directly through companies that deal specifically with the insurance of animals and some indirectly through organisations such as The Kennel Club and BASC (British Association for Shooting and Conservation).

Policies can include vets' fees, perhaps herbal and homeopathic medicines and other complementary treatments. Also, death from illness or accidental death; loss by theft or straying; recovery costs such as advertising; kennel fees; transportation costs if a vet refers your dog to another practice or school of veterinary studies; legal costs, holiday cancellation costs; accidental damage; burglar reward; third party liability; and brood bitch cover. Inoculations, boosters, elbow, hip and eye tests for breeding are not covered by any policy.

I would strongly recommend that you take out insurance because, if your Golden becomes ill or has an accident, your anxiety will be even greater if you have to worry about how much treatment you can afford. Costs vary, but most policies carry an excess or pre-payment of about 10–15% of the total claim for each illness or condition.

If you decide not to take out an overall policy I strongly recommend that you have third party insurance to cover you for legal liability up to the sum of £1–2 million. This may be included in a house contents insurance policy so that you are covered for damage to other people's property or accidents caused by your dog straying into a road.

If you are a breeder and do not already offer insurance cover for puppies, it would certainly be advisable to start and give yourself the peace of mind of knowing that, in the most vulnerable period of a new puppy's life, he is covered should anything go wrong with his health or he has a mishap. Although a fee used to be charged for this, most companies do not make a charge nowadays. It also gives confidence to the new owners to know their puppy has cover. All puppies that have left our kennel since the 1960s have been insured, except the few that have been exported, as cover is not available for puppies going abroad.

Food

An enormous variety of products is available from the different outlets, such as supermarkets, pet shops and wholesalers selling pet food. The breeder should let you know what to feed the puppy for the first 6 months, where the products are available and an idea of how much it costs to feed an adult. Puppies cost more to feed than adults as they do have additional feeding requirements.

I would not necessarily recommend the most expensive brands. I have used several moderately-priced products for many years, and have been entirely satisfied. Much will also depend on whether your dog has any special dietary requirements during his lifetime and what suits his palate. I have found most Goldens are good eaters but occasionally have encountered a fussy one. If you can buy in bulk it will help to keep costs down.

Dog Bowls and Stands

You will require at least two adult dog bowls - one for food and one for water. The latter should be accessible at all times, wherever your Golden is. Bowls are available in plastic, ceramic and metal. Metal (usually stainless steel) is the most durable and long lasting and is what I use mainly. It is more costly than plastic but all are fairly cheap and available from pet shops and other dog food outlets.

A new young puppy may find it very difficult to eat and drink out of large adult bowls so you may need to acquire slightly smaller bowls for him initially. Look at the size the breeder uses to see what the pups are coping with, and purchase slightly larger ones for the fast-growing puppy.

A non-spill water bowl - useful for car journeys or for dogs that try to paw water out of bowls.

Veterinary Fees

Costs vary from one veterinary practice to another and from one part of the country to another. Inoculations/vaccinations should be your first expenditure when your pup is between the ages of 8 to 12 weeks.

Collar

Legally, a dog must always wear a collar in a public place, so it is essential to purchase one for your puppy and a larger one for his adult life. If the collar is looked after carefully you should not need to replace it during your dog's lifetime. I find leather collars are the strongest and the best. A chain collar should not be used on a Golden Retriever as it cuts the hair, leaving an unsightly line around the dog's neck and a grey-black stain mark from the metal. If a Golden is trained correctly he should not need anything other than a leather collar. Check the collar's strength and stitching periodically and make sure that your dog does not outgrow it. As a rough guide, you should be able to slip two fingers between your dog's collar and his neck. Saddlesoap is very useful to preserve leather collars, especially if they become wet, as it prevents them from hardening.

Disc

It is also a legal requirement for a name tag or identity disc to be fitted to the collar, engraved with your surname, telephone number and/or post code. Cost of discs and engraving are very reasonable. Personally, I do not include the dog's name on the disc to prevent him responding by his name to an unscrupulous person who may decide to take him in rather than help to reunite him with his owner.

Other collar attachments are available such as barrels or tubes containing slips of paper on which the information is written. No matter how much I have tightened them, they always work loose and the paper is lost. However, when you go on holiday, it may be worth using this type to list your temporary address, in addition to the disc.

Lead

Many types of lead are available from pet shops, dog food wholesalers and vets, made of nylon, chainlink, leather and rope that clip onto collars or are slip leads.

I have tried all types and recommend a substantial slip lead which can be used for basic training and walking your Golden under normal circumstances. This type of lead is machine

washable, and does not cut the hair around the dog's neck as do chain leads. I have found that nylon leads wear much more quickly and need replacing more regularly. The chainlink lead is less suitable because it could be painful if it catches your dog's face. Any lead which is insubstantial will snap, which could have grave consequences, so do ensure the lead you choose is strong enough for your Golden. Whatever make you buy, check its strength and condition at intervals to ensure your Golden's safety at all times.

The slip lead loosens when the dog is walking to heel but, if the dog starts to pull, the lead tightens and checks the dog gently. It is not possible to do this with a lead clipped to a collar and I find that the dog simply continues to pull.

Excess force should never be used with any lead and collar arrangement as

A Golden with his collar and disc.

damage can be done to the dog's throat. In recent years the Halti has helped many owners to have more control over their dogs. It is based on the principle of a horse's headcollar and can be a useful aid in preventing the dog from pulling.

If the dog fails to return to his owner once off lead, an extended (flexible) lead can be used so that the dog can have some freedom but is not let off the lead until he is reliable.

The cost of leads is not extortionate but does vary slightly. It may be possible to obtain them more reasonably from stalls at dog shows.

Bones and Toys

Great care should be taken over the types of bones and toys Goldens are allowed to have, from puppyhood to old age. Goldens enjoy them to play with, for relieving boredom and for keeping their teeth clean.

Bones

I do not permit my dogs to have meat bones of any description, cooked or uncooked, as they can become fragmented and cause major illness and sometimes life-threatening problems. Some people believe that marrow bones from the butcher are safe but, having nearly lost a Golden when a minor splinter became embedded in an intestine, marrow bones are not allowed in our household. In addition, I know of many dogs that have had upset stomachs after chewing and gnawing on a marrow bone. Perhaps this is because the bone is very greasy when new and picks up a lot of dirt from the garden, where dogs are usually permitted to have them. They can become very fly-blown, particularly in the hotter months, and are almost impossible to clean, so harbour germs.

However, most pet shops do sell treated bones, such as calcium bones that have no smell, and those impregnated with an attractive flavour. They are not greasy and, whilst a dog is able to chew off the ends, the pieces crumble and are digestible. They last a reasonable amount of time. I use them throughout to help keep the dog's teeth clean, but particularly for puppies whilst they are teething. They are easily cleaned in hot or cold water and can be sterilised to prevent germs passing from one dog to another.

Wearing a 'Halti'.

As soon as the bones become smaller than 8cm (3in) in length I dispose of them and buy new ones. This prevents a dog from swallowing them accidentally or the bone becoming stuck at the back of the throat.

Manufactured bones, such as those in the Nylabone range, are available to help with teeth cleaning. These cost slightly more but can be washed and sterilised if necessary. It is claimed they prevent wear on the teeth and also slow down the build-up of tartar on the teeth.

Toys

Many types of toys are available but some are unsuitable for the larger breeds such as Goldens, as they can be easily destroyed by chewing or are too small and can be swallowed. I have found very hard rubber rings and balls are best; they can be cleaned and last many years. The balls must be larger than tennis balls for a fully-grown Golden not to run the risk of swallowing them. Rope toys are also durable, machine washable and teeth cleaners.

Fabric and soft toys, and squeaky plastic toys should not be purchased until you know for certain that your dog will not destroy and eat them. Plastic balls, tennis balls or any smaller balls used for golf or table tennis should never be used as toys for Goldens. If swallowed, they may cause asphyxiation at the worst or, at best, have to be removed surgically. Household articles, children's toys or pet toys made of metal, hard plastic or wood should not be given to Goldens, due to their potentially dangerous nature and to prevent a Golden losing his soft mouth (that is, his undamaging hold on an article which is a well-known breed characteristic). The more durable the toy the more expensive it is likely to be.

I have found that many puppies enjoy playing with cardboard boxes, empty toilet and kitchen rolls and screwed–up newspaper which, of course, cost nothing, but do ensure the boxes and papers have no tape or staples on them.

Never throw sticks for your dog. It can be very dangerous; if your dog catches a stick awkwardly in his mouth it will cause much damage and sometimes surgery will be required.

Grooming Aids
Brush, comb, nail clippers

These three items are essential when grooming your dog. Various types are available from pet shops, stalls at large organised dog events, or by mail order and generally cost very little. I prefer to use a wire brush with handle, a metal comb and nail clippers. Scissors are needed to keep pets tidy but household scissors are adequate for this purpose.

Dog shampoos

Again, many sorts are available and you should choose a type to suit your dog's coat and condition. They last quite a long time as most Goldens do not require bathing regularly unless it is on veterinary recommendation. Do *not* use human shampoos. See Chapters 4 and 8 for more details about keeping your Golden tidy and groomed.

Bedding

Most Goldens adore having some form of bedding to lie in or on. Many options are available and what you buy really depends on how much you are prepared to spend. Remember, however, that it is better to buy something which is not easily chewable or destructible for a young puppy, such as a hard plastic bed which can be easily cleaned, or the fabric vet beds, which are machine washable. The latter have lasted my Goldens 8 years or more.

There are cheaper fabrics similar to vet beds; they are more easily chewed but I have found most of my puppies and adults have not attempted to chew these either. Other kinds of bedding are dog duvets, quilts, bean bags, padded and wicker baskets. I have also seen advertisements for heat pads for bedding, which may be useful for elderly or arthritic dogs.

If at any time you are replacing your bed duvet or a single mattress, you could cover either with old, washable sheets or blankets, and use them for your dog, especially a mattress if you have the space. I have used a covered single mattress on the floor and a duvet in the car. The dogs have greatly enjoyed the comfort of both.

Crates and Pet Carriers

These are quite expensive items and are available in various sizes from specialist companies, which you will find in the classified section of the dog journals and shooting magazines. Argos also sell a basic folding crate which is suitable for most sizes of dog at a very reasonable price. Like baby gates, crates can be used for puppyhood and the growing months and then sold afterwards if required.

If you want to have more than one dog or intend to breed a litter, I have found a folding crate invaluable. For instance, when you buy a new puppy and introduce him to other dogs at home, a portable crate means that you can place the pup in any room with the other dogs so he can have their company without being a nuisance. This helps him to acclimatise more quickly and gives you peace of mind, knowing that the puppy can come to no harm. The crate can also be used if you are unavailable to the pup for a short time; he can be left with his favourite piece of bedding and some toys in safety, without being tempted to chew, dig or make a mess in your absence. Some people also use the crate overnight so that the pup learns to be clean in his surroundings

Pet carriers, folding crates and dog bedding are all useful items of equipment.

and asks (by whining) to go out. Be fair to the pup, however, and *never* leave him longer in the crate than is absolutely necessary, once he has been gradually introduced and accustomed to it.

I also found use for a folding crate when two puppies in a litter had upset stomachs and needed to be isolated for a few days.

Whether you consider a crate or pet carrier, check that the bars or mesh do not have any sharp edges or parts where tails and paws can get trapped. Also you will find those made mostly of solid plastic with only a wire mesh door can become very hot and may not be the most practical buy.

Dog Guards

Dog guards can be purchased from specialist companies or acquired second-hand, and fixed in vehicles manually. Some vehicle manufacturers make and fix their own. They are extremely useful to prevent a dog jumping into parts of the vehicle where he is unwelcome but, from personal experience, I have found that you cannot always use them immediately for puppies. The guard is used to keep the puppy/dog at the back of the vehicle, but this is where the motion of travelling is felt most and the puppy suffering from travel sickness will be worse off. Other solutions should be found until the puppy has overcome the problem.

A tailgate guard provides a secure way of ventilating your car (see also page 64).

Travel Harnesses

These are specially designed for dogs. A friend resorted to their use after having an accident in a saloon car and seeing his Golden thrown into the front of the car from the back seat on which he was sitting. The harness is like a seat belt so it may take a little patience before your young Golden gets used to wearing it. Travel harnesses can be bought from most pet shops.

Your dog will soon get used to wearing his travel harness, with a little patience and perseverance.

Baby Gates

These are not essential items, but many dog owners do find them useful in doorways as they contain a dog in a room without having to have the door closed. Dogs will also settle more easily behind a gate than a closed door, as they still feel in contact with their owners in the next room. Not only can they hear their owner, but they can see them going to and fro. One of the best uses for a gate is at the bottom of the stairs to prevent puppies and dogs going upstairs. This is particularly important whilst the puppy is still growing and his bones and joints are setting, up to 18 months of age. It will also prevent the puppy having accidents on the staircase, collecting items of clothing, children's toys and so on, and sleeping on the beds.

It may be necessary for the bars to be covered temporarily to prevent the puppy trying to squeeze through them. Baby gates are available from most baby equipment shops and can also be purchased second-hand. Purpose-built dog gates are available which are taller than the standard baby gate but which are also rather more costly. These are usually advertised in the dog press.

Going Away

If you go away and are unable either to take your dog with you or leave him with friends, family or with a dog sitter, you will need to budget for him to go into a boarding kennel. Most kennels charge similar fees for daily rates per dog. Two or more dogs can usually be boarded together so they have one another's company. You will need to check with the kennel's owners whether this would result in any price reductions. You should also warn the kennel owners if your bitch is due in season. Generally Goldens board easily, but there are a few exceptions to the rule. It may be worth letting your dog spend a day in a boarding kennel in advance of your holiday, to reassure yourself that he will settle okay.

Kennel owners require that your dog is fully vaccinated which, in most cases, also includes Kennel Cough. Vaccination certificates/cards need to be shown as evidence. To find a good kennel, ask fellow dog-owners or your vet which one they recommend. Also visit the kennel before booking in your dog to make sure you approve of the facilities.

An alternative to kennels is to use a dog sitter who can look after your dog in your own home. If you do not know of one, you may find someone through an advertisement, but you do need to investigate them carefully and check their references.

It is worth ensuring that your dog is fully vaccinated at all times in case an emergency (such as the owner being admitted to hospital) requires him to go into boarding kennels. In some cases, your insurance policy may cover some or all of the boarding fees, depending on the circumstances.

Details on the Pet Passport scheme, which came into force in Spring 2000, can be obtained from MAFF, Room 222, 10 Whitehall Place, London SW1A 2HH.

Training Equipment

Equipment costs for showing and working your dog are mainly very reasonable as only a few items are required and most last many years. The two exceptions are Agility and Flyball. For these most owners can use club equipment under supervision, but those who want to become involved competitively need to train privately or have the equipment to practise on at home. Equipment can be built, rather than purchased, but must be sturdy and completely safe for dog and handler to use. Overall, the cost of Agility and Flyball equipment is high compared to other types of work you can choose to do with your dog.

The most essential, but most costly, item is waterproof clothing, as most activities for Golden Retrievers are held outside. This also includes showing, as Golden Retriever breed classes are more frequently judged outside in all weathers, all year round, rather than in the halls and centres used for small breeds.

Travel costs to competitive events

As the price of fuel has increased enormously, the cost of travelling to events is frequently higher than entry fees and all the other costs put together. I believe the same situation is reflected in many other countries. In North America, for instance, the cost of travelling the vast distances between shows has led to the use of professional handlers as they can help to keep costs lower by transporting and showing a number of dogs at a time.

I seriously wonder what the long-term outcome will be in the United Kingdom for the dog show fraternity if motorway tolls are ever charged.

Dog or Bitch?

People within the breed define the difference between the sexes as: a dog gives love, a bitch takes love. It is a much-discussed topic in my household as my husband loves bitches and I love dogs!

The Dog

A male Golden Retriever:
- Is likely to be larger and heavier than a bitch.
- Generally moults less regularly than a bitch.
- May mark territory with urine. This behaviour is mainly confined to outdoors although I have known the occasional male Golden do this indoors, especially if kept with other bitches and stud dogs. It would be unusual for a male pet Golden to behave like this.
- May roam to find an in-season bitch although, as stated previously, I have not experienced this.

A male also:
- May kill your garden shrubs by urinating on them.
- Is capable of siring a litter from 6 months onwards until he dies, subject to his health and fertility.
- May howl for a neighbouring in-season bitch.
- May perform sexually with his bedding (no worries) or toys but will need correcting if he does this on people's legs.
- May mock-mate a bitch who is not in season, if she allows, or another male depending on the pecking order in the pack.
- Is more prone to certain diseases such as osteochrondosis dissecans (OCD) in the elbow.
- Has marginally lower average hip scores (by 2 approximately).
- Is usually more trainable than a bitch at an earlier age, especially for gundog work.
- If shown must be entire, with two testicles fully descended in the scrotum. The Kennel Club has said it would consider giving permission for a neutered dog to show if the operation was done on medical grounds but, as the Breed Standard still requires two testicles, this places judges in great difficulty.
- Uncastrated males may develop testicular cancer or prostate disorders.

- May show rivalry towards other male dogs.
- May show a more dominant temperament and require firmer control.

If you do not plan to show or breed from a male Golden and he is hyper-active and/or hyper-sexual, there are three options you can consider:

Hormone treatment is administered by injection. The preparation mimics the effect of castration in respect of the dog's behaviour, but it may not affect his fertility. Some owners try this to see if it would be worth going ahead with castration.

Vasectomy involves the tube that transports the sperm from the testicles being cut. The operation prevents the dog from being able to sire puppies but it will not affect his behaviour or curb his desire to mate. This option offers little help for family pet problems.

Castration involves the removal of the testes from the scrotum. It prevents the dog from fathering puppies and may help to overcome behaviour problems such as roaming and aggression towards other dogs. The expected behaviour changes may take as long as 4–6 months to have full effect.

In the case of any medical treatment, it would be wise to check if there are known side effects to ensure the results outweigh the problem.

A neutered dog may be more prone to weight gain. His coat may also change. It may become softer, thicker and woolly, require more grooming and trimming to keep tidy and prevent knotting (especially under the ears, chest, stomach, tail, inside the back legs and the feathering on the hindquarters), or become thinner.

The Bitch

- Is more likely to be smaller and weigh less than a male.
- Is likely to moult more frequently than a male.
- May enter into mock-mate play with females in and out of season and males when out of season. It is usually not a problem but some bitches may be irritated by this behaviour and want to fight.
- May escape when reaching her height of fertility to invite a dog to mate her.
- May call for a mate when reaching her appropriate mating time.
- Will come into season at regular intervals any time from 6 months onwards, unless preventative action is taken (see below).

A female also:

- May cover other bitches' urine, especially if kept with others, which can burn the lawn. She may also get used to urinating on a particular surface at home and will only do so away from home on a similar surface.
- Is capable of producing puppies from her first season onwards, subject to her health and fertility.
- May become more trainable for gundog work aged 2 and over.
- May have mood swings whilst in season.
- May have minor changes in her disposition anything up to eight weeks prior to coming into season, which in turn may affect any training or competitive work being undertaken.
- Can have pyometra or mammary tumours, usually in the latter half of her life but it is possible even under 12 months, particularly in the case of pyometra if she is not spayed. Tumours are unlikely to occur in a bitch under the age of one year old.

- When in season will probably lose a discharge for some, if not all, of the 21 days, which may stain furnishings unless the heat is controlled. Knickers are available but, not having used them on my dogs, I am not sure of their practicality.
- May have a false pregnancy(s), including milk production, if not mated or spayed.
- May stimulate others she lives with to come into season earlier than their usual cycle.
- Is reputed to be more easy to train, and better with children. I do not believe this is true of Golden Retrievers as I think it depends on each Golden and her/his owner but, in the main, both dogs and bitches are easy to train and trust with children.
- Must be kept under careful supervision whilst in season if puppies are not wanted. This can be difficult if you also have children and even more so if you keep males and females on the same premises and especially indoors.
- Cannot take part in any competitive competition on the working side whilst in season.
- Can be shown whilst in season in the United Kingdom as there is no Kennel Club ruling against it, but this is both inadvisable and unfair. There is the risk of infection and, of course, the bitch may feel vulnerable and irritable near other dogs. It is also grossly unfair to males, whether used at stud or not. There are many opportunities for Goldens to be shown so the etiquette expected of Golden exhibitors is not to show. Missing one or two shows usually is no hardship and should be expected as one of the disadvantages of owning a bitch.
- In most other countries is not permitted to be shown or enter the showground when in season.
- Can be shown if spayed, subject to Kennel Club permission.

Various forms of heat control are available:

Sprays prevent the smell of an in-season bitch encouraging a dog. I have found them to be useless but they may disguise any bitch odour unpleasant to the human nose.

Hormone treatment/heat suppressants must be discussed with your vet, as they may be inappropriate for some bitches.

Hind view of a spayed bitch's coat.

Profile of 9-year-old spayed bitch, showing profuse coat.

Spaying involves removal of the uterus and ovaries. If the operation is performed when the bitch is healthy, recovery is usually much quicker. However, if carried out due to a pyometra there will be more health risks involved and her recovery may take longer. There are various professional opinions as to whether a bitch should be spayed before or after her first season, so discuss this with your own vet if you want your Golden bitch spayed as soon as possible.

Most of the advantages have been referred to above, but the disadvantages are: the coat texture will change and become more difficult to manage; incontinence may occur after the operation or in old age; hormonal changes may result in a bitch gaining weight more easily, so her diet needs more care; a bitch with epilepsy may have more problems afterwards.

Acquiring a Second Dog

Whatever the reason for considering having a second dog, it is a serious undertaking and requires an even greater commitment than owning a single dog.

Most of the costs will be duplicated. The only possible exceptions are a food bowl, grooming equipment, dog guard and folding crate (if you have one; if not, the need is even greater to buy one. The same applies to a baby gate). Food may be marginally cheaper if purchased in greater quantities. Insurance premiums for a second animal may be a fraction less but some companies do not make premium deductions for less than three animals. Kennelling fees are sometimes reduced if the two dogs share a kennel.

Other things you will need to consider are:

- What you will do with the older dog until the puppy is fully vaccinated.
- Holiday arrangements if you do not take the dogs with you.
- If you take the dogs on holiday, will the places you intend to visit accept two large dogs? Some will make charges.
- People's attitudes to taking two large dogs into public places, given so much anti-dog lobbying in recent years.
- Will your first dog accept a Golden Retriever?
- Is your first dog of a suitable age to accept another dog? The best age to accept another dog is generally regarded to be 4–5 years. I cannot say I have found difficulties with Goldens meeting one another at any age, provided care is taken with the introductions, sleeping and living arrangements, particularly up to 6 months of age. If you have a slightly infirm, elderly or ill Golden it may be best to wait until after he has died or made a recovery.

I would strongly recommend you *never* have two of the same age together, and that the first dog is at least 18 months old before you acquire a second dog. This will give you time to have built a bond with him and to have established basic control. Two dogs of the same age will play together, look to one another, and totally ignore their owner when being trained. It also means that you need double the amount of time to train and socialise them individually. Another drawback is that when puppies of similar ages are kept together, one will usually become dominant and the other one submissive. This can interfere greatly with their training and general development, especially for the submissive dog who is likely to require even more socialisation training. The submissive dog may be affected for his whole life although, if you are lucky, he will outgrow it by the age of 2–3 years.

I have known many breeders run on two puppies from a litter, find that one has become very submissive and then have difficulties ring training and showing him. The disappointment is often doubled, as frequently the submissive dog is the better specimen of the two! Gender does not appear to have a bearing on the matter.

By leaving a minimum of 18 months before getting a second dog, you should have had time to fully train and socialise your first dog; he should be fully responsive to you and have gone through the adolescent stage.

- If you are acquiring an adult dog, take even greater care over the introductions (which should be done on neutral territory), and sleeping and living arrangements until you are entirely happy the two animals have bonded. Both dogs are likely to feel vulnerable for a while and each may require protection from the other.
- Will your Golden accept another breed of dog? My experiences have been that they accept other Goldens far more easily, but rivalry and jealousy are possible, whatever the breed and gender. This is not always apparent at the outset; it can develop later.
- Will your second dog be of the same sex as your first?
- Will you have both your dogs neutered/spayed, or one of them? If you have different sexes and you do not wish to spay or neuter either, will you be able to make arrangements for them to be kept separately when the bitch is in season?
- If one is ill, have you the facilities to isolate the other?
- If you plan to show two breeds which are both in the gundog group, their classes will be on the same day at Championship shows but they may have separate benching areas. If they are from different groups, their classes may be held on different days.
- If you plan to show both, it is unlikely that you will enter both at every show so you will have to leave one at home which will need looking after. The same situation needs to be considered if a bitch comes into season, one is out of coat or has an injury.
- If one of the two dogs has contracted or been knowingly exposed to any infections or contagious disease during 21 days prior to the show day, you cannot take the other. The owner signs a declaration to this effect every time he enters a show.
- One may pine if the other dies.
- If you are planning on having a number of dogs, what is your upper limit and how much time will there be between each one you introduce, to prevent yourself from having too many?

The adult dog as a training aid

Do not assume that an adult dog can train or house train a puppy, no matter if they are playmates and companions. All the training must be done by the owner and, usually, separately from the other dog, as the puppy's concentration span is limited and he will be easily distracted by his companion. It may be possible, however, to use an adult dog for assistance in a couple of matters:

(a) *lead training your puppy off your premises.* An older dog will help to give confidence to a young puppy so that he walks forward and battles less with a lead. Only use an adult dog for this purpose if he is well lead-trained, otherwise the puppy is more likely to pick up bad habits!

(b) *as an example in training.* When a puppy or adolescent does not seem to know what to do on some training issue, carry out the exercise with the older dog first, whilst another person holds the youngster. Friendly rivalry and jealousy may then encourage the youngster to do the exercise. I have used this technique very effectively with a few of my Goldens which have been slow to pick up feather or enter water.

Are you prepared for a commitment that may last twelve years or more?

Acquiring an Adult

Many of the points I have already made about puppies are also relevant to the acquisition of an adult Golden Retriever. If over a year old he may have had his elbows, hips and eyes tested and, of course, he should have been vaccinated. Ask for the vaccination record, health record and any other details if tested. It will also be helpful to see the Golden in his home environment to see his temperament and character traits and what he is used to in the domestic situation. The older the dog, the more likely he is to have a set routine. It would be best to observe and take notes of as much as possible if you decide to rehome an adult. Mimicking the situation, if possible, will assist with the dog's transition and settlement. It would also be wise to take into consideration many of the suggestions and recommendations given for puppies on preparation and the collection journey (Chapter 2), as they may apply or help with an adult.

In Conclusion

I have pointed out many of the issues, most of which appear to be disadvantages to owning dogs or Goldens in particular but, having lived with numerous Goldens for many years, I have felt the joys and happiness have far outweighed these.

CHAPTER TWO

Choosing Your Puppy

Where to Buy a Puppy

I would always recommend that you buy from a specialist dog breeder. Why? Most specialist breeders breed selectively; rear their puppies with more care; only breed from dogs that have been checked for the hereditary problems within the breed through official schemes; and provide Kennel Club registration, pedigree, insurance cover, diet sheets and advice and help for the dog's lifetime.

An agent or dealer buys puppies of any breed from sources around the country, sometimes from the commercial breeder but mainly puppy farmers, to sell on to the unsuspecting puppy purchaser purely as a business enterprise. I would define a commercial breeder as someone who breeds many litters of the same or different breeds for profit, but on their own premises from their own stock, with some care and consideration for their welfare, whereas the puppy farmer produces puppies with no care for the welfare of the puppies or their mother.

There is a greater risk of infectious disease and stress-induced illnesses when puppies have travelled long distances at an early age to an agent/dealer and been mixed with other pups.

It is unlikely, particularly when dealing with agents and dealers, that you will be able to see the puppy's dam to check whether she is in reasonable health and, especially, whether she is of good temperament. Some dealers do produce a bitch if you ask but do check it is the one that has had the puppies – she should be bonded to the puppies and her undercarriage will be lower than normal, showing signs of having fed or feeding the puppies.

You may also have difficulties with obtaining paperwork, support and further help and advice if you buy the puppy from someone who is selling puppies merely as a business.

How Do You Tell the Difference?

It is certainly easier to tell from a visit to the breeder's premises than by a telephone call. However, as the first contact is usually by telephone, check whether they keep many different breeds, if the sire and dam have been screened for hereditary problems and if they will have current certificates available for inspection on your visit. Ask whether the puppies will be Kennel Club registered, have insurance cover, whether you will receive a pedigree and diet sheet and be able to see the dam with the puppies.

If the puppy seller breeds many different breeds, acts evasively to any of those lines of enquiry, fails to provide an answer or states that it is unnecessary to carry out the hereditary checks, your suspicions should be aroused and you should look elsewhere for a puppy.

Guarantees that any breed of dog will have a totally trouble-free life cannot be given, no matter where you buy your puppy, but you have more chance of having a healthy, happy puppy with help from a specialist breeder than elsewhere.

A confident, well-adjusted puppy.

How to Locate a Puppy

Breed club secretaries, veterinary practices, The Kennel Club, Pet Plan Puppy Line, dog journals, shooting magazines, Exchange and Mart and local newspapers, and speaking to someone who owns a Golden Retriever are all possible ways of finding a puppy!

Breed Club Secretaries

Contact your nearest breed club secretary (see Appendix 2 or via The Kennel Club) to find out if any litters are registered on their 'puppies for sale' lists.

Most British breed clubs run a puppy line which means the breeders should comply with their club's rules and code of ethics. Most clubs require that both the sire and dam have their hips X-rayed and scored for Hip Dysplasia, and eyes tested and cleared for cataract, Multi-focal Retinal Dysplasia and Progressive Retinal Atrophy (both central and general) through The Kennel Club/British Veterinary Association Scheme, before a breeder's litter is registered on the puppy line. The secretary may have this information available. If not, you will need to ask the breeder for this information. Do ask to see the certificates when you visit. Dogs born after March 1997 are also eligible for x-ray under the Elbow Dysplasia scheme. Some breeders may be members of more than one club and have a litter registered with several secretaries.

Some countries have different breeding requirements imposed either by their Kennel Club and/or breed clubs, so check with the breed club secretary what these requirements are and the breeding restrictions imposed.

You should not expect any guarantees that a puppy or adult offered for sale will be free of those diseases or problems known to affect Goldens. No one can do this, no matter how well the puppies are bred and reared. Breeding is genetically unpredictable with many external influences such as diet, exercise and environment also possibly affecting the outcome.

Once in contact with the breeder(s), you will find they are often in close touch with one another. If they no longer have any puppies for sale, they might be able to recommend someone else or put you in contact with a breed club secretary.

Veterinary Practices

Vets do not always know of breeders who have puppies, but can often recommend a breeder who has been using their practice for several years who may be planning a litter.

Kennel Club

In the United Kingdom, The Kennel Club produces an information pack for prospective puppy purchasers which contains a list of anyone who is likely to have puppies for sale. There are no specific criteria for inclusion on the list other than payment of a service fee when the puppies are registered and a declaration by the breeder to abide by The Kennel Club's Code of Ethics. The breeder could be of any status and there is no specific requirement for the puppy's parents to be tested for any condition affecting a breed for which there are KC/BVA testing schemes. In view of this you will need to be vigilant.

For details, contact The Kennel Club, 1-5 Clarges Street, Piccadilly, London W1Y 8AB.

Pet Plan Puppy Line

This insurance company operates a register for breeders currently with puppies to sell, and will provide details of breeders to those actively looking for a puppy of a particular breed.

It is well worth waiting for the puppy of your choice.

Once again, the list contains anyone who pays a litter registration fee to the company, provided they declare the puppies are from a bitch they own and are their property at the time of sale. The company advertises extensively in Yellow Pages, Exchange and Mart, dog journals, veterinary surgeries and pet shops.

The Press

Dog journals: Some of the dog journals contain advertisements of puppies for sale. These journals can all be obtained through your local newsagent, but it will probably be necessary to place an order or contact the publishers direct (see Appendix 1, Useful Addresses).

The growing pup will get into plenty of mischief.

Dog World, Our Dogs, Dog Training Weekly and *Obedience Info* are weekly publications; the last two deal mainly with obedience, agility, working trials, flyball and training and are only available on subscription.

Gundogs, Dogs Monthly, Pet Dogs, Dogs Today and The Kennel Club publication, the *Kennel Gazette*, are published monthly. Annual publications are *Dog World Annual* and *Our Dogs Annual*.

Other owners: Goldens can often be seen out with their owners and I am sure most people would be pleased to let you know how they came by their pet. You need to be vigilant when pursuing a line of enquiry through this method to check the breeder is not a commercial breeder and that he fulfils the expectations of a specialist breeder as outlined.

Finding Your Golden Retriever

You may wish to consider finding a local breeder if you want a Golden Retriever as a pet, as it will be less distance to travel to visit the puppies and also less distance for the puppy to travel to its new home. If you are looking for some special breeding, distances will probably need to be disregarded.

Once you have selected one or more specialist breeders you then need to ascertain:

- When and if they have some puppies for sale.
- What sexes are available.
- What the sire's and dam's temperaments are like.
- What colour the parents and puppies are, if you have a preference.
- Whether the parents both have current clear eye certificates for cataract, Multi-focal Retinal Dysplasia and Progressive Retinal Atrophy (both central and general) and if you can have sight of the certificates when visiting the puppies.
- Whether the parents have had their hips X-rayed and what their scores are. The lower the hip score for each hip the better (see Chapter 6). Currently the Golden Retriever breed average total for both hips is 19.6 (9.8 per hip). Again you should also check that you will be allowed to have sight of the score sheet. (In some countries, hips are sometimes graded rather than given scores, so find out from breed clubs, kennel clubs or breeders what the hip status is for Golden Retrievers in your country. The same applies to any other known condition that is tested for other than hips, elbows and eyes.)
- Whether the parents have had their elbows x-rayed and what the scores are. The lower the elbow score, the better (see Chapter 6). Possible scores are 0, 1, 2 or 3. The KVC/BVA Scheme for elbows has only been operational in the United Kingdom since March 1998, so it is unlikely that this information will be available for all breeding stock for some years yet. It is more likely to be available for younger breeding stock and, again, you should ask to have sight of the score sheet, if the information is available.

- Whether you will see the mother of the puppies. This is important as it will help to establish whether you are dealing with a bona-fide breeder and not an agent or dealer. You will also want to assess the dam's temperament as a possible guide to the puppy's temperament in the future. Nervousness or aggression in the bitch does not bode well.
- Whether you will see the father of the puppies. This is only likely if the breeder has used his own stud dog but, hopefully, you may be able to see a photograph instead.

- When it will be convenient to visit the puppies and mother. Most breeders arrange for you to visit for the first time when the puppies are about 3–4 weeks old. It is unlikely that an appointment will be made earlier, as the puppies' eyes are not fully open until about 3 weeks and they are only just getting up on to their feet. Also breeders have to consider the risk of infection. Although the puppies may have immunity early on from their mother, the mother could be infected and pass a problem to the puppies through her milk. If the puppies have not been born, the breeder may invite you to see the mother of the pups-to-be and any of his other dogs to determine if he is happy with you having a puppy from him. Equally, you can decide if you feel comfortable about the breeder you hope to buy from and the mother's temperament and looks.
- What price the breeder is charging for a puppy.
- What the price includes, for instance: KC registration, a pedigree, insurance for 6 weeks, tattooing, diet sheet, general care information on the breed, any vaccinations, food for a few days after purchase and anything else.
- Whether any extras will be charged for anything above the initial purchase price. Most breeders will volunteer this information rather than having to be asked.

It may be wise for you to contact more than one breeder to try to locate a puppy of the type, temperament, sex and colour you want, particularly if the puppies have not yet been born and you only require a pet. Many breeders have had to disappoint people because insufficient puppies of either sex have been born to the number of enquiries received.

Generally, I have found bitches are in greater demand than males, so supplying them tends to cause the difficulties. If several people are on my waiting list and I foresee the litter will be small, I usually advise those lower on the list to look elsewhere but to keep me, and any other breeder they have contacted, informed of the position. However, if you are seeking a puppy from a particular breeder or combination of parents for showing or working, then you will have to be prepared to wait until a puppy becomes available. Some people have been known to wait 2–3 years for the puppy of their choice.

Any other questions you may have can all be covered when you visit the breeder to see the puppies. However, if anything particularly concerns you, do not hesitate to contact the breeder immediately to resolve the matter. He would rather know sooner than later if you may have to withdraw from purchasing a puppy from him.

What to Expect

Puppies are normally sold at 7–8 weeks of age and most reputable breeders would expect you to visit at least once, if not two or three times, before collecting your puppy to sort out all you need to know about each other. Most reputable breeders do provide the information and documentary evidence mentioned above without having to be asked.

Do not expect to be allowed to handle the puppies on your first visit or whilst they are under 5 weeks of age. Apart from the risk of infection this is also so that no harm comes to them whilst they are so young. They will be more interesting, active and larger at 6–7 weeks old. You may be required to remove your footwear or disinfect it on entering the breeder's premises to help prevent the risk of infection.

Do not expect an automatic choice of puppy unless you have arranged specifically to have, say, first or second choice of a particular sex. Many breeders will not commit themselves, mainly because they prefer to observe the puppies closely and question the prospective purchasers to try and match them suitably. For example, they may be reluctant to offer a puppy that was obviously going to be an extrovert and require a lot of handling to a very quiet couple, or the less outgoing puppy to a large, busy family.

Visiting the Litter

If you already own a dog, when you visit the young puppies, wear clothes that have had no contact with your own animal to prevent any chance of cross infection. Your dog may appear perfectly fit and well because he has built up antibodies to give him immunity but, in fact, he could have an infection. Many diseases can be carried by water and air, so why not on clothes and footwear?

On arrival you will make your own judgement on the breeder's domestic standards based on your own, but you should expect to find happy, healthy, lively and relatively clean puppies. The puppies will be less active if they have just been fed or have been sleeping. Whether or not you are buying a pet puppy, generally you should be looking for a healthy, outgoing, alert and sturdy animal. If he needs coaxing or is naughty, he will need more patience and/or firmness, respectively.

If after your first visit you and the breeder are happy with each other, a second visit is normally arranged, perhaps for you to make a choice if this is an option.

The breeder may inform you at any stage of the proceedings if there is something that concerns him and he is not prepared to sell you a puppy. Equally you have the right to withdraw your request for a puppy, but please be courteous and inform the breeder rather than failing to arrive for an appointment.

On either visit you will need to glean the following information: how best to transfer the puppy to his new home; what food to buy in; a copy of the diet sheet; tips on general care, management and training; details of vaccinations, if any; whether a deposit will be required (10–20% of the purchase price is normal), and whether there will be any paperwork other than the registration, pedigree and insurance, such as the tattoo transfer and sales documents.

I usually provide a copy of the diet sheet, general notes on care, training and management, and a sales document for the puppy purchasers to take away and study before collection day so that they are able to raise any questions about the contents beforehand.

If you are buying a puppy for the first time for a special purpose, such as showing or working, I suggest you ask an independent specialist breeder for help. It would be preferable if they owned or knew the breed, but they could probably still be of assistance even if they are in another breed of dog. Most breeders would not object to you bringing an additional person, provided you inform them first. This will be particularly helpful if you have the opportunity of making a choice.

If you are unable to obtain the help of a specialist, in most cases the breeder will help you as it is in his/her own interests for specimens with the best conformation to be shown. You should be looking for a conformation as close to the Breed Standard as possible, as well as taking the puppy's temperament into consideration. There will never be a perfect specimen, as many aspects of the Breed Standard are a matter of personal judgement. I have found the optimum time to select on most (but not all) breeding lines is 6 weeks. You may, however, have to fit in with the breeder and anyone else who is buying a puppy for showing, whether or not you have first choice.

I believe selection for working is more difficult, because temperament and character

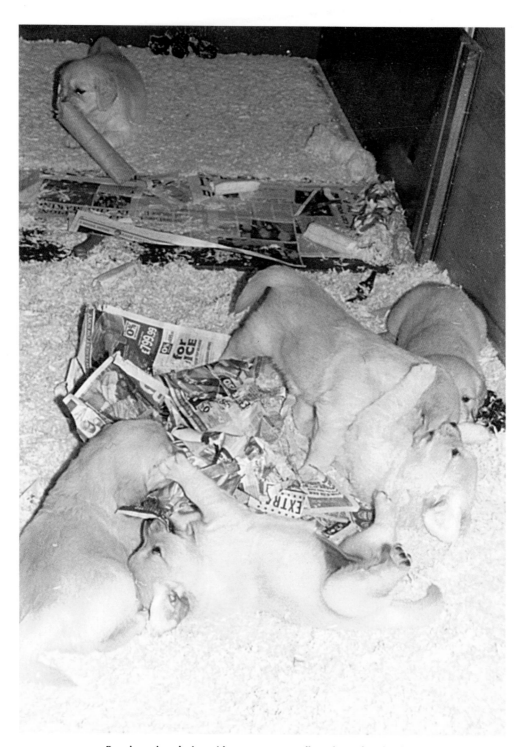

Puppies enjoy playing with newspaper, cardboard – and each other.

feature more highly than conformation in the assessment of the puppies, and because choices have to be made by 8 weeks before these traits are fully developed. In both work and show cases the achievements of the parents will be indicators as to how well the puppies may do, but it must be remembered these are just indicators – not a guarantee. In addition to his genetic makeup and parentage, much will depend on the puppy's overall care, socialisation, feeding, training, environmental exposures and his new owner's ability to understand his individual needs during his upbringing in his new home.

The cost of show and working puppies is not usually more than that charged for pets in the breed, but there are always exceptions to the rule. You must establish how the breeder wants to be paid for the puppy. Most prefer cash. Make sure you obtain a receipt of payment.

Some breeders may ask you to consider entering into a 'conditions of sale' agreement over the sale of the puppy, which may result in the reduction of the price of the puppy. For instance, they may wish to use a dog's stud services free of charge if he develops into a sound breed specimen and has a low hip and elbow score and an eye clearance certificate. In the case of a bitch, you may be required to have a litter with the breeder having one or more puppies of their choice or free of charge, subject to her hip, elbow and eye status. Whatever is suggested, make certain everything is fully explained and confirmed in writing with both parties signing, dating and retaining a copy of the agreement. Do not enter into any agreement if you have any concerns about honouring the arrangement, or you do not want any involvement. It is much easier to say **no** at the outset than to end up in litigation several years later.

Preparing for Your Puppy's Arrival

Buy a small collar, slip lead, identification disc, bedding, food and water bowls, bone, toys and perhaps a dog guard, travel harness, crate and baby gates if required (see Chapter 1).

Choose a local veterinary practice, check at what age the puppy will need his first and second vaccinations and make the appropriate appointments. Usually the first is done sometime between 8 and 10 weeks of age, then the second one at 12 weeks. My veterinary surgeon will do the first vaccination at 8 weeks, as I have other dogs, but usually vets prefer to give the first at 10 weeks.

If the breeder has had the first vaccination done, which is unlikely if the puppy is purchased before he is 8 weeks old, obtain details so your own veterinary surgeon can use the same type of vaccination. You must let the vet know in advance, otherwise he may have to start the vaccination procedure again. Do not invite pet-owning friends or relations to your house until your puppy is fully inoculated as his resistance is lower than an adult dog's until he is about 16 weeks old.

Ensure your garden is escape proof, including fences, hedges, walls and gates. It is important not to have gaps at a lower level, or fencing or gates the puppy can dig or push under or through. A Golden pup is only approximately 15–18cm (6–7in) tall at the age of 7 weeks. If necessary, as an interim measure make a small area safe for your pup to play in. Golden Retriever puppies grow very fast; by the age of 6 months they almost will have reached their full height so it is also important to ensure the gates and fencing are strong and of an adequate height. To prevent the digger escaping, fencing may have to be buried or cemented into the ground. I would recommend solid fencing with a minimum height of 2m (6ft), particularly if you have neighbours with pets (to help prevent confrontations, vocal

"Hello, Dad? When are you coming to see me?!"

or otherwise). In a more rural setting, I have found 1.4m (4ft) wire mesh fencing to be perfectly adequate.

Prevent access to poisonous shrubs and plants, ponds and swimming pools. Many ponds and pools have no exit points and a puppy could tire and drown before he is found.

Decide where in your home the puppy will be permitted to live and sleep until he is house-trained and you can trust him when he is left alone. If necessary, temporarily segregate these areas with a baby gate. Remove or barricade from the puppy's reach anything that you do not want chewed, stolen or which is particularly dangerous to the puppy. This includes precious furniture and carpets, household waste bins and bags, and small articles which can be swallowed, such as children's toys, plants, electrical cable and wires, fires, candles, cigarette butts, food, medication, needles and pins.

Inform your neighbours about your new arrival and ask them not to feed your puppy over the fence or throw any objects into your garden for him. Also the pup should not be enticed into your neighbours' gardens as their premises may not be as secure as yours.

Cigarette butts can lead to nicotine poisoning. Antifreeze is highly toxic and its scent attracts puppies so this should be kept out of your pup's reach and any drips should be cleared up. Other exposed toxins such as fly-paper hanging strips must also be kept out of reach. Toilet cleaners are mostly strong alkaline solutions which puppies are tempted to drink so keep toilet lids down.

Remember: Prevention is easier than cure or repair, is far less costly and may prevent a tragedy occurring.

Collecting Your Puppy

The Paperwork

- A diet sheet.
- General advice sheet(s) which should also give details of how many times the puppy has been wormed.
- KC Registration. Litter registrations are normally processed within 2–4 weeks. Therefore, provided that the breeder has applied for the puppies' registrations within the first 3 weeks after they were born and there have been no complications or errors on the registrations, the papers should be available for collection when your puppy is 7–8 weeks of age. The breeder will need to sign and date section A to enable you to transfer the puppy into your ownership. The breeder may have imposed certain restrictions with the registration such as: Export Pedigree Not Allowed or Progeny Not To Be Registered. If this has been done, he should explain why and under what circumstances, if any, he would be prepared to lift the restrictions. I recommend that you obtain signed details of this in writing from the breeder, to prevent any misunderstandings at a future date by either party, a copy of which should be retained by each of you.
- Copies of current clear eye certificates used to be provided by the breeder but, as The Kennel Club now includes a note on the registration document of both the sire's and dam's eye status, I do not feel it is necessary to provide them unless the Registration documents are not available. The same applies to hip and elbow scores, provided the parents were scored after 1991 and 1998 respectively. The information appears immediately below the sire and dam's names.
- The pedigree may be handwritten, typed or produced on a computer by the breeder and signed. Quite often champions are printed in red or highlighted, and abbreviated to Ch or FT Ch (Field Trial Champion), Sh Ch (Show Champion) and Ob Ch (Obedience Champion). Foreign champions may also have an abbreviation for the country, such as NL Ch (Dutch Champion). Usually four or five generations are included on the pedigree. Three-generation and five generation pedigrees can also be obtained from The Kennel Club. I still prefer to write my puppies' pedigrees by hand and include all known hip-scores of the ancestry at the time of sale.
- Signed Insurance Puppy Cover Note for a period of 6 weeks, which takes effect immediately the puppy leaves the premises.
- Signed receipt of payment.
- Copy of sales agreement outlining any terms and conditions imposed by the breeder. The breeder also retains a copy. Both copies should be signed and dated by both parties on the day of purchase.
- Information and/or certification of any identification processes carried out (for example, tattoos).
- Vaccination certification, if any have been carried out.
- A diet sheet and dog food for 2–7 days of the food the puppy is currently being fed. I also provide a new calcium bone for the puppy to chew; owners then know what to buy when it needs to be replaced.

You may also receive some useful free dog literature and promotional products from some leading pet food manufacturers via the breeder.

If you are purchasing an older puppy or adult Golden, you would expect to receive all this information and documentation and maybe the food and vitamins. The only exception may be the insurance.

The Journey

Puppies aged 7–8 weeks are unlikely to have travelled anywhere so you will not know whether or not they get travel sick. With care and good luck I have known most puppies to arrive home without a problem. Nevertheless, I always ask puppy buyers to come prepared for all eventualities. It may not just be travel sickness that has to be dealt with; the puppy may decide to relieve himself, as a result of stress from travelling, being removed from the puppy pack and his mother, or merely because of the length of the journey to his new destination.

Most breeders will delay or reschedule the puppy's meal times on departure day so that he is fed at least 2 hours before he leaves. My tips are:

- Take another adult to hold or look after the puppy whilst you are driving, or get someone else to drive whilst you hold the puppy.
- Never place a puppy in a crate, pet carrier or box, unless absolutely necessary; you do not want his first car journey to be unduly stressful.
- Allow the puppy to travel as near to the front of the vehicle as possible, perhaps in the foot-well, to prevent as much motion and vision as you can. Try to prevent the dog from looking out of the car. It has been suggested that seeing the world speeding past the windows may cause dogs to have travel sickness.
- Keep the vehicle ventilated and not too hot.
- Take several old towels for the puppy to lie on, either on someone's lap or in the foot-well. It may also be advantageous to cover the seats with an old sheet. Take old newspapers, kitchen roll and a refuse sack so that you can clean up and place anything in the sack, which can be tied up for disposal. This will help to remove offensive smells.
- Take a wet flannel for wiping the puppy, if necessary, wipes for cleaning your hands, and a towel.
- A small lead, to have control over the puppy in case it is necessary to take him out of the vehicle. **Never** let the puppy out of the car without a lead. Remember, great care should also be taken where you stop, as it is unlikely the puppy will have had any vaccinations. Try to avoid areas that look as though they have been fouled or used by other dogs, especially at motorway services, roadside cafés and public parks. Also do not stop where there is heavy traffic as it may be dangerous and frightening for the puppy.
- Some water in a container and a water bowl, in case of long journeys or emergencies such as traffic jams.
- On short journeys, avoid giving the puppy anything to eat or drink.
- Keep calm if your puppy does have a problem. Some children will panic if a puppy is sick which will cause the puppy more stress. This is why I do not think young children should accompany you to collect a puppy, even though they will be looking forward with great excitement to their new arrival.
- Try to pick the straightest roads and shortest journeys; avoid well-known areas of traffic congestion.
- Drive as smoothly as possible, especially around corners, and avoid excessive braking.

I believe this first journey is very important as it can establish the trend of whether the puppy associates the car with pleasantness or travel sickness. If the latter, it can take a long time to break what so easily can become a habit, and may make you reluctant to take the puppy in the vehicle other than for an essential journey to the vet. Having another dog who enjoys travelling in the car may help the younger one to adopt a more positive attitude, as may the other suggestions listed at the end of this chapter.

Some Goldens may grow out of the problem after 8–9 months of age or after a bitch has had her first season, others may need the care described above and help from pet travel sickness pills which usually are obtainable from pet shops. Most pills need to be given at least 2 hours prior to a journey to be effective. If you go out for several hours with a journey break it may be necessary to give another tablet or dosage two hours before your return journey.

A homeopathic remedy for travel sickness, panting, yawning and dribbling is Cocculus. It does not have the sedative effect that some conventional medications may have. One tablet is given one hour before a journey, followed by another half an hour later. A third may be required for a long journey.

Dogs can sometimes develop a hatred of travelling in a car, for example, due to sickness problems or because they have been involved in an accident. In such cases you need to encourage the dog to associate the vehicle with pleasure. To do this you can:

- Feed the dog one of his meals occasionally in the parked car.
- Let him sleep in the car when you are close at hand, or with another dog that does enjoy being in the vehicle.
- Take him on a short journey, say 5 minutes, to a park or field where he can safely have a gallop or go for a walk.

Keeping the dog in a confined space, preferably in the front or middle of the car until the sickness difficulties are overcome, will prevent it feeling the vehicle motion. If you want to find out how uncomfortable it is in the rear of an estate car, try a 5-minute journey yourself – I have. You will have far greater respect for how your dog feels afterwards.

Good luck!

Now the fun begins.....

CHAPTER THREE

Puppy Care

The First Day

As a breeder I try to prepare my puppies for their new home to lessen the trauma. I do not let the dam feed the puppies after they are 6 weeks old and only allow her to play with them occasionally, to reduce the bond they have with her. All my litters are kept indoors both summer and winter, and exposed to household noises such as radios, televisions, vacuum cleaners and so on. I also let them out of their indoor pen, together and separately, on grass, concrete and in the kitchen. However, leaving their first home with its familiar smells, litter mates, dam and daily routine can be a culture shock for some puppies no matter how outgoing they are. Therefore do not be alarmed if for a day or two your puppy is a little wary of his new surroundings and scents, as he no longer has his siblings or mum to play with or for support.

Firstly you must decide what to call your puppy and begin to use the name as soon as possible to help him respond to you and accept your family as his substitute pack.

On arriving home, place the puppy in the safe area outside where he can relieve himself if he wishes. Stay with him so he does not become alarmed. You will then know for certain if he has urinated and you can clear up any faeces immediately.

Allow your puppy to explore some of his new environment indoors under your supervision, including his feeding and sleeping areas, so that he becomes familiar with these areas.

Even if he is due for a meal according to the breeder's feeding routine, wait for about one hour after a journey before offering a meal. Your puppy is more likely to eat after a break or a short period of exploring and sleeping. Immediately after feeding any meal, go outside with your puppy to allow him to urinate and defecate. This should be done regularly throughout the day, and last thing at night.

Do not overdo it on the first day as it is not advisable to overtire a young pup. Young puppies require many short, undisturbed naps between their play and investigating periods, so choose a quiet area where he can sleep away from all the busy family life. Even on the first day, your puppy should be encouraged to sleep in the day time, and to develop a routine.

Keep introductions to a minimum and involve only the immediate family. Friends and neighbours can be introduced at a later date. The same applies to most of the family's pets if you have any, such as cats, rabbits and guinea pigs. However, if you have a dog, you may like to see how the two react to one another as the older dog's company may help the puppy adapt more quickly to his new home.

Some owners believe it is prudent to have a newly-purchased puppy checked by their vet as soon as possible, but not necessarily on the day of arrival. Others will wait until the first vaccination is due, unless something concerns them in the interim.

Always supervise playtime until the older dog is used to his new friend.

The First Night

This may be your puppy's first crisis. If your plan was to leave your puppy with another dog for the night, you must introduce them earlier in the day and judge the chemistry between them. In my experience, the older the dog, the longer it takes to accept a new puppy and therefore it may not be wise nor safe to leave the two together for several nights, weeks or even months until the chemistry is right between them. You could place the puppy behind a baby gate so that he can see the older dog for comfort, or in a sealed crate with bedding near the older dog. The only disadvantage to using a crate is that the puppy may soil his bedding. If the older dog does react badly to the puppy, do not be too harsh or judge him unfairly.

Initially most puppies will go off to sleep after a tiring day and their supper but they may wake up in the night and feel lost and alone. They may also want to relieve themselves, especially to urinate, as their bladders are small and control comes only as they grow. However, I have known some puppies to be clean at night from the outset.

If your pup wakes up, he may cry and/or bark and you must judge whether you go to resettle him. It is difficult sometimes to know what is best, as going to him may make the pup think he has succeeded in gaining human attention and he will cry and bark all the more when you try to leave him. Of course, he may be asking to go out as he does not wish to soil his bedding or indoor sleeping quarters. I often leave a pup for 5–10 minutes to see if he goes off to sleep again but, if he persists, I will attend to him. Having several Goldens means I can usually find one that will sleep with him safely.

Ensure that your puppy is warm throughout the night, but not too warm. You may like to experiment by playing a radio quietly and/or leaving on lights. You could place some old newspaper or wood shavings close to an exit door for the puppy to use if he needs to urinate during the night. Some owners leave a back/kitchen door open at night for the puppy but this is not always practical if the weather is bad or for security reasons. The alternatives are that the puppy sleeps near you (in his crate) or you sleep near your puppy. It may only be for the first few nights, but you may then find that he wants to sleep with you for the rest of his life.

Family Introductions

To Children

- Make sure your children are sitting down quietly, preferably on the floor.
- Try to prevent them from picking up a puppy in case of accidents. Goldens grow very fast so it will be only a few weeks before the weight increase will prevent this from being possible.
- Teach the children the correct way to hold a puppy, in case they have to pick him up for any special reason. They must support his body fully and never hold him by his legs, skin or tail.
- Teach the children how to stroke a puppy correctly (gently and the way the hair grows), respect him and talk to him quietly.
- Keep the children's and dog's feeding areas separate and never leave either unsupervised when eating, to prevent food sharing.
- Do not allow your children to train your dog unsupervised and only then when they understand what is required.
- Discourage your dog from licking the children.
- Do not allow the children to pull the dog's ears and tail or tease him.
- Do not allow the children to give treats to the dog unless they are supervised.
- Do not allow the children to wake a dog when he is resting. This is particularly important in the case of puppies, who need many small rest periods. Providing a quiet place in the home will assist the puppy.
- Do not allow a dog to play with a small child unsupervised as he may hurt the child accidentally.
- Never allow children to walk a dog unsupervised. A dog's strength may be too much for them to cope with if he becomes excited or sees another dog. It can be very distressing for a child to lose the dog or see their pet attacked by another animal.

To a New Baby

Treat the puppy or adult dog as usual and, as far as possible, continue his routine without alteration, including exercise, even though a new baby will make many demands on your time. When your baby is in bed it may help to allow your dog some extra privileges. Let your dog become accustomed to a baby's cry. Discourage your dog from licking the baby or jumping up to his or her cot or pram. Never leave a dog with a new infant unsupervised or tie him to the pram in or out of doors; take one or the other with you to be safe.

To Another Dog

- Introductions should take place as soon as possible so that the older dog does not feel unsettled by a new arrival which may take up more of your time. At 7 weeks, the puppy is more likely to be confident than at 8–12 weeks when he enters a critical period of sensitivity.

An older and wiser paw keeps the youngster in check.

- Supervise socialisation sessions and keep them brief to begin with.
- Supervise feed sessions.
- Ensure your puppy does not steal the older dog's toys and bedding. If jealousy or strong reactions are shown by the older dog, removing the articles temporarily should help.
- Treat them equally in all respects, so that the older dog does not feel he is being neglected in any way.
- Do not allow the two dogs to sleep together unsupervised until their body language indicates they have bonded. Points to look for are toy and bed sharing, and if the adult dog accepts the puppy's possible submissive behaviour.

Whilst most animal behaviourists advocate that dogs should resolve their own problems without human interference, this is certainly not wise initially as the older dog may react if the puppy ignores its warning growls and snaps. An adult dog can also cause a damaging injury to a pup which may affect its show prospects, or cause some incapacity, for example, blindness if an eye is caught.

To a Cat

A cat's reaction to a puppy will be unpredictable. Most will avoid the puppy's presence initially, until they realise the newcomer has come to stay. Unfortunately, some may also urine mark indoors. Many cats and dogs will cuddle up together eventually.

Many of the points given for dog introductions can be applied in the case of the cat. It may also help if you provide your cat with eating and resting areas at a higher level out of the puppy's reach, and also move his litter tray out of reach. If a cat door presents a security problem for your puppy, you will need to make alternative arrangements for your cat.

There may be additional difficulties if you are rehoming an adult dog that may have already developed a dislike for cats or become a chaser. It will be necessary to praise and reward the dog when he behaves correctly or chastise him if he behaves improperly. Changing a dog's developed characteristics may be a lengthy process, or impossible if the dog has become too set in its ways. Both animals will then require their own space.

To Other Animals

Be it mice, rats, rabbits, guinea pigs, fish, fowl or caged birds, care must be taken not to allow the puppy to be over-enthusiastic and bark or jump at them or their cages. A pup may frighten and shock small animals or even try to retrieve them if they are loose. It would probably be wise if the pup is denied access to them until he ignores their presence. Aquarium fish present a great fascination for some Goldens, who may try to paw the tank and cause accidental damage if left unsupervised.

A word of warning if you have an uncovered fish pond. I have had several Goldens with the skills of a cat who have scooped the fish out of the water with their paws. The fish have then been carried undamaged to the back door. I wonder if this has any connection with the Golden's part-Tweed Water Spaniel ancestry, a breed which was thought to help men net salmon on the north-east coast of England at the beginning of the 20th century.

The main anxiety with larger animals, such as horses, is more for the dog in case it is kicked. Dogs should be introduced carefully and only allowed supervised contact with larger animals until a mutual respect is established. I have occasionally seen dogs exercised freely in public places by horseriders. The potential dangers this conjures up for dog, horse and rider appals me because of the lack of control in the event of the unexpected happening.

It would be wise not to exercise your dog near sheep in case he is taken for a sheep worrier by the farmer.

Feeding

There are some 'Golden' rules to remember!

- Keep to the diet plan provided by the breeder for as long as possible, and at least 2 weeks. This includes the food, number of meals and schedule. Maintaining the same routine will help the puppy to become used to his new home.
- Ensure that fresh drinking water is accessible and available at all times.
- Clean dishes after meals and water bowls, at least once a day.
- If you decide to change the puppy's food, consult the breeder first for advice on alternatives. There may be very good reasons why certain foods have not been recommended on the diet sheet.
- If your puppy will not eat the food listed on the diet sheet, consult the breeder first for advice on how to get the puppy to eat, and on alternative foods if necessary.
- If you visit the veterinary surgeon for the puppy's first vaccination and he recommends a different food product, which many do, consult the breeder for advice on the product. Again, there may be good reasons why the puppy was not reared on this product. (This does not apply in the case of a serious dietary problem where prescription diets are recommended.) Loose stools may be due to a change of home, change of water, worms, eating garden rubbish/plants, or the introduction of a new food into the puppy's diet.

Your pup should acclimatise to the water and new foods in time, but do make sure he cannot reach any rubbish. You can get worming tablets from the vet. Please follow the instructions very carefully.

- Do not free-feed Goldens or leave bowls of food down after a mealtime. This is for reasons of hygiene, prevents the puppy becoming fussy and stops flies from proliferating.
- If your puppy vomits other than to bring up a foreign body, or has diarrhoea, starve him for 12 hours. Give him small quantities of boiled rice to start with, then rice with a cooked white meat such as fish or chicken. Provided the sickness and diarrhoea do not continue, gradually re-introduce the normal foods. Live yoghurt is very useful to replace lost enzymes. If vomiting or diarrhoea persists, consult a vet.
- Do not overfeed your puppy, as this is likely to give him diarrhoea.
- Do not force feed your puppy to produce rapid growth as this is likely to lead to bone disorders.
- Do not over-supplement your puppy's diet, if it is necessary at all. Again this may cause bone disorders.
- If the diet does not include vitamins, supplementation will be necessary to prevent disorders, especially during the dog's growing stages.
- If your puppy is a fussy eater, try not to make an issue or a crisis out of this and never scold him for not eating. Some sensitive Golden Retrievers pick up on their owner's exasperation or anxiety, which often makes matters worse.
- See if you can make mealtimes fun, even though it may be the furthest thought from your mind at the time.
- The aim is to keep your puppy round and firm with a waistline, not fat or flabby.
- Puppies require a large amount of food to supply them with the nutrients for growth, energy and maintenance. Due to their small stomach capacity it is necessary for puppies to be fed at four or five regularly-spaced intervals during the day at the usual age they arrive at their new homes. As puppies grow and their stomach capacity increases the meals can be reduced.

- With the wide range of products now available on the pet food market, breeders are spoilt for choice. Many will use feeds they have tried for many years and that are easily available for pet owners to buy.

Three feeding regime options are possible:

(a) the original method, using raw meat such as tripe and biscuit with added vitamins as the main base and, perhaps, milk feeds.

Follow the breeder's diet sheet to avoid your puppy having an upset tummy.

(b) the modern method using all-in-one balanced dry foods or tinned meat products to which no supplementation should be necessary as this already has been included.

(c) the combination method, using a mixture of (a) and (b).

There are advantages and disadvantages with all methods. For instance, dogs may find tripe very appetising but normally you need to have freezer space to store it and you may not find the defrosted tripe so appealing! Freeflow tripe is available in packets. A quantity can be allowed to defrost overnight and then cooked in the microwave in a matter of minutes, ready for eating. Dry foods usually result in the dog producing less stools but some dogs may eat it too fast, causing choking or bloat if the food is not soaked. I would not recommend that Golden Retriever puppies are reared solely on complete dry foods, as the breed is quite fast growing. From the age of 2 years, once the dog has completely grown, I would have no hesitation in using this food as recommended by manufacturers, provided that it is soaked for the fast eaters. If method (c) is used, care must be taken not to unbalance the daily nutritional requirements by over- or under-supplementing the vitamins.

For many years method (a) was used at our kennel and later puppy tinned meat was substituted for tripe for storage convenience. However, following three successive litters where some puppies had an intolerance to milk feeds, I have recently succumbed to using the dry puppy foods, but combined with puppy tinned foods, light meals as described below and Vitamin C supplementation (see Chapter 7 for quantities).

Feeding Guide for 7-week-old Puppy

(a) Original method
8.00 am 85g (3oz) raw meat/tripe, 2 draining spoons of soaked mixer/biscuit, vitamins and calcium.

11.00am 0.3 litre (0.5pt) full cream milk or goat's milk. Cow's milk is too weak. Milk products are available from most pet shops; goat's milk is available in some supermarkets. Alternatively, use condensed milk made up with water at a 50/50 strength.

1.00pm light meal which can consist of scrambled egg, half a small tin of sardines/mackerel fillet, with oil drained off, with brown bread (use a teaspoon of the oil on another meal on other days). Alternatively, 3 tbsp cooked pasta with half a hard-boiled egg or half a tin of fish (rice can be used instead of pasta), or 1–2 tbsp of tinned rice pudding. Do not use tinned fish daily as it is a rich food.

6.00pm as for breakfast.

10.00pm 0.3 litre (0.5 pt) milk mixed with Farex, Weetabix, Ready Brek or porridge oats.

(b) Modern method
8.00am dry food – the quantity needs to be calculated accurately according to puppy's age and weight, as detailed on the product. I prefer to soak it, preferably with warm water. Check that it has cooled before feeding. The daily quantity needs to be divided into equal amounts for the four meals per day.

1.00pm as for 8.00am meal.

6.00pm as for 8.00am meal.

10.00pm as for 8.00am meal.

(c) Combination method

8.00am 85g (3oz) tinned puppy meat and 2 draining spoons of mixer.

1.00pm light meals as in method (a).

6.00pm as for breakfast.

10.00pm soaked dried food, one-third of daily quantity.

NB: No milk or calcium to be added to method (b). No milk to be added to method (c) but some vitamins or calcium may be required to balance the variety of food being fed.

I also offer a Farley's Rusk or one large biscuit to the puppy at bed-time or if he has to be shut in and left for a short period.

I prefer to start the puppy off each day with a meat meal as he has gone 10 hours since his last meal. If milk is used, a maximum of one pint per day is all that is necessary. Eggs should always be cooked, never given raw, with a maximum of 4 per week.

The number of daily meals should be reduced to four meals at 8 weeks (exclude 11am), three meals at 12 weeks (exclude 10pm), 2 meals at 6 months (exclude 1pm) and then, if you prefer, just one meal per day from 18 months onwards. Some people feed their dog twice daily, which does give them something more to look forward to and is less stressful on the digestive system.

The main components of any diet will need to be increased on a weekly basis up to 6 months unless stated otherwise and the appropriate age range should be used when feeding manufactured food. A guideline is: increase meat by 30gms (1oz), biscuit and mixer by 30gms (1oz) up to 455gms (1lb) maximum, rice and pasta by half to one draining spoon up to 12 weeks, rice pudding half a tablespoonful fortnightly, not weekly, up to 12 weeks, and brown bread by half a slice up to 12 weeks.

The puppy should remain on the six month quantity until he is around 9 months old. Then the biscuit/mixer may need to be reduced by about 115gms (4oz). At 12-18 months the meat should be reduced to approximately 455gms (1lb) or to one large tin or whatever allows him to maintain his optimum weight.

For dry foods and vitamin supplements, follow the manufacturers guidelines throughout.

Loss of Appetite

It is quite possible that a puppy arriving in a new home may suffer a loss of appetite for a short period (1–2 meals) due to the transition and new distractions, but often because he no longer has the competition of eating alongside littermates. Most overcome this within half a day or so. I would not become unduly concerned unless the fasting lasts for more than 24 hours. If he refuses to take liquids for 12–24 hours, then I would contact the breeder immediately for advice or the veterinary surgeon if necessary.

If you can feed your puppy alongside another dog or a cat, it may help to improve the competition element but this must be done under supervision. Under no circumstances leave the animals unattended for any reason as one may take the other's food. This may cause difficulties between them in the future and you will not know if the puppy has had his full quota of food. One difficulty with this is that a puppy aged 8–12 weeks will be on four meals a day and an adult one to two. You could give your adult smaller meals but do take care that he does not begin to put on weight under a new feeding programme.

Other things to check out with a fussy puppy or non-eater are whether:

- Your puppy is overtired, exhausted or just had a car journey.
- He is reacting to his first or second vaccination.
- The food is too moist, too dry or too rich (the latter is more likely to be responsible for a puppy vomiting or having diarrhoea).
- He is teething. Many puppies have discomfort during this period (usually between the age of 3-6 months) and their gums can swell. Soft foods may be more appropriate until his denture is complete.
- You have added anything such as a vitamin supplement or oil which may have put the pup off due to the texture, taste or smell.
- You are feeding the puppy too much. Even within the breed, the adult sizes can vary by 10cm (4in) or 14kg (30lb) and I never feed the same quantities to dogs and bitches.
- The food is fresh and has not become rank.
- The puppy may require one less meal a day a week or two earlier than the breeder's recommendation.
- The food dish is too small or too large. A small dish or one with a lip may be difficult for a puppy to eat from. Conversely, a large dish may allow the ears to flap in the food or touch the sides of the dish, which a pup might find off-putting.
- He prefers plastic, china, metal bowls, or none at all and would prefer to eat off the floor. This may not be very hygienic but might help him through a fussy stage.

Where the adult goes, the pup is sure to follow.

- The floor surface. Some food bowls make a lot of noise on stone floors. Place them on an old towel or cloth to muffle the noise and prevent the dish moving about, or wedge the dish in a corner. If the pup's identity disc knocks against the side of the dish, the noise may also be off-putting. If so, remember to remove his collar at mealtimes.
- The bowl is too low for him. Try a food stand for the food bowl or metal ring to fit the bowl attached to a wall at a height of around 30cm (1ft). Alternatively, place the bowl on a step for the pup to eat from.
- There are too many noises or distractions where the puppy eats or there is an object which is frightening him.
- You need to change the feeding place or timing.
- The puppy needs to relieve himself prior to eating.
- The addition of gravy may make the meal more appealing and pet food suppliers sell appetising liquids, but I have not tried these myself.

Alternative foods can be expensive and may affect the puppy's stomach. If you do resort to offering alternative foods based on the breeder's or vet's recommendation, buy small quantities for a week or two in case your puppy decides to quickly become bored with it

Products are available which may help to improve a loss of appetite. The only one I have tried and found successful is Malted Kelp tablets, available from Dorwest Herbs. Several homeopathic remedies are also available: Arsenicum Album (commonly known as Arsen Alb), Carbo Vegetabilis (Carbo Veg) and Nux Vomica (Nux Vom).

Sickness, Diarrhoea, Dehydration and Constipation

Your puppy may encounter many problems as he grows up but the most common in the early weeks are sickness and diarrhoea and, perhaps, dehydration as a result of these and constipation. Diarrhoea is the passing of food with too high a water content.

Sickness and diarrhoea can occur after food changes, eating garden debris or as a brief reaction to the puppy's vaccination. If so, report the matter to your vet for your dog's records in case he has further reactions to the annual boosters. However, most cases are caused by minor problems involving the small intestine. Poor diet and food sensitivities such as a wheat allergen can also result in malabsorption, causing the intestine to become inflamed and irritated. This results in food passing through more quickly with insufficient water being removed in the process.

If the condition persists after you have tried the 12-hour starvation-reintroduction of foods, or there are traces of blood, you must consult your veterinary surgeon, whether it is a vaccination reaction or not. The puppy should be wrapped warmly for the journey and carried, not walked. If the condition lasts even after 24-hours starvation in adult dogs, a vet must be consulted.

Other serious signs that you need to consult your vet about immediately are: an arched back, intestinal pain, crying when moved and the passing of blood in either vomit or diarrhoea.

In order to make the correct diagnosis, your vet will need as much background information as possible. On feeding: how often; quantities; foods used; diet changes; whether the dog has eaten or drunk anything that he should not have done such as contaminated water, plants, shrubs, manure, faeces, rabbit pellets, dog excrement, poisons, wood, stones, toys, any other household articles or substances; whether he can keep water down and/or is drinking excessively; time of last meal.

Also generally: the time when the last bout of sickness and diarrhoea occurred and its regularity; signs of illness; temperature (if you have been able to take it); when the dog was last wormed; habit changes; colour and consistency of vomit and diarrhoea; whether the food has been digested or not.

If a foreign body has been swallowed the vet will probably have to X-ray the puppy and operate to remove the object, but drugs will be prescribed in most other cases.

Dehydration can occur much faster in puppies than in adults due to their size, continual sickness, and/or diarrhoea and if they are unable to keep water down, even with glucose.

To check for dehydration, pinch a fold of skin on the pup's back. If it falls back into place without delay the pup is not dehydrated but check regularly if the symptoms continue. If the skin fold tends to stay up or falls slowly into place, you need to consult your vet without delay.

The vet may find it necessary to prescribe anti-sickness, anti-inflammatory and antibiotic drugs. You may be given lectade powder sachets to make up at home into a liquid containing minerals to replace any your puppy may have lost due to the condition. In the worst cases the puppy may be required to stay at the surgery for observation and to be placed on a drip to rehydrate him until the symptoms of illness have subsided.

Water should never be withheld. Glucose could also be added to the water to help with your puppy's energy maintenance.

One easy way to control the quantity of liquid intake is to use a 24ml syringe, available from the vet, to give small quantities regularly into the side of the mouth, not down the back of the throat. Ask your vet to let you know the quantity of liquid (water or lectade) he would expect your puppy to consume during a day for his age, size and weight and then you can calculate how much to administer and the time intervals.

Constipation can be caused by a number of things including a stricture and incorrect feeding. Ensure the diet contains some carbohydrates, for example, biscuits and add about 10% bran. A small dose of liquid paraffin may cure the problem, but if it continues or the puppy is in pain, seek veterinary attention (see Chapter 6 for further details).

When you think a puppy is failing to pass any faeces, he may not be constipated but consuming his own stools, a habit known as coprophagy. This is regarded as natural and normal behaviour in a bitch with puppies until weaning has commenced and puppies will occasionally imitate their mother. Of course, a companion dog may be eating the puppy's faeces. Try to ensure this does not happen by cleaning up immediately after the puppy has passed faeces (further information is given on coprophagy in Chapter 6).

House Training

Most people interpret this purely as teaching a dog to be clean inside the home, but it also includes other behaviour such as whether he is allowed to jump up and whether he is permitted in bedrooms, the kitchen, on settees, behaviour with strangers, and so on. The family should agree collectively what the house rules are; everyone should know them and the dog is not permitted to break them. If different rules are applied by different family members, the dog will be confused and this is unfair, especially if he is chastised for something one person allows that another does not. The pup will not be able to differentiate between standards set by different people. It is particularly important that children are included in this process once they are old enough to understand. A common set of basic training commands should be used by everyone to assist the dog's learning process (see below). It is important that the family learn to use the same commands to avoid confusion.

Close supervision helps greatly for all sorts of house training. Firstly, it helps to correct the dog immediately he has done something wrong. There is little point telling him the error of his ways after the event, he needs to associate your disapproval with the event itself. Secondly, with close contact owners begin to foresee situations and can prevent the dog committing an error.

Young puppies need much closer supervision than older dogs and should not be expected to behave perfectly in a few days or even weeks. It helps to reduce the area they are permitted to live in until they are trained and clean. Temptation should be removed until the dog can be trusted to leave things alone and not damage them. This also includes keeping food out of reach at all times.

Remember, Goldens do love to carry articles around as part of their natural instinct. Except when teething or if left for long periods, most Goldens soon accept and learn not to destroy belongings. If you wish to retain your Golden's retrieving instinct and will to please, never snatch anything from his mouth or play tug-of-war games and always replace an article he should not have with one that he is allowed. This will build his trust and rapport with you. There should be no difficulty in removing any object from a dog if he is taught a simple exercise when young: to 'hold and then give' an article he likes and is allowed to have. The exercise can be repeated three times every few days until he understands. This usually prevents possessiveness developing over toys, food bowls and so on. Everyone in the family should carry out the hold/give exercise to ensure the trust applies to them all. Again, it is important to include the children so the dog does not regard them as lower in the pack order.

Suggested Training Vocabulary

No

Leave

Good dog (or name) to praise

Sit (not 'sit down') or an equivalent. If I intend to work and show a dog I use 'hup' so the command is not confused with 'stand'

Down

Stay the dog to remain in the same position until you return to release him

Wait (before being called to come to you)

Come

Off

Give

Hold

Several principles should be followed in training which are even more important with youngsters. They are to:

* Keep training simple, brief and fun.
* Never train a tired dog or one just fed if it involves exercise (see bloat, Chapter 6).
* Make sure you are in the right frame of mind and not tired.
* Never reward a dog for doing something wrong.

• End training sessions on a positive note. Give the dog something that he can do so you can finish by praising him.

Treat rewards can be offered to train puppies and adults of any age and praise - physical, verbal or both - should always be given as soon as a command or exercise has been completed correctly.

Often a dog fails to carry out a command because the message is not clear enough for him to understand, but not always – some just take longer to learn or understand or have a short concentration span. Always ensure the command is obeyed if you know the dog understands. Gently remind the dog what you want, praise, release and try again later.

Teaching a puppy to be clean becomes easier for him physically the older he is, as the bladder has greater capacity and becomes stronger, but puppies under six months may not be clean for long periods. This process can be assisted greatly by routining the pup and remembering always to let him out immediately after being awoken; first thing in the morning; after every meal time; last thing at night before he goes to bed; and last thing before he is shut in if you have to go out.

It is also wise to observe him either through a window or accompany him to ensure he has done all that is necessary. Most Goldens can be taught to relieve themselves on command.

First select one or two words to cover the act of being clean and use them when you accompany the pup outdoors and he begins the action. He will associate the word(s) with the activity, but the words must be used frequently.

When you use the word(s) later on when you are out with him, it will help the dog to concentrate and/or encourage him to go to toilet. This can help enormously when taking the dog to unfamiliar places later in life.

If problems persist, the routine may need to be altered. Residual smells from previous urination/defecation accidents (remember that a dog's sense of smell is very acute) may remain after cleaning, causing confusion, as the puppy believes that there is the right place to go. To remove these smells it may be necessary to use a strong bleach. I have found the Betterware Pet Sanitary Accident Cleaner to be very effective and it leaves a more pleasant smell than most disinfectants. I have also found it safe to use on all my hard and soft furnishings.

Accidents can sometimes occur due to illness or a bitch coming into or being in season. If you suspect illness, seek veterinary attention. Also, submissiveness can give rise to involuntary emission of urine, particularly in puppies. It can be triggered by fear, punishment, or even pleasure and greetings. Most youngsters grow out of this but may require their confidence to be boosted in the process.

Smacking or any form of punishment that causes suffering to a dog is not only inappropriate but ineffective for all sorts of training. It is more likely to induce fear, submissiveness and sometimes aggression if continually applied rather than corrective behaviour. This applies even more to dogs that are nervous, sensitive and shy and puppies from 7–16 weeks in their critical period of sensitivity. Most puppies or older dogs will respond to the word 'no', a grumbly voice and a tap on the backside, but if anything further is required, it is best to apply the methods used by dogs themselves such as social isolation, a direct eye contact stare, a shake of the skin around the neck, or holding the dog's front feet off the ground.

Will you allow your dog on the bed?

Simply ignoring the dog for 10 minutes or so can be used for young puppies up to 16 weeks, especially those of a shy or nervous disposition who might be unduly stressed by verbal correction. Always remember to make friends again after any punishment when a suitable amount of time has elapsed. Ask the dog to do something that you can praise him for (such as sitting or coming to you when called) and then make a fuss of him.

Routine

It is important for dogs to have a daily routine. This includes times for exercising, feeding, playing and sleeping, and should be worked out to fit in with your and their requirements. Within a short while their body clocks will tell them what they ought to be doing! Faeces should be disposed of daily and outside hard surfaces which are soiled by the dog should be washed and disinfected daily.

Socialising

This is also very important. Everything expected of the dog, or everything it is likely to encounter, should be dealt with by the age of 16 weeks if the dog is expected not to react unfavourably later in life. It may be necessary to risk some socialisation prior to the dog being inoculated. Much depends on each person's individual or family life style but some of the important things are:

- Learning to walk on a lead.
- Some physical restraint, such as grooming.
- Coping with some mechanical household apparatus (cleaners, washing machines).
- Strangers, children if you have none.
- Dogs and other animals.
- Shops, shopping trolleys, prams, bicycles.

- Traffic including lorries and buses.
- Car journeys and/or public transport.

Socialising can and should be continued after the pup is 4 months old, but it is more difficult and time consuming and less effective if the basics have not been put in place.

Care should be taken during the 8–12 week period which is regarded as the critical period of sensitivity. Bad experiences occurring in this time may result in fear affecting the dog for the rest of his life, and more so if the dog has an inherited problem.

Breeders running on a pup of their own breeding should let the pup go for a short break to a friend with or without other dogs, between 8–12 weeks for 2–7 days so he can learn how to deal and cope with stress. Many breeders have had nervousness problems, particularly one of a pair, whereas the littermates in their new homes are fine. The difference is that the ones that have gone to new homes have had to cope with that transition. If you have two pups, they should go individually for a break, not together.

Handling

Handling and touching a puppy gently and frequently on all parts of his anatomy has many advantages. It can include grooming, offering affection and praise or any other pleasing physical contact and must occasionally include looking at the teeth and touching gums.

Playing and handling puppies gently helps to build the bond and trust between dog and owner.

Its main value is that it helps to build the bond of trust between you and the puppy and enables you to carry out the regular check ups required throughout his lifetime, for example, ears, nails, trimming or when he is hurt or ill. It also enables the vet to examine the dog at any time without a problem.

If an aggressive reaction occurs to any form of handling the dog should be rebuked firmly but mildly. Some Goldens do 'talk' or 'smile' with their lips raised or quivering or may be ticklish if their feet are touched, but their other body language should help you differentiate between these traits and signs of aggression such as a low sounding, threatening growl, lips drawn back and raised in creases, standing on tip-toe, the hair along the spine raised up, tail waving slowly, sometimes in a high position (not wagging). In cases of aggression brought on by fear, the eyes may become glazed and blackened.

Some very young puppies may snap and bite hands and ankles. There can be several reasons for this, but it is rarely due to bad temperament as many new dog owners believe. Nevertheless it should be discouraged, particularly if the puppy is likely to have contact with young children who are more likely to snatch their hand away from the pup's sharp teeth and be scratched, and elderly people who have more delicate skin and prominent veins. Older Goldens may try to carry your arm around in their mouth.

Grooming and Trimming

Grooming should be done every 2–3 days. It will enable you to keep an eye on the dog's coat, condition, skin and so on, and any minor ailments can be dealt with before they become a major problem. Carry out spot checks on:

- Eyes for discharge or damage.
- Ears for discharge or swelling.
- Teeth and gums for plaque, inflammation (gingivitis) and foreign bodies.
- Paws for cuts.
- Nails for length.
- Hair for condition and knots.
- Skin for spots, lumps, insect bites and parasites.
- Genitals for wounds, inflammation and discharge.
- Mammary glands for tumours, and milk about 8 weeks after a season.

Do consult a vet if anything gives you cause for concern.

Very little needs to be trimmed on a young puppy under 6 months of age. The hair around the feet may need tidying a few times to the shape of the foot. An ordinary pair of straight edge scissors will suffice at this age. No feathering on the backs of any legs or under the brisket should be cut and, as the tail hair is often still growing and unfolding at this age, I often snip only the excess length off of the tip (a thumb's length from the tail end).

As the coat continues to grow, by about 6 months it will gradually require more attention. As well as the feet, the hair on the ears and around the neck may need thinning so that the ears can breathe to prevent infection. The tail will also need to be fanned with scissors from 2.5cm (1in) beyond the tail tip to about 13cm (5in) in length at the base to prevent the hair becoming too straggly. This also encourages the tail hair to thicken. If the hair on the back of the hocks becomes very thick it will require shortening. Straight edge scissors can be used for all this, unless the dog is going to be shown (see Chapter 8).

When a dog begins a change of coat, brush daily to remove the dead hair. Less will then have to be cleaned off your furnishings.

Nail trimming is important for every Golden. This includes all feet and maybe the dew claws. A few breeders remove these still, but most do not. Keeping the nails short will ensure that your dog is comfortable and does not develop splayed feet.

You will need proper nail trimmers which can be purchased at most pet shops or from traders at shows. It is easier to trim the nails on young pups as they are not so large or hard as on adults. Care must be taken not to cut into the quick as this will cause bleeding and the dog will be reluctant to allow you to cut the nails again. Do a little at a time if the quick is not visible. You should be able to see it on grey/pink nails but it is more difficult to see on black nails. It sometimes helps to wet the nails first.

Teething

Your pup will change his teeth between 3–6 months. Try to avoid handling the mouth too much at this time. The pup may find hard foods a little difficult to eat during the change.

Teething toys and flavoured/sterilised bones can help to prevent the puppy chewing and damaging household belongings whilst he is teething. Try not to let him chew objects that will splinter and become lodged in his throat or small articles which can be easily swallowed and rest in his intestines or stomach or damage his teeth or bite. Keep a check on the teeth to make certain all the first teeth come out or are pushed out by the new teeth. Some of the canines do take a little longer. If any remain in or become a problem consult your vet.

Teeth also need to be kept clean. Chewing of bones and certain toys designed for this purpose were discussed in Chapter 1. Most vets will only descale teeth under anaesthetic so,

A young pup will try most things to see if they taste nice or are worth a chew!

for this reason, I prefer to use a descaler which can be purchased from trade stands at shows. Toothbrushes and toothpaste specifically designed for dogs have also become more readily available in recent years.

Exercising

Dogs enjoy being exercised for many reasons, such as time spent with their owner, playing games, and being out in the fresh air in different surroundings. It also helps to keep them fit (mentally and physically) and to burn up their energy. If you have more than one dog and they play together frequently this helps to provide some of the exercise needed but should never be a substitute for free running (in the case of adults) in a safe environment.

Playing regularly provides much of the exercise a very young puppy needs. Too much exercise too soon must be avoided. Running up and down stairs and jumping on and off furniture is not to be encouraged during the pup's main growth period, which is up to 9 months. Care should also be taken from 9–18 months when the bones and joints are finally setting. For the same reason young children are not allowed to run marathons!

Sleep is also important for the growing pup. If possible, the pup should have several uninterrupted sleeping periods during the day. It is particularly important to maintain this until the pup is about 6 months, especially if you have children or regular visitors.

Exercise should be avoided one hour before and after meal times throughout the dog's life. This is to prevent bloat which Goldens can get occasionally (see Chapter 6). An approximate exercise guide is:

7–14 weeks: (until the puppy is fully inoculated and can go out into public places) free exercise in the garden for 10–15 min periods, 3–4 times per day and as weather permits. If your puppy gets wet, dry him with a towel, especially his undercarriage.

14–20 weeks: free exercise in the garden can be extended within the daily routine. Hard surfaces help to keep nails shorter and feet more 'cat like'. Exercise on a lead along paths and roads should be limited to 2 x 5 min sessions per day.

20 weeks–9 months: exercise can be increased to 2 x 10 min sessions per day.

9–12 months: exercise can be increased to 2 x 15 min sessions per day.

12 months +: increase gradually to fit in with the dog's requirements and your own timetable.

Only let your dog off a lead in a public place once you have trained him to return to you when called. Initially, an extending lead can be used to ensure obedience to your commands but it should never take the place of free running once the dog has been taught to respond to you. Never call the dog solely to put his lead on at the end of the walk as he will soon learn that the fun ends when the lead appears and then he will be less likely to obey. Try calling him several times during the walk, praising him, giving him a toy or titbit and then releasing him to do his own thing again. You will probably find that he doesn't take his eyes off you! Care should be taken if you are likely to meet adults, children or other dogs on your walks that your dog does not jump up or run towards them.

Training

Many of the comments made under the house training and socialising sections are relevant to general and specialised training. Learn to understand your dog and gain his respect. When you take your dog out you want him to be under control if the need arises. The basic requirements are for him to:

- Heel on lead and remain in close proximity off lead if required.
- Sit on or off lead.
- Stay on or off lead.
- Come when called.
- Instant down (this could save your dog's life in an emergency).

All this training can begin in the garden or home prior to the puppy being fully inoculated. The commands required for this are: Heel, Sit/Down, Wait and Come. When using commands, say the dog's name first, then the command and then praise and/or reward.

With puppies aged up to 5 months, I would only do about five minutes training each day interspersed with lots of play and praise.

Is this what you mean by 'Down Stay'?

To help a puppy get used to wearing a lead, place a small collar on him for short periods whilst he is at home, but do not leave him unattended in case the collar catches on an object and strangles him (this also applies to adult dogs). Do this before a meal time so he associates the experience with something pleasant. Then put a lead on him in the garden, encourage him to walk to heel for a treat and praise him if he walks forward with you. As the territory is familiar, few problems are usually experienced. Problems can occur when leaving familiar territory. Initially select a quiet place with few distractions and use treats to encourage the puppy to walk forward. If you have another dog who walks to heel already on a lead, a puppy

**With a clear hand signal and verbal command 'wait', teach your dog to remain or 'wait'
in the car until you tell him to come out.**

will enjoy walking with him and this will build up his confidence. Once the puppy is confident, try him on his own. When he is used to the lead and heeling in a reasonably controlled manner, introduce other distractions, such as traffic but take care not to overwhelm your puppy (for example, by walking him beside a busy dual carriageway before he is old enough to handle the experience).

Collars should be checked periodically to make sure that they are not too tight for the growing puppy.

Dogs have to be taught to sit. The most effective way is to place a treat under the pup's nose, say the dog's name and 'Sit', and get him to lift his head, at the same time applying a little pressure on his rump with your other hand. If this does not work, place one hand at the back of his thighs with a little forward pressure. Leave him in the sitting position for a few seconds before praising him.

'Down' can be taught by offering a treat on the ground when the dog is already sitting. Most dogs will lie down to pick up the treat. Say the dog's name and 'Down' and keep him in the down for a few seconds before releasing him. If necessary apply a little pressure with your free hand to keep him on the ground. Once the exercise has been completed allow him to have the reward.

The stay can be taught in any position but it is easier to teach the dog when he is either sitting or lying down. The dog should be on a lead so he can be corrected easily if necessarily. Step away from your dog for a few seconds and then return. Avoid making eye contact. If he moves, replace him on the same spot and repeat the exercise briefly several times until success is achieved. Gradually increase the distance you walk away and the time you are away until you can eventually move out of sight.

Once the dog has learnt to stay you can begin the recalls. The recall commands are 'Sit', 'Wait' and 'Come'. Treats or a favourite toy can be used to ensure a prompt response. If the dog fails to return immediately never chase him; either lie down flat on the ground or run backwards away from the dog. Most will come to you, out of curiosity if nothing else!

Your pup also needs to be trained with other dogs so that he is not worried by seeing other dogs when out, thus disobeying your commands. If you want to show your dog and do basic obedience, it is wise not to teach your dog to sit all the time otherwise he will try to sit in the breed ring when he should be standing. Tell the trainer, and most will permit your dog to stand instead. To retain your dog's interest never allow training to become boring and too repetitive. Lessons should be kept short and interesting. A number of clubs also take part in the Kennel Club Good Citizen Dog scheme.

Playing

Most Goldens are very young at heart and enjoy playing into their older years and some for their whole lifetime. They have been nicknamed the 'Peter Pans' of dogdom.

Playing can help their development but take care not to overtire or over-exercise a young puppy, and do not let him be teased by adults or children. Tug-of-war games should not be permitted for several reasons:

- I have found that it can build up excess neck muscle, causing heaviness across the shoulders – this only need be of concern for show dogs or those with show potential.
- There is always the worry that teeth may be pulled out of line or damaged, especially in the front – again this is mainly a concern for show dogs or those with show potential.
- If the dog is permitted to win the tug-of-war games, it may lead to him being more dominant and believing he is higher in the pack order than the person playing the game.
- It may make him 'hard mouthed' and unwilling to give up an object. This may result in problems if he finds a treasured object or you wish your dog to become a gundog worker.

Worming

Your puppy should have been wormed several times before collection. You should check when it was done last, so you can prepare for it to be done at 4-weekly intervals up to the age of 6 months and twice yearly thereafter or if signs or symptoms occur.

Try to avoid worming your puppy at the same time as he has the vaccination. If the pup has a reaction you will not know whether it is to the injection or the worming.

Some vets recommend that puppies are wormed at 2-weekly intervals up to 6 months. From my experience this is excessive (unless the puppy shows signs of worms) and it can upset their stomachs.

Only use worming products obtained through your veterinary practice. Do not use products obtained elsewhere, whether or not they are cheaper (unless they are the same brands dispensed by the vet), as they may scour out the puppy's stomach.

Faeces should be disposed of after as soon as possible after worming, especially if you have children.

CHAPTER FOUR

Adult Care

Maturity

From the age of 12 months onwards, no dog is regarded as a puppy but, given his disposition, a Golden is likely to act like one for some time after. He will not grow any taller but the processes of growing up mentally and maturing physically are very gradual and generally take place between the ages of 1–3 years. On some slower-maturing lines, physical maturity may not be complete until the dog is 4–6 years old.

Feeding

Much of this has been covered in Chapter 3. At 12 months your Golden will be on two meals per day and, by 18 months, either one or two meals depending on the feeding regime you choose. Remember, if a diet change is required for any reason, even only because the dog loses interest, introduce any new foods over a 5–10 day period to prevent stomach upsets. This is difficult if a dog suddenly refuses to eat a brand of food. You may be able to prevent loose stools by adding boiled rice to a new food.

Goldens over a year old do not require very high protein foods and most ordinary diets will suffice. Special diets are readily available nowadays for dogs being worked and leading a very active life style, bitches to be bred from or animals with particular requirements.

Training

If you wish to pursue some form of working activity, basic obedience on and off the lead is essential, as most trainers do not have the time when taking a class to wait whilst you catch your runaway dog. It will embarrass you and, if it happens often, will make you and your dog unpopular, not only because of the disruption but because bad behaviour can be infectious.

Generally, males respond to gradual specialist training from about 12 months and bitches from about 15–18 months. I do not expect miracles from either but especially from bitches until they are 2+ years old due to the Golden's slow mental development compared to some other breeds. Very experienced handlers may be able to achieve far better results far more quickly from lines bred purely for working but this usually follows many years of observation, living with and training of the breed.

Do remember that some bitches may be less trainable or responsive 6–8 weeks prior to a season. A few males may also be affected by hormone imbalance,. Hormone injections or castration may help or cure the problem. There are no restrictions on neutered animals competing in working events in the United Kingdom. In the United Kingdom, bitches in season are not permitted to enter or attend working events. This rule does not apply to breed shows, though I know many stud dog owners who wish it did.

Car Travel and Holidays

Never leave a dog in a car in warm weather or if the sun is focused on the back window, whether a window is open or not. Cars heat up very quickly and dogs can become very distressed and die from heat exhaustion. Car travel on hot days can also present difficulties unless the car is fitted with air-conditioning. Small fans can be fitted inside to help keep dogs cooler. Always carry spare drinking water for the dog, no matter how short your journey, in case you become stuck in a traffic jam or break down. Non-spill water bowls are also available for use in cars. A wet flannel or the sprays which are used to mist plants are very useful items to have in the car for your dogs during summer journeys.

Most of these points are very relevant if you holiday in hotter months and your dogs are not permitted on beaches, in pubs, restaurants and so on. It is possible to purchase tailgate guards (see photo on page 18), not to be confused with dog guards. These allow the tailgate to be left up - thus allowing air to circulate - and can be secured so that the dog cannot escape or be removed unless by the owner. Many people who take part in canine activities have these fitted to their cars, or use car cages, so that their dogs can attend events in safety and comfort. Sheets can also be used to cover the car (which absorb some of the sun's rays) together with window grills and a non-spill water bowl. Regular checks on the car and its occupants is, of course vital, whatever the conditions. Manufacturers of tailgate guards and car cages advertise in the dog press and canine magazines.

If you take your dog to the beach, remember that some local authorities limit access to dogs, for part of or even the whole year. You should ensure your dog has toileted prior to going on a beach but, if he soils the sand, remove the faeces. Some authorities provide such facilities for dog owners, but always go prepared with polythene bags. Keep your dog on a lead, especially if the area is crowded. If not, only let him off the lead if he is controllable and can be supervised so that he will not make a nuisance of himself with children, adults and other dogs, or become lost due to unfamiliar surroundings.

If you allow your dog to paddle or swim in the sea, remember that excess salt water will flush the dog out and he will require plenty of fresh drinking water. Do not permit your dog to gulp or drink the fresh water too fast as he is likely to bring it up again.

Whatever the time of year you holiday, check whether you are allowed to take a dog into your accommodation. Mention his size, whether he sleeps in a crate, the number if you have more than one, and ascertain if any charges will be incurred. A car can get very cold if you expect your pet to sleep in it overnight in the cooler months.

Grooming, Care and Trimming

As Goldens mature, the feathering on their legs and brisket continues to grow, adding to their beauty. Their feet and tail hair and nails will continue to grow unless trimmed as described in Chapter 3. Regular grooming is important because it:
- Keeps dogs cleaner.
- Keeps your home cleaner if dogs are kept mainly indoors.
- Maintains the bond with your Golden and provides him with quality time.
- Helps to find exterior health problems sooner.
  Frequency is also important. I recommend :
- Grooming at least once a week.

- Spot checks at least once a week.
- Trimming at least once a month.
- Bathing at least twice a year or as situations dictate.
  There are several methods in addition to grooming that help keep dogs clean. They are:
- See Chapter 8 for details of shampoos and cleaners.
- Using wet and dry towels instead of bathing.
- Using dry chamois leather to absorb moisture.
- Using baby powder to absorb moisture. When it is dry you brush it out and most of the dirt is removed.
- Using baby oil to remove grease or tar.

Make sure that any shampoos and conditioners are thoroughly rinsed out of the coat, as any residue will cause skin irritation and dullness of coat. To prevent water or shampoo entering the ear canal, or shampoo getting into the eyes, I do not bath the dog's head or ears. If these areas need to be cleaned, they can be wiped with a wet towel or sponge.

Damp hands, sellotape and rubber gloves can all be used to help remove dog hair from clothes and furnishings.

Vaccinations

Booster injections are due annually from the date of the pup's second vaccination. Kennel Cough nasal drops have to be given twice a year to keep your dog fully protected.

Worming

I recommend that worming is done twice a year or as required if signs are seen in a dog's faeces or if his general condition and health make you suspect infestation (see Chapter 3).

A Bitch's Seasons

The first season is not normally very heavy but probably will last the full 21 days. Take note of the first day the bitch shows colour on each occasion, confine her to home and garden for the duration and check the season finishes on day 21. Some do last a little longer. It is also useful to make a note of the time difference between each bitch's season. Most keep to a fairly regular pattern. My experience is that the shorter the period the more reliable the regularity. This information helps you to plan for holidays, shows and so on.

Confinement can result in a bitch putting on a little weight, so watch her diet or reduce it marginally. Her nails may grow due to lack of road work, so it may be necessary to clip them.

Dealing with Emergencies

Many of the emergencies described below may result in a dog becoming unconscious or shocked. Neither artificial respiration nor cardiac massage must be used unless the dog is unconscious and it would appear that he may die without your aid. First attempt to find out if your dog is unconscious. Check for responses to:

- Calling his name.
- Heartbeat.
- Blinking.

- Retraction of a pulled limb.
- Gum colour after it is pressed. The gum should be pink and return to being pink almost immediately if the heart is beating. If this does not happen, or the gums are blue or very pale, cardiac massage may be required to restore circulation, and immediately if you cannot detect the heart beating.

Second, look for shock. Blue or pale gums are a symptom indicating circulation failure. Shock can be life-threatening and needs to be dealt with before injuries. It may affect the heart rate either by lowering or raising the rate. (The normal rate is about 70–100 beats per minute.) Other signs include weakness and cold extremities such as the feet. The treatment of shock is dealt with in Chapter 6.

Artificial Respiration

1. Lay the dog on his side – if possible with his head lower than his rump, so that the blood travels to the brain more easily.
2. Clear the airway by ensuring the neck is straight.
3. Check that both the mouth and nose airways are clear by pulling the tongue forward and by using two fingers in the mouth to remove any debris or excess saliva.
4. Kneel on the ground behind the dog. Lift up the dog's head slightly onto your knees to extend the neck and assist the opening of the airways to the lungs.
5. Gently clasping the muzzle shut with both hands, place your mouth over the nose and blow until you see the chest expand. Pause to let the lungs deflate. The procedure needs to be repeated about 15–20 times per minute. Check the pulse rate every other breath to ensure the heart is beating. (Normal respiration is 15–30 breaths per minute.)

Cardiac Massage

1. Lay the dog on its side as for **1.** above, unless the dog is very fat in which case he should be placed on his back.
2. Kneel behind the dog's back and lean slightly forward. Place the palm of one hand on the chest behind the elbow, with the other hand on top at right angles. In the case of a fat dog on his back, press on the chest.
3. Press down and forward firmly about 70–100 times per minute. This pumping action assists the blood to travel to the brain.

Both procedures can be applied to restart breathing, the heart beating and improve circulation until the gums return to their normal colour.

Apply 10 seconds of mouth-to-nose artificial respiration and alternate with 25 cardiac massages until the heart beats and gum colour returns. The artificial respiration should be continued until the dog begins to breathe.

Collapse or Comatose State

There can be many reasons why a dog collapses, including airway obstructions (see below), serious illness, and so on. When it happens to a dog that has enjoyed good health:

1. Check the airways are clear of obstructions and discharges.
2. If the dog is unconscious, the gums remain blue or pale and you believe the dog will die without aid, carry out cardiac massage to try to restore circulation.
3. If this fails, try mouth-to-nose artificial respiration.

4.   Keep the dog warm.
5.   Seek veterinary attention immediately and continue the artificial respiration on the way if you have secured the help of a person to drive.

Dog Fights

This is a subject few people in Goldens wish to discuss as the breed mainly has a good temperament. However, fighting is a natural dog trait and a few Goldens may fight if they wish to establish supremacy over food, because of a bitch in season or to defend themselves. By watching the body language between your own dogs and establishing yourself as pack leader you can prevent it occurring.

Fortunately, most Golden owners will never encounter such an incident during their dog ownership, but every owner should know what to do as parting fighting dogs can be very difficult and distressing.

Firstly, remove any dogs not involved from the scene. See if the dogs will respond to you by shouting the command to 'leave'. If this works, segregate the dogs quickly before they can begin again. If it does not work, do not continue as shouting or screaming will excite the dogs further and make matters worse. Using water from a nearby container, such as a water bowl, bucket or a hose can be very effective. Hitting dogs will not work as they do not respond to pain. Other alternatives are to lift the dog's back feet off the ground. This causes him to have less power, and the surprise is enough usually to make him break or loosen his grip. Never lift the dog up by his front feet and show the underside of his belly to the other dog.

Dog fights are unlikely to occur between individuals who know and accept their place in the pack order.

Alternatively, try to move the dogs to a doorway and, with one dog either side of the threshold, close the door.

If collars are being worn, find a stick, place it in one of the collars and twist it so that it tightens and cuts the dog's air supply momentarily. This should be sufficient to ensure that the grip is released and the dogs can be parted. For subsequent action and treatment see Chapter 6, Dog Bites.

Take care if you become involved in parting fighting dogs because they will be oblivious to anyone but the other dog and you may get bitten. If you are caught in their crossfire, it will be accidental and they should not be blamed for this. Tetanus protection must be up-to-date if the dogs have broken your skin with their teeth.

If the dogs involved in the fight live on the premises together, they should be kept apart whilst they calm down and are cleaned up and treated. Try to mix them carefully after this as soon as possible but, if their body language indicates they still have a problem, leave it for a day and try again. It is not always possible to house dogs together after such an incident.

Drowning

Water can be a lot of fun for Goldens but it also presents dangers. Only allow your dog to enter water under supervision and when it is safe to do so. Some Goldens love water and are able to sense it even if you are unaware of its presence. If a river is in flood or has dangerous currents and your dog is uncontrollable near water, keep him on the lead. Do not allow a dog to walk on ice-covered ponds, pools or rivers; he may become submerged and trapped beneath the ice. There is also a risk at the seaside. If a dog swims further and further out from land and refuses to return to his handler, he can eventually become too tired to return.

If your dog is in trouble, try to obtain help, professional if possible. Do not try to rescue the dog yourself unless you will be in no danger. Great thought needs to be taken over this decision as you may be thinking irrationally. Each year, tragedies occur when owners drown attempting to retrieve their dogs, yet the dogs have survived.

Never enter deep water in the colder months as the dog can exist for longer in the colder temperature than man before hypothermia affects him. Never walk on ice to retrieve your dog.

Never allow your dog to enter water with a collar on, in case it becomes entangled in weed or hooked up on anything below the water line. It is also dangerous to allow your dog to jump into water, regardless of how spectacular the sight is, in case he should accidentally impale himself on an object hidden below the water line.

If you are able to remove the dog from water, near-drowning is suspected and the dog appears unconscious, you should

1. Check his airway.
2. Remove any debris from around his mouth.
3. Drain water out of his lungs by holding him up off the ground by his hind legs for about 30 seconds.
4. If he is not breathing, carry out cardiac massage and mouth-to-nose artificial resuscitation until he begins to breathe.
5. Begin drying and keeping the dog warm in case he is also affected by hypothermia and take him to the vet.

Electrocution

As with everything, prevention is easier than cure but should this occur:

1. Switch off the electricity.
2. If this is not possible, do not touch the dog, but find a wooden object long and strong enough to enable you to move the dog away from the source of electricity.
3. If the dog is unconscious and his gums are blue or pale, carry out cardiac massage to try to restore circulation.
4. If (3) fails, carry out mouth-to-nose resuscitation until you arrive at the vets.

Eye Injury or Foreign Body in the Eye

1. Prevent the dog from rubbing or scratching his affected eye.
2. If the dog is in pain apply a cold wet pad.
3. Take the dog to the vet immediately.

Falls

My only experience has been with my parents' first Golden, when Simon fell over a low sand cliff. The fall was about 30ft but luckily he was only winded and dazed and we could get to him. Where the dog is accessible:

1. Check him for injuries. If any are visible, transport him to a vet quickly. You may need to move the dog on a board if you suspect spinal injuries or fractures.
2. Comfort the dog as he may be disoriented or in shock (see Chapter 6, 'Shock').
3. If the dog appears unconscious, check him out by following the procedures described above. If necessary, carry out cardiac massage or mouth-to-nose artificial respiration. Where a dog is inaccessible:
1. If there is time, find someone to stay at the site.
2. If not, make a note of as many landmarks as possible to describe to rescuers.
3. Notify the police and any other professional rescue services that operate in the vicinity.
4. Once the dog is retrieved, follow whatever procedure is required as described above.

Loss of Blood

1. Check any wounds for extraneous material that can be moved easily.
2. Apply a large dressing and pressure to the wound, but not too much if the wound still has small pieces of debris in it. Replace as necessary.
3. If blood is spurting, apply a tourniquet above the wound. The pressure must be released every 15 minutes.
4. Keep the dog warm and get him to a vet immediately.

Obstructions

Obstructions in airways caused by foreign bodies can occur in:

The mouth

Signs are excess salivation and pawing or rubbing at the face. Inspect the mouth and all round the teeth, remove the article if safe and possible to do so. If not, seek veterinary attention quickly.

The nose

Signs are a runny or bleeding nose, pus discharge from nostrils, head shaking and nose rubbing. Inspect the nostrils but, as the article is unlikely to be visible, it is most likely that veterinary attention will be required quickly.

The throat

Signs are choking and/or unconsciousness. The most common obstruction is a small ball.

1. Try to find someone to help if there is time, as removal is likely to require the aid of a second person.
2. Hold the dog's mouth open as wide as possible. Do not prevent the dog breathing through his nose.
3. Hold the tongue as far forward as it will go and check if you can see the object.
4. If the object is a ball, round or smooth and unlikely to inflict damage by removal, pull the object forward - either with a hand, tongs or forceps. If there is a risk of pushing it back further or causing damage, you may have to leave well alone and seek veterinary help immediately. The dog may need to be anaesthetised to ensure the object's safe removal. Alternatively, it may be possible to dislodge the object by pressing the ribs with force.

Trapped by Barbed Wire

1. Keep the dog calm and as still as possible.
2. Protect your hands with any available thing so that you can try to remove the wire.
3. You may need to protect yourself from the dog if he is reacting badly.
4. Use wire cutters if any are close at hand.
5. Deal with the wounds (see Chapter 6).

Stolen and Lost Dogs

Stolen Dogs

1. Notify the police and give an accurate description of your Golden with a photograph if possible and say whether he had any identification.
2. Give details of how and when he was stolen.
3. Notify the breed's rescue services (see Breed Club secretaries, Appendix 2).
4. If your dog has been microchipped or tattooed notify the appropriate registrars.
5. Inform your insurance company if your Golden is insured. Some policies include a reward or offer other financial assistance to help you find your dog. If not, offer a reward.
6. Check every other day with the police, local veterinary surgeons, local dog/civic warden and rescue kennels to see if they have any news of your Golden or had a dog brought in matching his description. There is often some confusion over identification between Golden Retrievers and yellow Labradors. Every possibility is worth following up.
7. Have a sheet printed with a description of your dog, including a photograph, details of any reward and a contact name and telephone number and circulate it as widely as possible in all veterinary surgeries, pet shops, shops, on lamp posts and so on.
8. Use the local press and radio. They sometimes have a lost and found pets column/notice.
9. If you do become reunited with your dog, notify the authorities you alerted to his disappearance.

Lost Dogs

Some dogs may bolt from home if they are frightened by fireworks or thunder. If the fear subsides the dog should be able to trace his way home by scent, but if he becomes too disoriented he may get really lost and searches will be required.

1. If a dog is lost whilst out walking, retrace your route to the starting point. A dog will usually find his way back to this point.
2. If you have to leave the area to report the loss, leave an article with your scent on, or return with one if you have nothing on you at the time.
3. Return regularly and keep checking the surrounding area, as dogs are often found close to where they were lost even up to several weeks later. If people unknown to the dog are helping in your search, instruct them not to startle or approach the dog quickly as he may panic and run off again. If he becomes disoriented he may try to hide. A disoriented dog may not recognise or acknowledge his owner for several hours or days but, with much reassurance, love, warmth and food, he should return to normal.
4. If you do not find your dog after searching the area for about an hour, follow the procedures 1–8 for a stolen dog.

    If a dog escapes from the car after an accident and you are some distance away from home, note the exact area as most dogs will return to the site (if not too badly hurt), even though they are unfamiliar with their surroundings.

    Your dog's return will be aided if he is wearing his collar and name tag (a legal requirement if you are in a public place) and if he is microchipped or tattooed.

Traffic Accident

1. Try to hold up the traffic, or ask someone else to do so whilst you deal with the dog.
2. If the dog is badly injured and immobile, place a coat or blanket over him to keep him warm. If he appears to be mobile, he will probably be distressed, panicky and try to run away. You may need to improvise in order to restrain him with a make-shift lead.
3. The dog may act out of character and bite anyone who touches him, so you will need to:
    (a) wear gloves if possible, to protect yourself.
    (b) find something soft to loop gently over the dog's muzzle, but not so that his breathing is restricted.
4. Move the dog to the side of the road as soon as possible. A blanket is very practical for this purpose but, if you suspect dislocations, fractures or spinal injuries, the dog should only be moved on a board.
5. If there is a loss of blood or the dog is unconscious follow the procedures described above.
6. Ascertain where the nearest veterinary surgery is and transport the dog, on a board if necessary. If the dog does not belong to you, see if any identification is visible, such as on a collar or a tattoo number in the ear, so that you or the appropriate authorities can notify the owner.
7. If you are responsible for the accident you must report it to the police.

First Aid/Medicine Chest

When you have your first dog it is unlikely you will give any thought to this, but it does help to be prepared for certain emergencies and minor ailments the dog will experience during his lifetime. Your own experiences will guide you, but it may help if I share how I have dealt with this aspect of dog ownership. Listed below are items I like to have at hand.

Adhesive tape	*Lectade – mineral, salt replacement
*Antibiotic – cream, powder	Liquid paraffin – constipation
*Antihistamine	Meat tenderiser – stings
Antiseptic - Savlon, TCP	New skin – foot wounds
Aspirin – pain reliever	Olive oil – tar remover
Baby talcum powder	Potassium Permanganate - to stem
Benylin (chesty coughs) – tonsillitis,	bleeding nails, when mixed with water
gulping	Sterile, airtight containers for
Cotton wool	urine/faeces samples (eg 35mm film roll
Crepe bandage 5cm (2in) wide for	holders)
emergency muzzle (see overleaf)	Sterile dressing
Disposable gloves	*Syringes (see photo on page 73)
*Ear cleaner	Thermometer – digitals are the easiest
*Elizabethan collar - prevents scratching	to use and read and can be used on
or chewing of wounds	very young puppies
*Eye ointment - conjunctivitis	*Tooth cleaner/brush/paste or
*Flea treatments	bicarbonate of soda
Glucose for energy	Tweezers
*Kaogel	Washing soda crystals – emetic
Kaolin – stomach upsets	*Available from veterinary surgeries.

Any equipment used for administering medicine should be sterilised before use. Always wash your hands before and after administering any medicine.

Administering Medicine
Liquids
Use a syringe if the liquid cannot be added to food, but it is better to place it on the dog's tongue. It is much easier to use a syringe when measuring quantities, preventing spillage and administering into a dog's mouth. This should always be done through the side of the mouth, not down the back of the throat which may cause choking and the liquid getting into the lungs.

Tablets
If they cannot be added to meals, hide them in a knob of butter, slip into the back of the throat, and rub the dog's neck to make him swallow. I find placing the tablet on the tongue and making the dog swallow does not work very well.

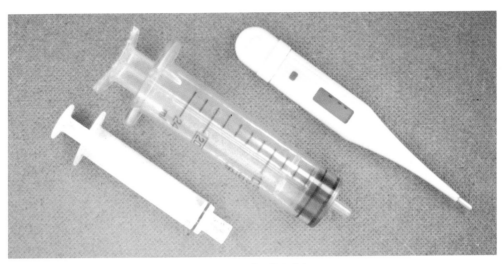

Example of syringes and a digital thermometer.

How to administer a liquid medicine into the side of the mouth.

Place the tablet on the very back of the dog's tongue or in his throat and rub the throat to make the dog swallow.

Emergency Muzzle

Take approximately 1m (3ft) strip of crepe bandage. Place the middle across the bridge of the muzzle, cross underneath, bring back up and tie half a knot, applying enough pressure to prevent the dog being able to open his jaw fully, but not so much that he cannot breathe. Cross underneath and then take behind the back of the neck near the ears and tie two reef knots.

Making Provision for your Dog

Another topic owners find difficult to think about, discuss and arrange is what will happen to their dog in the event of their mental and/or physical incapacitation and death, but everyone owes it to their pets to make appropriate arrangements in their will. This will ensure your wishes are carried out. You should also inform the family or close friends to prevent any delay in the dog being looked after. If you have no-one to look after the dog, contact a breed rescue service who should be able to advise you. You may also wish to make some financial provision.

Ch Tokeida Temptress of Mossburn (aged 8 years).

CHAPTER FIVE

Elderly Care

Ageing – What Is It?

Each dog will age at his own rate depending on a number of factors that have affected his life such as care, feeding, illnesses, wear and tear on joints, environment and his genetic makeup. Ageing may be very gradual or rapid.

Golden Retrievers can begin to show signs of ageing as early as 4 years when the hair on their muzzle or in their coat begins to turn grey, but others may be 8 or more before any outward signs begin to show. This shows up particularly on the golden coats as opposed to the cream. Inwardly, however, a dog in good health will be about eight before his organs begin to work less effectively. Better nutrition, veterinary care and knowledge are generally increasing the life expectancy of dogs.

General Visible Signs of Ageing

- anaemia
- bad breath
- calluses on pressure points (elbows and hocks)
- confusion if the daily routine is altered and particularly if objects are moved when poor eyesight is a factor
- constipation and/or straining
- cystitis
- dehydration
- dental problems
- diarrhoea with or without traces of blood
- eyesight, cataract, cloudiness on the lens
- hearing
- incontinence – urinary or faecal
- increased thirst
- intolerance, due to the dog believing he is wiser than his owner!
- lack of coordination
- less active, slower, calmer, may sleep more
- muscle wastage – mainly on the hind quarters and over the skull and spine
- persistent or occasional lack of bladder control without signs of remorse
- poor coat, thinner, less shiny and greying
- senility, forgetfulness, a whimpering bark for no apparent reason
- sickness with or without traces of blood
- skin greasy, dandruff and warts
- smaller or increased appetite
- stiffness after long periods of rest and substantial or lively exercise
- weight loss

Males

- perineal hernia, where the rectum and anus muscles shrink and rupture, which may allow a hernia to develop. If it affects the rectum, constipation is likely with traces of blood in faeces. If the bladder passes into the hernia, urination may be difficult or impossible.
- prostrate gland enlargement
- testicular cancer – affects more than half the males where a testicle has been retained since puppyhood. This is why vets recommend early removal.

Bitches

- pyometra (see Chapter 11)
- mammary tumours

Non Visible Signs of Ageing

- arthritis
- full or impacted anal glands
- blood vessel and heart problems
- hormonal imbalances
- immune system problems
- kidney failure
- liver disease
- respiratory problems
- spondylosis

Signs of Ageing

A list of potential visible signs of an ageing dog is given in the table on page 75, but some of these may be the result of an illness or disease not directly linked to the ageing process. See Chapters 6 and 11.

Well-being of Your Elderly Golden

There are a number of ways owners can assist their Golden's general well-being once they begin to notice the signs of ageing, although many procedures should have been followed from the beginning.

Weight Watching

One of the most important rules to follow is never to allow the dog to become overweight or obese. This places additional stress on the dog's structure, organs and systems at any time of his life but obesity in an ageing dog can result in an acceleration of many diseases and conditions, premature and accelerated ageing and a shorter life expectancy. Weight reduction can frequently reduce the symptoms of a condition, but obesity is much easier to prevent than cure.

The domestic dog depends entirely on his owner for his food, so the position should be completely controllable with no excuse for overfeeding.

A number of other major risks for an overweight dog include: overheating (because fat is an insulator), anaesthetic, and over-exertion leading to heat-stroke. The last two can, of course, be fatal. An easy way to detect that your Golden is overweight is to:
- Check that you can feel the dog's ribs easily, making minor allowances for a dog with a thick coat.
- Observe whether he has lost his waistline.
- Observe and feel if he is carrying excess rolls of fat across the top of his shoulders.
- Observe the dog when he is moving to see if he rolls from side to side. Some vastly overweight dogs will move towards you with an extremely wide front leg action.

The only way a dog can lose weight is to receive less food than he requires for his daily intake. As a guide to reducing weight, give about two-thirds of the maintenance level per day and nothing else between meals. Most canned dog foods and tripe are less than one-third the calorie content of dry complete meals and biscuit. Alternatively, low-calorie balanced prescription diets are available from the vet. If your dog likes boiled cabbage you can add some to the meals to increase their bulk. The calorie content of this is negligible. I have used this method successfully with no problems. Boiled rice is also a good substitute for biscuit.

The other suggestion is to feed the meal(s) earlier in the day so that the dog can burn off the calorie content. Feeding in the evening, when most dogs tend to be less active, only assists the fat build-up process. Exercise should not be used as a method of reducing weight, as it may be a health risk for an obese dog and it only burns off a few calories.

If you need to reduce your dog's weight:
- Weigh your dog initially.
- Decide on an optimum target weight based on professional advice.
- Work out a feeding regime with some exercise.

- Weekly weight loss should not exceed about 1kg (2.2lb).
- Weigh the dog every two weeks to monitor the weight loss.
- If there is no decrease after two weeks, reduce the meal quantity to one-half of the maintenance weight. If the decrease is too great, increase the food quantity marginally.
- Continue the regime until target weight is achieved. It should then be safe to return to the appropriate maintenance quantity.
- If weight gain is again observed, follow the same process and lower the maintenance quantity to find the optimum amount to prevent further weight gain.

Hormonal problems and neutering may sometimes lead to weight gain. Neutering can sometimes reduce the metabolic rate, meaning that the dog will require anything up to a third less food. Preventing obesity is an act of kindness.

Routine Weekly Inspections

Inspections help to detect problems as they arise rather than allowing them to take hold before symptoms are noticed. This includes the arrival of parasites such as fleas and ticks. The inspection should include bottom, coat, ears, skin and teeth. Eyes should be very obvious and not require inspection.

Maintenance Grooming and Care

The regularity of this will depend on the individual requirements of each dog. Some may require care several times a day, sometimes only weekly or even less. It should include: ear cleaning, eye cleaning, coat grooming, trimming, cleaning and inspecting for knots (especially if the dog has been neutered), nail trimming, teeth cleaning and emptying the anal glands.

Some elderly dogs may need to sit or lie down rather than stand whilst the grooming is carried out.

General Care

- Ensure that annual boosters and veterinary check-ups are maintained.
- Provide a healthy, quality-controlled diet appropriate to the dog's age, activity level and any specific medical conditions. Like older humans, some Golden oldies may require 2–3 meals a day, either due to a condition or just simply for their well-being. Raising the food bowl may also assist an elderly dog. Elderly dogs usually require lower protein and salt levels but highly digestible diets. Essential fatty acids are helpful to maintain a good coat and skin condition. If your dog has a poor appetite, supplementing with Vitamin B may help to improve it. Other vitamins may be required but seek advice so as not to over-supplement the diet.
- Provide manageable exercise more frequently but for shorter periods. This may include a walk round the garden on a lead. One of my oldies, who adored his daily walk, would always turn around once he had had enough and wanted to return home. Regular, gentle exercise helps to stimulate appetite, bowels, heart, lungs and joints.
- Provide stimuli to prevent boredom, lethargy and mental depression arising from being left out of activities during their declining years. There are a number of ways

Signs of ageing often show first on the muzzle and face.
Ch Scotangus of Mossburn (aged 9 years).

Mossburn Sandpiper, a typical elderly Golden of 12 years in full coat.

this can be achieved: grooming, physical contact, exercise, feeding two or three times a day, short car journeys, not to be excluded from visitors (caution may need to be taken, however, with young children if the dog's disposition has changed due to illness, pain, a condition such as impaired sight or just ageing intolerance and frustration arising from a disability).

- Maintain routines and familiar surroundings.
- Allow the dog to sleep undisturbed, which he will do more as he gets older, but not excessively if it is due to boredom.
- Provide comfortable, clean, dry, easily-washable bedding in draught-free surroundings. Vet beds are very suitable and useful if the dog is incontinent, as the urine passes through the fabric leaving a dry surface to lie on. Bean bags are also comfortable, supportive and good insulators.
- Provide a companion, given that the dog is not ill, infirm or too intolerant to cope.
- If the elderly Golden shows any signs of senility, physical immobility or hearing and sight impairment, consider any potential hazards indoors and out such as stairs, slippery floors, new or moved furniture, fires, heaters, swimming pools, steps and ponds. Even more care needs to be taken off home premises, particularly off the lead. Almost anything can be a hazard, from traffic to a cliff drop to a river. The dog might also become lost if allowed to disappear from sight. You will need to have both compassion and patience for any senile dog.
- In cases of incontinence or strong body odour, allow the dog to sleep in or use a warm room which is the least likely to cause a cleaning problem. If possible, acclimatise him to the room gradually if he has not used it much beforehand as otherwise he is likely

to feel dejected. Use a non-carpeted room if possible but, if the surface is too slippery this may be impractical, especially if the dog is also unsound or lacking strength. More frequent toileting opportunities, less rich meals, and not feeding late meals may also help you to cope with faecal and urine incontinence. Restricting water intake is not an option – water must be available at all times, otherwise dehydration may occur or an illness may worsen.

- If you have to leave the elderly dog for any period of time for any reason, try to arrange for a neighbour to let him out to toilet, feed if necessary and have some contact with him to prevent him feeling stress and guilt if he has incomplete control of his bladder and bowel. If you take a holiday without your elderly Golden, you may like to consider leaving him at home in familiar surroundings with a dog sitter, or at a friend's home with which the dog is closely acquainted, rather than put him in a kennel. Most dogs can cope with kennelling when they are young, but may find it stressful in their twilight years even if they are in good health, as the routine and environment will be so different to their normal circumstances. If, however, they are ill or infirm, kennelling is likely to be totally impossible.
- If you have more than one dog, it may be kinder to feed the elderly one separately to prevent him feeling stressed by his inability to eat his food quickly, being knocked or threatened.
- If signs of serious illness or diseases are detected, seek veterinary advice or treatment urgently. Delay may allow a rapid deterioration to occur in an elderly dog. For more general matters make a veterinary appointment as soon as possible. If surgery is required, there may be risks depending on the dog's condition but if it is advised or the only option, do not be reluctant to proceed. The vet will always take your dog's age and condition into consideration, and there has been much improvement in techniques and anaesthetics in recent years. Veterinary methods of detecting illness include testing of urine, faeces, blood tests, ECGs and ultra-sound scans.

Euthanasia

My husband states that 'the sad part about owning dogs is the ones we outlive'.

Making the Decision

Making decisions about the end of your dog's life is never easy, no matter how many times you may need to do it. I myself, like most others, would prefer a dog to die in his sleep, peacefully, without distress and pain. Sadly, very few of us are spared the responsibility of making the decision to have our dogs put to sleep.

Most dogs die or are put to sleep aged 10 and over so, as an owner, it is unlikely you will have to consider the position for many years. However, it is best to be prepared, as accidental tragedies, illness and disease can take its toll on a dog at any time of his life.

In some cases, euthanasia is the only option to prevent the dog's pain or where the life expectancy is only a few days due to chronic, incurable diseases or conditions. However, for those who are not ill or in pain, but old or senile, the decision can be very difficult because you have to try to decide, maybe with professional advice, when is the right time to have it done.

The searching questions that you may need to ask are:

- Has the dog an acceptable quality of life?
- Is there any likelihood of improvement in the illness or condition with or without medication?
- What is his possible life expectancy?
- What quality of life does the future hold for him?
- Are you keeping the dog alive for you or the dog? (Probably the most difficult of all.)

The person who makes the final decision usually feels alone and guilty as the act is so final. This is quite a natural feeling. In most cases after the owner has had the opportunity to grieve, he or she knows that they have performed the last kindness for their long-standing companion.

How It Is Done

In most cases the vet injects a barbiturate anaesthetic solution into a vein in the foreleg. In a few seconds the dog loses consciousness and, within a few minutes, the breathing and heart also stop. Sometimes reflex actions may occur afterwards but this cannot be prevented. The bladder and bowels usually empty after death and eyes often remain open. The vet will check that the heart has stopped.

Occasionally the vet may have difficulty in locating a vein if the dog is very ill and it has collapsed. In such cases the dog will be given a strong sedative to put him into a deep sleep. It will then be necessary for the vet to stop the heart functioning by an injection into the heart muscle. If this method is necessary, the vet is likely to ask you to say your goodbyes and leave the room whilst he carries out the last part of the procedure.

The third scenario is when your dog may be undergoing major or exploratory surgery. If the vet finds the condition is inoperable or the dog's life expectancy is very poor he will contact you immediately whilst the dog remains under anaesthetic to inform you of the prognosis, recommending that he does not bring the dog round and euthanases him whilst he is still asleep. Hopefully, if this situation arises, it will not have been unexpected. Whilst the above is the kindest way in such circumstances, the vet will respect your decision if you wish him to bring the dog round for you to say your goodbyes. You must again ask yourself if that is the kindest thing you can do for your dog.

Some of the points you will need to consider are:

- Whether the euthanasia will take place at home, the surgery or even in the car if it is difficult to take the dog into the surgery. If it is at home, and you wish the vet to dispose of the body, the dog may need to be transported back to the surgery by the vet in a specially-designed sack; this is because the bladder and bowels normally empty after death. If it is to be at the surgery, try to arrange a time when you can be seen discreetly without other people about and arrange for payment beforehand. There can be nothing worse for a distressed owner than having to pay immediately after their dog has been put to sleep.
- Whether you wish to stay with your dog whilst euthanasia is carried out by the vet. Many owners like to stay with their dogs to prevent them having further distress. However, if you are emotional yourself, this may upset the dog as he is likely to sense your state of mind. It is not a sin to show your emotions or to be unable to cope with staying with your dog. Vets and their staff are sympathetic.

- Whether you have a friend who can take you and your dog or only your dog to the vet for you, who will not be so emotionally involved. I know this has helped some people greatly, and they have been able to offer a reciprocal arrangement when required to do so.
- Whether you want to have the dog cremated by the vet, cremated separately, or you want to take the dog home to bury him. Most dogs are cremated at the veterinary surgery. If it is done communally the ashes may be buried at a pet crematorium. Separate cremation is likely to cost more. If you have any concerns about your dog's body, ask your vet about the normal disposal arrangements. For further reading, see Bibliography, **The Ageing Dog**.

Dealing with Bereavement

Everyone has his or her own way of coping with the loss of a long-loved family companion. I find keeping a little lock of their hair helps me in the long term. Initially guilt, anguish and sadness are normally felt. As time passes these emotions are likely to be replaced by others and, hopefully, eventually you will be able to recall the happier times you spent together. Having other dogs can help greatly as the home will not be devoid of companions, and for them life carries on. Some dogs can also feel the loss of a dog with whom they may have developed a close rapport. You may have to deal with this situation separately (see Chapter 7). If you do not have another dog, acquiring one can assist your loss but you will have to decide whether to replace him immediately or let some time pass. Acquiring another dog can also help a dog who is pining over the loss of a companion.

Let the dog's quality of life always be your guide.

CHAPTER SIX

Ailments and Illnesses

The author wishes to acknowledge Mr J Sauvage MRCVS BA (Hons) BVet Med Cert SAC for his assistance and advice when checking this chapter.

Abscess
Definition: Swelling beneath the skin containing pus encompassed by fibrous tissue.
Symptoms: Pain and swelling may occur anywhere and develop over several days. Usually bursts to disperse pus.
Cause: Bacterial infection, normally following a wound.
Action/treatment: Seek prompt veterinary advice. The abscess may need surgical drainage and a course of antibiotics.

Allergy
Definition: Over sensitivity to one or more 'allergens'.
Symptoms: May vary accordingly to cause and severity, normally affecting the skin which may appear as raised areas. Commonly affects eyelids and lips and may result in a temporary loss of pigment. Can also result in haemorrhage and gastro-enteritis.
Cause: May include pollen, household dust mites, in food (colourings, gluten) and so on.
Action/treatment: In severe or recurring cases, seek veterinary advice to determine cause and treatment. A blood sample can be tested to identify the cause. Diet may need to be changed or contact with environmental cause prevented to stop recurrence. Animal anti-histamine may be given or prescribed according to the dog's weight to reduce the effect of symptoms.
Comments: Household Dust Mite Allergy – this skin irritation occurred in one of my Golden bitches when she was out of coat and came into contact with coarse grasses and stubble, and only in the summer, when out working or exercising. I found that wiping her stomach and inner thighs with cotton wool soaked in diluted Savlon antiseptic prior to taking her out prevented skin inflammation recurring.

Anal Glands
Definition/cause: Anal gland sacs become over-full. One small gland is placed internally either side of the anus and, when a dog passes faeces, these should empty. If the diet does not contain sufficient bulk, this may not happen. Worm infestations are not normally the cause. If the dog is not constipated or suffering from diarrhoea, Anal Saculitis is unlikely to be dietary – often it is just a chronic infection of the gland.
Symptoms: Excessive licking and biting the tail and around the rectum. Rubbing the bottom on the ground, mainly after passing faeces, but it may occur at other times. Abscess in severe cases. Benign tumour lumps.

Action/treatment: Your dog's glands should be checked and emptied at least once a year. No anaesthetic is required and it only takes a few minutes. If you do it yourself, you will need to wear protective or disposable surgical gloves and have some cotton wool to collect the fluid. Hold the tail up high with one hand and empty the sacs by pressing firmly on both sides. Add more bulk to the dog's diet. In severe cases, veterinary advice must be sought immediately as the glands may become impacted and lumps become sore and require medication to heal or remove. The vet may decide to remove the glands, which is unlikely to cause the dog any difficulties.

Arthritis

Definition: Joint inflammation and degeneration. The 10 areas most commonly affected are backs, elbows, fore-paws, hind-paws, hips, hocks, neck, shoulders, stifles and wrists.

Symptoms: In severe cases pain, lameness, stiffness and swollen joints. In less severe cases, a Golden may show little or no signs to the naked eye but the condition may be detected by a vet examining the flexibility of the limbs and joints or by X-ray(s). Incontinence due to poor mobility.

Causes: Infection, injury, joint deformity (this may be caused by hereditary factors, diet, exercise, hormone imbalance, and carrying excess weight during the pup's growth, especially up to nine months). Wear and tear due to age.

Action/treatment: The vet will determine the joints affected, the severity, and the medication/drugs required to reduce the inflammation and pain and lubricate the joints. He also may suggest alternative natural remedies and therapies which can be used safely in conjunction with traditional medication. Occasionally an X-ray may be necessary under anaesthetic. In some cases an operation may be required. Dogs carrying excess weight need to be placed on a diet and kept to a target weight.

Add cod liver oil to food (maximum 1 teaspoonful a day). Instigate an exercise plan as directed by a vet. This usually consists of regular and gentle exercise. Put the food in a stand off the ground and ensure that the floor surfaces where the dog is kept have grip.

Auto Immune Disease

Definition/cause: The antibodies' reaction and destruction of own body tissues. The symptoms tend to develop more slowly if the dog's own tissue is the underlying problem as opposed to an external antigen such as pollen.

Symptoms: Skin blisters or sores – pemphigus, of which there are four variations, depending on where the blisters most commonly occur, for example on muzzle, face, lips (inside and edges). Possible loss of nails if feet and nail beds are affected. Red blood cell problems – coagulation and possible destruction May only occur in the cold extremities such as the ear tips. May be linked with subsequent kidney damage.

Other possible signs include: anaemia, depression, heart murmur, lethargy, loss of appetite and sensitivity to coldness.

Cause: The most likely cause is hereditary, as certain breeds and/or lines within breeds show a genetic predisposition. Stress is thought to trigger the platelet form or cause it to recur. Other possibilities are diet, infections, inoculations and medication. Diagnosis is very difficult as tissue changes resemble other illnesses or skin conditions.

Action/treatment: Seek veterinary advice for a correct diagnosis without delay, especially with the more elderly dogs, as they are more prone to disease and infections. Steroids are used firstly, either to control or to quieten the immune system. If they prove ineffective, immuno-suppressive medication will be used. In the red blood cell disorder, provided the cell coagulation and destruction has been halted, the anaemia may be dealt with by a blood transfusion.

Bloat (Gastric Dilation and Torsion)

Definition: Rapid enlargement of the stomach which is full either of fermenting food or gas due to an abnormal intake of air and inability to emit wind back through the mouth. If the stomach twists and both the throat entrance and small intestine exit become blocked, the condition is known as torsion and becomes even more serious and difficult, especially as the closure of the oesophagus prevents blood returning to the heart.

Symptoms: Hard, swollen abdomen, pain, distress, breathing difficulties, attempts to pass faeces and vomit before the torsion occurs – afterwards this would not be possible.

Causes: Further research is still required, so the causes are still not absolutely proven: excessive exercise after feeding or vice versa, excessive drinking after eating a dry meal, eating a dry meal too fast, consuming too large a meal, stomach blockage by an indigestible material, and excess stomach fermentation.

Action: This is an **emergency.** Contact a vet immediately as this condition can result in rapid death. When transporting the dog, take care when you load and unload him into the car to prevent torsion. If possible, place the dog on a board.

Treatment: The vet will need to empty the stomach to release the gas and treat the likely shock. Advice will be given on diet to aid the dog's recovery.

Comment: This is a condition where prevention is easier than cure as Goldens are susceptible. Always leave at least one hour between feeding and excessive exercise. Dogs trained for agility should have an even greater gap. If you have a susceptible dog, feed it two meals a day instead of one, soak the food, prevent excessive drinking after a meal, feed the dog separately if you have more than one dog and **never** leave a dog unaccompanied near package stored foods in case he decides to scavenge.

Burns (Major)

Symptoms: As for minor burns.

Action/treatment: If caused by hot fat, remove as much as possible with paper. Drench the burn with cold water only. Seek veterinary attention as soon as possible.

Burns (Minor)

Symptoms: Pain and inflammation.

Action/treatment: Cut hair around affected area, apply cold water to help the discomfort. Clean the area and continue to keep it clean. If after a few days the inflammation has not subsided consult your vet..

Cataract

Definition: Opacity of the lens or its capsule in the eye.

Symptom: Clouding of the lens. Onset is usually gradual but can result in total blindness. It can occur at any time in a dog's life in one or both eyes from birth onwards, but it is more commonly found in the older dog. It is not painful.

Causes: Mainly inherited. Can also occur as a secondary disease in the later stages of Generalised PRA, another inherited eye condition. The mode of inheritance has still to be established some 30 years after eye checks began, but it is thought to be a dominant gene with incomplete penetration. Genetic fingerprinting (DNA tests) may soon be able to determine carriers. Other causes are trauma injury to the eye, certain diseases such as diabetes, poor diet, toxic exposure to some drugs, glaucoma or as a complication of other primary eye diseases.

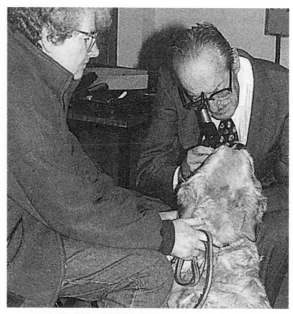

Dr Startup, BVA/KC/ISDS Eye Panel examiner (now retired), testing a Golden's eyes. The test would normally be conducted in a darkened room but, for demonstration purposes only, the photo was taken in daylight.

Action: Contact the BVA or ask your veterinary surgeon to put you in touch with a member of the BVA/KC Eye Panel. The eye panellists are the **only** vets who are qualified or permitted to give an official opinion and BVA/KC certificate. Inform the breeder. Do not breed from your dog if an inherited eye condition has been confirmed.

Treatment: Surgical removal is possible when the cataract is fully developed, but the dog's sight will not be totally restored. The operation is expensive and has about a 30% failure rate. A method with only a 15–20% failure rate is Phacoemulsification where the cataract is dealt with in the early stages. A drill is used to break it up and then fluid is passed into the eye to suck out the particles.

Post Polar Cataract is minute - a little larger than a pin head and may only be detectable using an opthalmascope. It does not usually develop or affect the dog's eyesight, in 95% of cases identified, but as 5% do so it will be classified as an eye failure if detected.

Comment: (a) Nuclear Sclerosis, which is the hardening of the lens occurring with age, should not be confused with cataract. To the lay person the blue-greyish clouding within the eye pupil may give the appearance of the early signs of a cataract. If you are concerned, consult a veterinary eye specialist. (b) See 'comment' under conjunctivitis.

Colitis

Definition/cause: Inflammation of the colon, but the rectum may be involved. About half the cases of persistent and recurrent diarrhoea are attributed to this condition. Golden Retrievers appear to have a pre-disposition to colitis; cases occur more frequently in this breed than other breeds. Males seem to be slightly more prone. It can occur at any time of life but mainly between the ages of 1–2 years. Sometimes referred to as 'irritable bowel syndrome'.

Symptoms: Motions are passed more frequently. Straining even after the rectum has been emptied may lead to pain. Higher quantities of jelly-like mucus are passed, sometimes as a coating around formed stools. Sometimes blood will be seen on or in the stools and, in severe cases, in the mucus. Lengthy cases and those not treated specifically for colitis are likely to recur more regularly until they become continuous. Vomiting is possible and means the stomach is affected because the colon nerve endings pass a message to the brain which induces the action of vomiting – similar to travel sickness. Unlike other causes of diarrhoea, the dog's appetite remains unaffected. In severe cases, there may be a temporary loss of appetite. Weight loss is negligible as the food contents have already been digested and absorbed in the small intestine. Any weight loss is likely to be the result of vomiting back food or short-term loss of appetite.

Causes: Distemper, mercury poisoning, bacteria, fungi, parasites (in America, most commonly whipworm), disorder of several parts of the body, such as kidney damage, scavenging, idiopathic (unknown). Also, a dietary allergy, stress, excitement, viral reaction, genetic predisposition or a combination of the causes.

Action/treatment: It may be difficult to detect if colitis is the condition, so immediately, treat for diarrhoea (see Chapter 3). If the case is severe, persistent and recurring, or the symptoms indicate it is colitis, consult your vet for specific treatment. Avoid giving bones to dogs affected or having a predisposition to the condition.

Conjunctivitis

Definition: Inflammation of the conjunctiva eye sac.

Symptoms: Discharge from the eye. In minor cases it may be clear and minimal, but in a more serious condition it will contain pus and may be painful. It will result in a tear stain on

A Golden with blocked tear ducts.

the dog's face which may become sore with continual eye cleaning. The whites are bloodshot.

Causes: If accompanied by other signs, it may be due to a major disease or illness. Other causes are: blocked tear ducts or tear ducts that are too small; other anatomical eye defects such as entropion; draughts; environmental (smoke, oilseed rape); viral or bacterial infections; injury; foreign bodies such as sand and grass seed.

Action/treatment: Seek veterinary attention to ascertain the cause as the dog's eyes are too important to delay action. An eye ointment is normally prescribed for minor cases. More severe cases may require surgical correction and medication and your vet may refer you to an eye specialist. A dye test is used for tear duct problems.

Comment: If your vet suggests corrective eye surgery, ask to be referred to an eye specialist as they will be more familiar with such conditions and the possible surgery required. Young Goldens are occasionally susceptible to this condition whilst their skull is still developing up to the age of two years, by which time the runny eyes will have disappeared. Corrective surgery on a young Golden may be unnecessary and leave a permanent scar.

Dogs that undergo corrective surgery should not be bred from and The Kennel Club, which may bar them from being shown, should be notified.

Constipation

Definition/symptoms: Failure to pass faeces – may be painful.

Causes: (a) unbalanced diet containing mainly meat and insufficient biscuit; (b) feeding bones; (c) being left indoors too long; (d) long car journeys accompanied by altered feeding schedule and (e) unfamiliar environment, lack of exercise; (f) lack of anal hygiene – matted hair and maybe faeces blocking the passage; (g) stricture; (h) enlarged prostrate gland, usually diagnosed in the older male.

Action/treatment: (a) to (e) can normally be overcome by providing a small dose of liquid paraffin (maximum dose 1 dessertspoonful per 13.6kg/20lb daily); altering the diet; not feeding bones; ensuring the dog has the opportunity to defecate every 4–5 hours and is regularly socialised on unfamiliar territory.

For (f) ensure hair is kept well groomed around the anus or, if necessary, washed and dried thoroughly to prevent a chill in the tail. Knots and matted hair can be removed with an ordinary pair of scissors to relieve any discomfort. In severe cases, a vet may be required to help remove the matted hair.

More serious are (g) and (h), and veterinary help should be sought quickly to prevent the dog continually straining.

Coprophagy

Definition: Ingestion of faeces, including the dog's own.

Symptoms: None, unless the faeces contain parasites such as worms and/or bacteria.

Causes: Imitation of dam who consumes puppies' faeces up to and partly during the weaning period (normal behaviour for the dam); inadequate diet or a diet with poor indigestibility; boredom and being left alone.

Action: Curing this condition is difficult and punishing a dog either caught in the act or afterwards will not resolve the problem. Prevention and preventative training are more likely to be effective.

(a) Worm the dog.
(b) Check that the diet contains the correct vitamins and nutrients but remember that overdosing may cause other difficulties.
(c) Feed a higher-fibre diet such as one of the the complete dry range diets, as long as this is not contradicted by any veterinary advice or treatment, or ask the breeder to recommend a suitable dry diet.
(d) Feed the dog more frequently, to prevent hunger.
(e) Clean up and dispose of your dog's faeces so that he has no opportunity to eat them.
(f) Teach the dog to toilet on command and, if necessary, on a lead to assist with (e). Praise the dog greatly after he has defecated but before removing the debris.
(g) Provide more regular exercise and play.
(h) Add an iron tablet to the meals to make the faeces less appetising, particularly if the dog eats his own. This is more difficult and costly if you have two or more dogs. (It is claimed that a few chunks of pineapple added to meals also make stools less attractive.)
(i) Peppering stools makes them more unpleasant.
(j) Use an extended lead to exercise and toilet-exercise your dog. Deliberately permit him to find dog faeces but immediately he shows an interest in eating them, gently but purposefully pull him away. **At the same time**, make a loud noise or spray the dog's head with water so that he associates the faeces with an unpleasant experience. Whilst the dog is distracted, tell him to sit or stay. As soon as he obeys, praise lavishly

Corneal Ulceration

Definition: Ulceration of the front of the eye.
Symptom: Opaque patch on eye surface.
Causes: Mainly through injury such as running into a twig or barbed wire fence. A film appears over the cornea as a result of tear production failure or inflammation.
Action/treatment: Consult a vet immediately.

Coughs

Comment: Some dogs cough briefly after barking, playing or pulling on a lead. This is quite normal but more regular, persistent coughs should be investigated.
Causes: Chest injury if accompanied by rapid breathing, rib pain and bruising; distemper; heart disease; irritants, such as paint fumes, if accompanied by rapid breathing depression and watery eyes; Kennel Cough; laryngitis and pharyngitis if accompanied by retching, depression, fever and possible loss of appetite. Poisoning (Paraquet and Warfarin). Respiratory disease. Tonsillitis, if accompanied by retching, depression, fever and possible loss of appetite. Worm infection.
Action/treatment: If you think your dog has inhaled an irritant, telephone for veterinary advice at once. If you suspect poison, take the dog immediately to the vet with any evidence of what has been eaten and a vomit sample for analysis.

A sudden and persistent cough may indicate an infection. If you have more than one dog, immediately isolate the affected animal and seek veterinary attention. Leave the dog in the car, explain to the veterinary nurse why and she will advise whether the vet will see your dog in or out of the surgery. The same applies if a cough continues intermittently over a few days.

Kennel Cough can last for several weeks and is associated with a persistent, hacking cough. It is caused by a number of viruses and bacteria. To prevent this highly contagious illness, administer a separate vaccine by placing drops in the nasal passages. For full cover these need to be given every six months. Transmission is from dog to dog through the air. The infection attacks the cells lining the respiratory tract.

If infection is confirmed, isolate the dog for three weeks after the condition has subsided to prevent further spread. This applies to public places where your dog may come into contact with other dogs, boarding kennels and dog events. It also applies to other dogs you own that have come into contact with an infected dog.

For other conditions the dog may need to undergo tests before receiving treatment, as the cough may be a symptom of another disease.

Coughs can be alleviated by the administration of Benylin for Chesty Coughs non-drowsy.

Cystitis

Definition: Bladder inflammation.

Symptoms: Dog adopts urinating position more regularly than normal; passing little or no water. Blood may be present in the water. The dog strains unsuccessfully.

Causes: Mainly bacterial infection, stones and growth.

Action/treatment: You will probably need to obtain antibiotics from the vet.

Comment: This condition can occur at any age, from young puppies in the nest to the old dog. I have also seen it in an 8-year-old bitch immediately prior to an open pyometra and another 12 hours prior to coming into season. Freshly chopped parsley mixed in the food was effective on this occasion.

Cysts

Definition: Fluid-filled swelling under the skin which can appear on the body, suddenly under the tongue or at the jaw joint (salivary cyst) or between the toes (interdigital cyst).

Symptoms: Ordinary cysts are usually slow growing; interdigital cysts can appear quickly and recur between toes, causing pain, lameness and soreness, and may become infected with a bacteria; salivary cysts cause drooling and tongue displacement.

Causes: Perhaps lack of condition; an interdigital cyst perhaps due to blocked sweat glands in the foot or grass seeds imbedded in the skin. The cause of salivary cysts is unknown.

Action/treatment: If the cyst begins to grow rapidly, ruptures or starts to bleed, seek veterinary attention immediately, and always in the case of interdigital cysts. The cysts can be lanced, bathed in salt water or diluted Savlon antiseptic several times a day and treated with antibiotics, both tablets and powder spray. Alternatively you can apply a compress and treat as described (without lancing) after the cyst has burst.

For salivary cysts, seek veterinary attention urgently, as surgery may be necessary.

Deafness

Symptom: Failure to respond to owner's voice, environmental noises and lack of interaction with kennel mates. There is a professional hearing test (BAER) available for adults and puppies over the age of four weeks old.

Causes: Ageing – deafness is usually progressive and is not uncommon in Goldens. There is no cure or treatment. Growths in the ear canal. Disease in the ear or elsewhere. Carbon monoxide poisoning, caused by fumes from solid fuel, calor gas or oil boilers or faulty car exhaust systems which stops oxygen reaching the lungs and blood. In severe cases the dog collapses with blue tinged tongue; in non-severe cases he will have bloodshot eyes and be sleepy. CMP can kill, so it is important to prevent such an occurrence.

Action/treatment: If you suspect CMP, consult your vet immediately. In any case it is worth consulting your vet to assess there is no underlying cause of the deafness where treatment or surgery may be required.

Comment: Like many breeds of dogs, the older the Golden the wiser, and the more likely to become deaf by choice. Young Goldens are also capable of pretending to be deaf!

Diabetes Mellitus

Definition/causes: A hormonal imbalance brought on either by the failure of the pancreas to produce sufficient insulin or the tissues' response to the effects of the hormone insulin.

Symptoms: Early signs are: excessive thirst, together with passing of excess urine in vast amounts. Rapid loss of condition. Appetite remains unaffected but vomiting is possible. If symptoms are not identified in the early stages the stomach becomes distended and cataracts may occur in the eyes eventually.

Action/treatment: Seek veterinary attention urgently if the early signs occur and provide a urine sample for analysis. A blood sample may also be taken. Severe cases will require daily insulin injection, whereas in minor cases an oral hypoglycaemic drug will be given with a decrease of carbohydrates in the dog's diet.

Distemper

Definition: Highly infectious disease which can be further complicated by secondary bacteria. Distemper can last up to eight weeks and result in damage to the nervous system.

Symptoms: Early signs are: depression, loss of appetite, diarrhoea (possibly), vomiting (possibly), high temperature 39.5°C/103°F or more, harsh cough with enlarged glands and inflamed tonsils, runny eyes, nose and noisy breathing, reddened eyes. Later signs are chorea (nervous twitching), fits, paralysis, hard pad - where the pads and nose harden and crack and the feet swell.

Cause: Virus. The incubation period is normally 7–21 days. It is transmitted in the air from infected dogs and perhaps birds, vermin and parasites that have come into contact with an infected dog or his faeces.

Action/treatment: Consult your vet immediately. Ask where your vet would like to see the dog – do not take him into the waiting area. Keep the dog warm and quiet. Wash all areas indoors and out to which the dog has had access, firstly with a detergent to remove dirt and grease and then with an effective disinfectant containing some form of chlorine.

Comment: Have puppies inoculated and adults boosted annually.

Dog Bites

Action: If incurred during a dog fight, part the dogs and isolate them as soon as possible in a car, room or kennel. Quickly check them to see if any have sustained injuries (which will be mainly puncture wounds) and deal first with the dog that has come off worse. If another party's dog is involved, exchange names and addresses as you would in a car accident, but do not indulge in any other form of exchanges!

Treatment: Stem the blood flow, if any (ears are more vulnerable and difficult). Bathe with a saline solution or diluted Savlon antiseptic. Dry with a clean towel or kitchen paper. Apply Savlon cream or any other antiseptic cream or powder. Repeat 2–4 times a day until the wound(s) heal. If the wound deteriorates, that is, enlarges or forms pus, seek veterinary advice as soon as possible.

Scratches are not always evident immediately as a Golden's skin is protected quite well by its double coat, but they may erupt under the coat and need treating with an antiseptic healing cream. They can result in eczema.

Major wounds may require cleaning and stitching by the vet and medication without delay. If they are painful, your dog may not want you to touch the wounds so take care until the vet has dealt with them

Breathing difficulties/eye injuries are likely to be serious and should be dealt with as an emergency. Go to the vet immediately and, if possible, ask someone to phone the surgery to warn them of your arrival.

Shock: see page 116.

Comment: If you are bitten, you will need to follow a similar procedure, depending on the severity of the wound. You will require a tetanus injection if you have not had one during the last five years, no matter how serious the puncture wound.

Ear Mites Infestation or Otodectic Mange

Symptoms: Ear scratching, discharge like canker (see Otitis) that is often dry and dark brown.

Cause: White mange mite – can be transmitted by cats from their ears.

Action/treatment: Obtain an ear cleaner and medication from the vet. Do not use cheaper ear preparations – it may be false economy. Great care should be taken with dogs' ears as hearing is one of their major senses and their ears are far more effective than humans. Treat both ears, even if only one appears to be infected. Treat any other animals in your household to prevent re-infection. Regular ear checks and use of ear cleaners can help prevent further ear disease.

Ectropion

Definition/symptoms: Out-turned lower eyelid exposing the conjunctiva. It can affect one or both eyes.

Other symptoms: Runny eyes, inflammation of the conjunctiva sac.

Cause: It is an anatomical defect which may be hereditary – probably polygenic (that is, controlled by more than one gene).

Action/treatment: Consult your vet and/or a veterinary eye specialist. See 'comment' under Conjunctivitis. Surgical correction may be required. Inform the breeder. It is inadvisable to breed from an affected dog

Comment: If the condition is hereditary, perhaps Golden cases are linked to Bloodhounds in which it is seen today, as they are partly behind the ancestry of our breed.

Eczema

Definition: Inflammation or eruption of the skin. Can occur anywhere.

Wet eczema symptoms: Temporary irritation, moisture, hair loss mainly to a dog licking, crust forms from exuded moisture.

Causes: Not always obvious but can be attributed to one or a combination of the following: contact with irritant (may affect one dog, not all will be susceptible), fleas, heat (mainly during the summer), foods such as maize causing blood to overheat, nerves and stress.

Comment: One of my dogs succumbed to this after a booster injection in the neck in summertime and several times another dog suffered when his major moult coincided with summer.

Action/treatment: Try to identify and deal with cause. Cut the hair away from the moist area before it crusts over and traps the long coat, to enable the skin to breathe, dry and heal. Clean the affected part with cotton wool soaked in Savlon antiseptic. Dab dry with kitchen paper, then apply Calendula with cotton wool (1 drop to 10 drops of water), 3 or 4 times daily. This allows the area to dry and heal, appears to remove the irritation and does not sting the skin so much as more old fashioned drying solutions. Add watercress and parsley to the dog's meals to reduce his blood heat.

Try to prevent the dog from scratching and nibbling the inflamed area as this will spread the problem. If the condition becomes unmanageable or infected, seek veterinary advice. Antibiotics and anti-inflammatory drugs will probably be prescribed.

Comment: Goldens seem susceptible to the condition on the face, behind the ears, along the back, on the flanks, on the tail and around the tail set. If a dog is permitted to scratch, wet eczema may soon spread or become infected. An Elizabethan collar, available from the vet, can be used to prevent a dog scratching his face, head and ears.

Dry eczema symptoms: Irritation, skin becomes red and sometimes blackish, temporary partial loss of hair.

Causes: Possibly lack of condition, poor health, under-nourishment, worms, demodectes mite associated with demodectic mange.

Action/treatment: As for wet eczema and add Savlon cream.

Comment: It commonly occurs on the legs, flank and tummy.

Entropion

Definition/symptoms: In-turned eyelid, with eyelid hair rubbing on the cornea. It can affect one or both eyes and tends mainly to be the lower eyelid in Goldens. Eye irritation, runny eyes, cornea damage leading to blindness if left untreated.

Causes: Anatomical defect, thought to be hereditary (recessive gene).

Action/treatment: Consult your vet and/or an eye specialist. See 'comment' under Conjunctivitis. Minor surgery may be required. Inform the breeder. Do not breed from an affected animal.

Epilepsy

Definition: It is a sign, not a disease, and is described as fits/convulsions/seizures and is not to be confused with the normal twitching and whimpering of a sleeping animal. It is called primary where there is no evidence of a specific cause, or secondary if there is.

Symptoms: May be preceded by a complete character change. Sudden collapse if not already asleep but frequently occurs when the dog is relaxed or asleep. Unconsciousness, frothing at the mouth, clamped jaws, stiff body and extended limbs. Shaking and paw paddling comes later. Vocalisation. When the dog relaxes he may lose control over his bladder and bowels and have involuntary evacuation. The convulsion can last from a couple of minutes to longer.

Recovery can vary from a few minutes to several hours after the seizure, during which time the dog may be dazed, unsteady, disoriented and his sight may be temporarily affected. Sight is often the last sense to return fully. After recovery, the dog is ravenous and sleepy.

Causes: Abnormal electrical discharges to the brain brought about by various reasons:

- Abdominal pain, especially in puppies.
- Accidents and trauma – onset may occur several weeks, months or even years later as a result of scar tissue forming on the brain.
- After operations or whelping.
- Brain tumours – such cases often result in vets having to recommend euthanasia.
- Wasting of temporal muscles is indicative of this condition.
- Distemper.
- Falls where the brain may have been damaged.
- Fear and stress.
- Heart disease.
- Heat suppression in a bitch.
- Hereditary, but insufficient research is available. The Golden Retriever is believed to have a predisposition to primary epilepsy. The exact mode of inheritance has yet to be determined. Early indications are that it may be of an autosomal multifactorial recessive mode which basically means it will be very difficult to eliminate with the current scientific means available.
- Hyperventilation.
- Infection.
- Inherited conditions such as water on the brain.
- Liver disease.
- Pain.
- Poisons, such as strychnine.
- Rabies.
- Sexual excitement.
- Teething from 3–6 months.
- Toxaemia.
- Worms – round or tape, the pup will appear pot-bellied.

Action:

- Do not force anything into the dog's mouth.
- Do not touch the dog during the seizure – he may bite you due to disorientation and fear.
- Remove any other dogs from the room.
- Remove anything near the collapsed dog that may cause him to injure himself.
- If the dog is in an unsafe place, move him carefully to safety using a blanket.
- Turn off any radios or televisions and keep the room quiet and dark.
- Try to remain calm. Do not ask the vet to visit as the fit will probably be over before he

arrives. Make a note of how long the fit lasted, whether the dog became unconscious, other symptoms, any circumstances that preceded it and how the dog behaved afterwards.

Emergency: If a dog with primary epilepsy has one fit after another for many hours *(status epilepticus)*, he must be taken to the surgery immediately for an anaesthetic if he is to have a chance of survival. Provided there is not too great a time lapse before anaesthesia is achieved, the dog can resume living a 'normal' life for many years.

Treatment: In less serious cases, contact the vet by telephone to report the incident and make an appointment to have the dog assessed for primary or secondary epilepsy. The dog may need to undergo tests before medication and therapy can be prescribed, or be referred to a specialist for further tests. Anti-convulsant drugs can control the condition but, in severe cases, the dog may not always respond to medication. If there is an underlying cause, such as a brain tumour, surgery may be another option.

Comment: Golden males appear more prone to primary epilepsy. It tends to occur by the age of three and not very often after six years. Normal activity need not be restricted.

Eyeball Prolapse

Action/treatment: This is an emergency – go to the vet immediately. Do not attempt to replace the eye. Gently apply a folded cloth soaked in water to cover the eyeball and socket.

Faints

Definition/symptoms: Temporary loss of consciousness.

Causes: Breathing difficulties, heat stroke, low blood sugar if the dog has worked hard, is distressed or fed irregularly (feed something sweet in this case).

Action: If condition recurs, report the matter to your vet.

Treatment: Stay with the dog whilst he recovers. Ensure airway is clear by pulling tongue forward. Apply cold water or ice to forehead and mouth.

Fractures

Definition: Breaking of a bone anywhere and in any direction. A compound fracture occurs when the bone protrudes through broken skin.

Symptoms: Sudden severe pain; the limb may appear deformed and unusable.

Causes: Fall or traffic accident.

Action: Take the dog to the vet as soon as practical. Care should be taken when moving the dog to prevent causing further pain and damage. The dog may bite due to pain, so loop a lead over his nose to restrain him. A dog can be moved gently and carried if rolled into a blanket.

Treatment: This may involve X-rays, and certainly surgery to repair the fracture. The success rate is good but the dog may suffer from arthritis in later years.

Gastro-enteritis

Definition: Combination of gastritis and enteritis; there is both diarrhoea and vomiting.

Cause: If the temperature rises to 39°–40.5°C (c. 102.5°F) or higher, the cause may be a virus and veterinary advice should be sought. See Chapter 3, Diarrhoea.

Glaucoma

Definition/cause: Increased fluid and pressure in the eye due to an inherent defect. The primary cause is a drainage problem, the mode of which has yet to be determined. Secondary glaucoma is linked to trauma and some eye conditions, for example uveitis, which is the inflammation of the uveal tract. Onset may be sudden.

Symptoms: Pain. Perhaps bulging, staring eye with a fully-open pupil resulting in blueing of the cornea in advanced cases. Vision impairment or loss of sight.

Action/treatment: Immediate veterinary assistance, preferably from an opthamologist, needs to be sought to prevent sight loss within 24–48 hours.

Comment: Primary glaucoma in the Golden Retriever is under investigation by the BVA/KC. It would be wise not to breed from an affected dog and to inform the breeder. Dogs can be examined for the condition at 5–6 months but, as specialist equipment is required, not every member of the panel can carry out the procedure, which is not part of the routine eye scheme checks. A fee is therefore charged according to the number of dogs examined. It is a once-in-a-lifetime test but does require anaesthetic drops applied to the eyes. Some dogs will require sedation for the procedure, involving extra cost.

Growths

Definition/symptoms: A growth of abnormal cells which are no longer under the body's control. They can be benign or malignant, of any size and can occur anywhere on the body, external or internal. They may be the size of a pimple, like a wart, or show as a large mammary tumour. An external growth appears as a hard lump under the skin. Internal growths often affect the organs and may go undetected for some time unless other signs of illness appear when the growth is malignant (cancerous) and it spreads. Severe weight loss is often a strong indication of some cancerous growths, or sores that do not heal or bleeding from the mouth, nose and rectum. Benign (non-cancerous) tumours do not spread.

Pain (mainly confined to bone cancer), nausea and general lack of well-being in advanced cancer cases.

Causes: Various and unknown or too difficult to detect in individual cases.

Action: To be on the safe side, seek veterinary advice on any growth found or suspected. No action may be taken immediately unless the growth increases rapidly in size, is a wart rubbing on the eye's cornea which is likely to cause damage, is on the vulva producing incontinence and irritation or is a mammary tumour. In these cases surgical removal will be required.

Treatment: Surgery – some growths can be surgically removed and tested to check whether they are benign or malignant, but it depends where and how advanced they are as to whether the vet will operate. Your vet will advise on your dog's prospects and the quality and possible length of life expected afterwards. Tissue testing cannot be carried out until the growth has been removed. Secondary tumours often occur in other vital organs, such as the lungs.

In cases where the growth tissue is identified as malignant further treatment may be required, such as:

Chemotherapy – that is, anti-cancer drugs. Frequently used for cancer of the lymphatics and in conjunction with other treatments. The side effects associated with humans, such as hair loss and vomiting, do not occur. If administered correctly, the drugs rarely produce toxicity. It is not a cure but can slow down or halt the cancer.

Cryosurgery – application of intense cold to kill the tumour. This is not upsetting or harmful to a dog. An offensive smell may occur as the tissue dies.

Hormones are useful for dogs with leukaemia or lymphoma to improve their appetite and general well being; also for thyroid cancer and tumours of the glands in the skin around the anus.

Radiotherapy is used for the following cancers: bone, (alleviates pain greatly), breast, lymphomas, mouth and skin tumours. Some tumours are cured, but some may recur and spread. Radiation sickness does not occur. A local loss of hair may follow treatment.

Comment: Cancer treatments other than surgery are slowly becoming available, but mainly at specialist centres. The feedback I have had on a few cases to date indicates that in all but one case the dog's quality of life deteriorated despite and because of the treatment. The whole aim of chemotherapy is to maintain quality of life as well as to prolong it. Treatments are improving all the time but are costly and are definitely 'buying time'.

Haematoma

Definition: A blood or fluid-filled swelling, following damage to blood vessels on the anatomy, but normally affects ear flaps.

Symptoms: Ears – head shaking or holding the head at a tilt. Hot soft swelling, which increases slowly over a few days. Pain. Other – soft swelling, perhaps pain.

Causes: Injury (fight or accident); scratching or shaking ear(s) due to an infection such as ear mites, irritation or foreign body, for example grass seed. Post-operation injury.

Action/treatment: Surgical treatment may be required. If an ear is involved, steroid injections will be given into the ear flap. Surgery will involve the vet shaving, draining the fluid and stitching the ear, and treating any condition or removing a foreign body. Post-operative cases may require a support bandage.

Comment: All but one case I have experienced involved earflaps, mostly due to head shaking and hitting ears on low tables. All the dogs made a recovery but had a few small, pimple-like scars, either from the stitching or the damaged blood vessel. All were hidden once the hair grew back.

The other case was almost at the top of the shoulder blade (cause unknown). It arrived suddenly and became the size of a large grape. My vet took no action, preferring to see if it went away of its own accord. Within 3–4 weeks it had totally disappeared and gave the dog no concern.

Heart Disease

It is estimated that about 5% of heart cases are present at birth and the other 95% of cardiac diseases are acquired later in life. Some cases can be prevented by giving a dog a healthy diet and ample exercise and keeping him at a sensible weight throughout his life. A dog that develops a problem in addition to the action/treatment suggested below may also have need to have his weight watched, to be given controlled, manageable exercise and to be placed on a low salt diet, prescription available from vets or pasta, potatoes, fresh meat or vegetables. However, too many carbohydrates may cause eczema. Small meals may also need to be given several times a day to prevent the stomach from becoming too large and placing indirect pressure on the heart function.

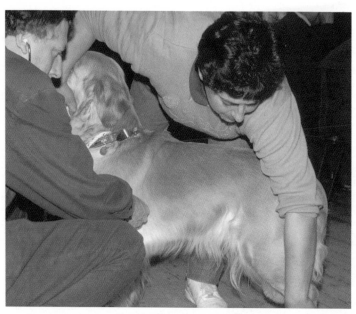

A Golden being heart-tested. Mr J Sauvage is seen here using a stethoscope to listen for a heart murmur.

Congestive heart failure

Definition: Chronic heart disease which reduces the heart's competence to pump blood at a rate and volume required for the body's needs.

Symptoms: Coughing, breathlessness, fluid in abdomen, intolerance to exercise, loss of weight.

Cause: Heart defect commonly resulting in a progressive condition.

Action/treatment: A veterinary consultation is recommended without delay. Many effective heart and circulation drugs now on the market can be prescribed to help heart conditions and their symptoms and increase life expectancy.

Congenital valvular

Definition/cause: Puppies born with ineffective working valves.

Symptoms: Sleepiness, sudden tiredness, tongue, mouth, eyes and nostrils turn blue.

Action/treatment: Consult a vet immediately as surgery is likely to be required.

Valvular

Definition/cause: Incompetent heart valve. This is rare in Goldens unless secondary to heart muscle weakness (cardiomyopathy).

Symptoms: As described above for congenital valvular. In adults the heart can bulge out, causing pain and the dog cries out for no obvious reason. Possible collapse during an attack for varying lengths of time.

Action/treatment: As for congestive heart failure above.

Comment: Conditions affecting heart valves used to occur mainly in older dogs that had had a strenuous working life. In the last decade a specific condition known as Sub Aortic Stenosis (SAS) has become a concern for the Golden breed in Britain as it appears the breed has a susceptibility to it at any age. In severe cases it can cause cardiac failure and result in death. It has been a real problem in North America for much longer but, despite much research, to date it has no proven inheritance. British breed clubs have held some heart screening sessions to provide statistical data for cardiologists to determine the breed's heart status. The matter has met with opposition from some breeders and the way forward has yet to be determined by the Golden Retriever Breed Council.

Heart attack/failure

Symptoms: Sudden collapse – the dog may appear to be dead. Possible involuntary bladder and bowel evacuation. Possible upward rotation of eyes.

Action: Leave the dog alone during the attack, keeping him quiet and in low light. Keep the dog warm, provided that the collapse is not due to heat stroke. Assess whether the dog is unconscious. Only if the dog is unconscious will it be safe to give him artificial respiration or heart massage to restore breathing circulation and heart beat (see Chapter 4). Arrange for someone else to seek urgent veterinary attention whilst you attend to the dog.

Heat Stroke

Definition: Collapse due to a high temperature.

Symptoms/causes: Mainly occurs in the summer when the dog is in an unventilated car; at other times of the year whether the car windows are open or not; and lying or working outside in high temperatures for long periods. Body temperature may be greater than 41°C (106°F).

Action/treatment: Cool the dog immediately, with cold water or ice for about 5–10 minutes maximum. The quickest way is to use a towel soaked in cold water, lay it over the dog and douse the head with cool (not cold) water. Offer the dog as much drinking water as he wants. A pinch of salt can be added to assist rehydration. (Also see Bicarbonate of Soda, Chapter 7.) As soon as it is practical, take the dog to your vet for a check up, even if all seems well.

Hepatitis

Definition: Inflammation of the liver. This is highly contagious but is unconnected to the disease of the same name in humans. Can affect dogs of any age but mainly puppies. Can have a rapid onset and be fatal, especially for puppies. Incubation period is 1–7 days.

Symptoms: Off-colour, loss of appetite, abdominal pain, diarrhoea, vomiting, high temperature, pale gums and conjunctivae, convulsions, pneumonia. May be jaundiced (yellowing of eye whites) and have blue eye (blue clouding of the cornea in one or both eyes). Mild cases in adults may only cause upset stomach and blue eye.

Causes: Bacterial virus caught by eating infected material such as excrement, urine and saliva from dogs with the disease or perhaps from those who have recovered several months earlier. It is possible for an affected dog to become a permanent carrier of the disease. Dogs may need to be segregated even after recovery, and blood tested to determine if they are carriers before mixing them with kennel mates and taking them to public places.

Action/treatment: As for Distemper.

Comment: This disease has been linked with 'fading puppy' referred to in Chapter 11. It is believed that hepatitis survivors that are bred from produce 'fading puppies' and any puppies lucky enough to survive will themselves produce 'fading puppies'. The seriousness of the disease and its possible consequences for survivors underline the need to prevent it by early vaccination of puppies and annual boosters for adults.

Hereditary Breed Defects

Screened by British Veterinary Association/Kennel Club: see Cataract, Elbow OCD, Hip Dysplasia, Multifocal Retinal Dysplasia and Progressive Retinal Atrophy.

Hip Dysplasia (HD)

Definition: Malformation of one or both hip joints due to developmental abnormalities related to growth (primary changes), and usage abnormalities attributed to wear and tear (secondary changes). Golden Retrievers are affected by this condition; it is not entirely hereditary but a multifactorial recessive genetic disorder (partly genetic) which may be influenced by other factors such as diet and exercise.

Symptoms: Mild cases may show no clinical signs and HD is only detected by an X-ray when the dog is assessed for possible breeding purposes. Good muscle tone may mask even severe cases. In the latter, the dog suffers from inflammation, pain, lameness and immobility. Osteoarthritis may occur later in the joint(s), causing further unsoundness.

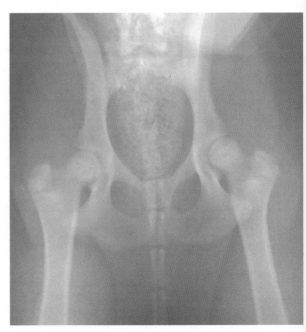

Hip x-ray. Example of a 3:4 score (total: 7). Scores which total 8 or less are considered as very good.

Causes: Injury, accident, inheritance (passed genetically by both the sire and dam to their offspring), rapid growth development, environment (rearing, diet, exercise, excess weight).

Action: Clinical cases need to be investigated by a vet who will X-ray the dog whilst he is anaesthetised or sedated. It is a treatable, but not a curable, condition.

Treatment: Can be complicated but may involve:

- Surgery on the muscles and or joints.
- Applied heat.
- Massage.
- Correct exercise (for example, swimming) as advised by the vet.
- Suitable bedding.
- Drugs to reduce inflammation and pain as prescribed by your vet.
- Natural alternative remedies to assist the dog's comfort, joint fluids and arthritis.

Hypothermia

Definition/cause: Drop in body temperature following exposure to intensely cold temperatures or cold temperatures for a lengthy period. Can occur in puppies, particularly after their birth, if insufficient insulation or heating is provided (see Chapter 11).

Symptoms: Inability or inclination to move a great deal; collapse; death (mainly in puppies).

Action: Do not administer any form of alcohol or subject the dog to very hot temperatures. Cover the dog with a light blanket and keep him warm. Vet beds or luke-warm water bottles can help. If the dog can drink at all, offer some warm milk.

Treatment: Seek veterinary attention immediately.

Hypothyroidism

Definition/cause: Inadequate thyroid hormone level.

Symptoms: Bi-lateral hair loss, lethargy, obesity, skin changes. Poor growth in youngsters.

Treatment: Daily administration of thyroid hormone pills will help re-balance the deficiency but your vet will have to blood test the affected dog to determine the quantities.

Comment: A bitch of mine had poor coat growth and infrequent seasons. Tablets helped both problems but a possible side-effect of the condition when an affected bitch is put into whelp can be uterine inertia. I was unaware of this when I mated my bitch. I nearly lost her through dehydration whilst she was undergoing a Caesarean section, and did lose eight of the 11 puppies. It was very distressing for all involved, including the bitch who was very aware her full brood was not present – a situation I would never repeat.

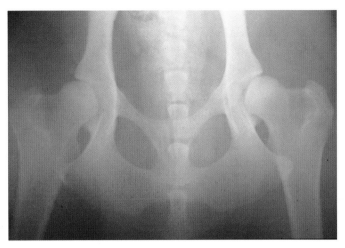

Hip x-ray. Example of a hip score 14:15 (total: 29) – 9 above the breed average.

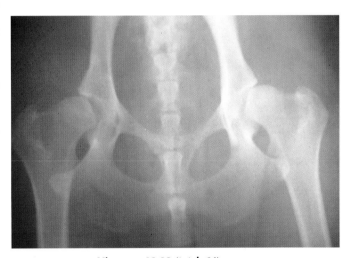

Hip score 32:32 (total: 64).

Incontinence

Definition/symptoms:
Involuntary passing of urine. This does not include puppies or adults not fully house-trained.

Causes: Illness, diseases resulting in excessive drinking, old age, immobility (arthritic dogs, for example, find it difficult to rise), paralysis, submissiveness brought about at times of fear and excitability, usually seen in young puppies. Most tend to outgrow this by 12 months. Bitches improve after their first season. Other causes of incontinence in bitches are: spaying, cystitis, and urinary system congenital defects such as ectopic ureter (see Chapter 11 Breeding Problems).

Action/treatment: The cause needs to be determined by you or your vet. Spayed bitches can be helped with hormone treatment. Urinary system problems are likely to require corrective surgery and your vet should advise you on the full recovery success rate and quality of life expectation for the dog. Submissiveness difficulties can be helped by improving the dog's confidence. Do not let old dogs become chilled or overweight. Provide a good quality low protein digestible diet and a Vitamin B supplement. Do not restrict water intake.

Comment: I have experienced fully house-trained bitches who have accidents several weeks prior to coming into season and during their season, and a male (not at stud) who has one accident nearly every time bitches have been in season – not territory marking.

Lameness

Definition: Inability to sustain some/all weight on one or more affected limbs.

Symptoms: Pain, perhaps swelling, deformity and breaks in the skin. The dog may hold the limb off the ground, turned outwards or inwards. If a front limb is affected, more weight will be placed on the sound leg and the head will drop almost to the level of the dog's back. When a hind leg is affected, the hindquarters appear to dip when weight is placed on the sound limb. An affected limb may also be dragged.

Causes: *Feet* – torn nail, internally under the skin or externally; damaged quick; infection in foot or under nail; impaled thorns, pins, nails, grass seeds, glass, etc; interdigital cysts; eczema between the toes; torn, cut or worn pad; dislocated and/or broken toe; embedded mud and snow between the toes and pads; oil, tar, stone chippings, chewing gum and other sticky substances; arthritis.

Leg/joints: arthritis and osteoarthritis; fractures or dislocations as a result of accidents or falls. Sprains and strains to ligaments, muscles and tendons which may have been overstretched, twisted or torn.

Comment: If the dog holds the foot off the ground, the problem is likely to be in the foot, otherwise it will be higher up the limb. Jumping out of cars can often be the cause of strains.

Action: If the cause is not obvious, examine the dog to identify the region of the difficulty or injury starting with the foot, working upwards.

Treatment: A dog in pain may snap and need restraining. Dogs in severe pain should be examined by the vet urgently, but most cases will require prompt veterinary advice unless only a minor foot ailment is involved. Remove mud and snow by soaking the foot in warm water. Gum and glue may need to be partly cut away from hair, then soaked and washed off using a dog shampoo. Remove tar by first applying another oil, such as olive or cooking oil, to dissolve it and then by washing the foot. Try a dog shampoo but, if this does not work, you may have to use washing-up liquid. If you do, be sure to rinse and dry the foot thoroughly to prevent any irritation.

Arthritis, eczema and interdigital cysts – see the appropriate sections.

Damage to pads and nails can be treated easily at home unless cuts require stitching. Bathe the foot in either a salt water solution or diluted Savlon antiseptic solution, dry, apply an antiseptic cream (Savlon or one obtained from the vet) or an antibiotic powder. Repeat 3–4 times daily until the condition has healed. New Skin, obtainable from the chemist for minor cuts, can be applied safely as it allows the skin or pads to breathe. Only apply after the foot has been treated as above. Several layers can be painted on to give added protection, but each layer must be thoroughly dry before a further coat is applied. Avoid walking the dog on hard ground and carpet pile as this is likely to aggravate the problem. Using this method I have dealt successfully with a minor pad cut which has healed within 3–4 days.

NB If at any time you notice an infection or swelling near the damaged area, take the dog to the vet for a course of antibiotic tablets and perhaps an injection. You may not think it serious but one of my dogs had a minor swelling behind a nail which resulted in tetanus, quite rare in dogs. Antibiotics were administered to the dog before signs of tetanus became apparent. The dog recovered, but the vet believed this was due only to the antibiotics.

Leptospirosis

Definition: Bacterial disease.
Cause: Leptospires (group of bacteria). The two organisms which can infect dogs are:
Leptospira icterhaemorrhagiae, transmitted by rat urine. Dogs can become infected when consuming an infected dead rat or something contaminated. The disease is carried by about 50% of rats. Incubation is between 5–15 days.
Leptospira canicola, transmitted from dog to dog via sniffing urine, also with a 5–15 day incubation period.

Leptospira icterhaemorrhagiae
Symptoms: Initially the dog may appear off-colour, off his food and have a high temperature (up to 41°C/106°F). After two days the temperature can drop to subnormal levels. Severe thirst, frequent urination, vomiting, diarrhoea (dark, foul-smelling and containing blood), abdominal pain, loss of condition. Jaundice can develop in the latter stage. Check the eye and mouth membranes in natural light for a yellow tinge in the eye whites, cheeks and gums. They may become bright yellow or gold if jaundice worsens. Death may result within two days if the acute form known as haemorrhagic enteritis is the cause.

Action: This condition is an emergency and needs to be caught in the early stages for there to be any chance of recovery. Consult the vet immediately for treatment and medication.
Treatment: Antiserum which may be preceded by laboratory tests; antibiotics; rehydration therapy in advanced cases; intensive nursing.
Comment: Prevention of this disease is very important for many reasons:
(a) It is a very difficult condition to treat.
(b) The Spirochaete organism can be passed on to humans if intensive hygiene is not practised.
(c) Dogs can excrete the organism in their urine for several months after recovery.
       Dogs should be vaccinated as early as possible and boostered annually. Take great care wherever rats may be found as they can infect ponds, drainage ditches, streams, water bowls, fallen fruit, grass and so on.
       I knew a man who became infected with the illness, known as Weils Disease in humans. He was seriously ill for a week before the disease was detected. He believed that the only place where he might have had contact with rats was when he sat fishing on a river bank wearing shorts and, possibly, contaminated grass made contact with a graze on his leg.

Leptospira canicola
Symptoms: Symptoms are similar to the above except that jaundice is less obvious and less frequent and the temperature may rise less and become normal after two days.

Kidney disease: see Nephritis, which may become more important as the dog ages. Advanced cases show foul-smelling mouth ulcers, uncontrollable vomiting. These are normally fatal.

Action: Isolate the infected dog and consult the vet immediately, especially if he is a puppy. Disinfection may be ineffective, so any recovered dog should be retained in the same living area for a minimum of six months as he could still pass the organism in his urine for up to a year following his recovery.

Treatment: If caught early, the disease will respond well to large doses of penicillin. Treatment becomes more difficult once the kidneys sustain damage.

Comment: Prompt inoculation and annual boosters are very important to prevent infection.

Megaoesophagus (Congenital)

Definition: Distended oesophagus where there is a breakdown in the mechanics passing food along it to the stomach. This condition is seen in Golden Retrievers.

Symptoms: Not all dogs have clinical symptoms. Affected weaned puppies may vomit or bring back food but within 2–4 months the clinical signs may disappear as the condition resolves itself.

Cause: May be hereditary.

Action: Feed soft moist/soaked foods in smaller quantities at regularly spaced intervals, for example, 3–4 meals every 4–6 hours. Feed the dog so his head is higher than his stomach. A food bowl stand is helpful (see Chapter 1).

Multifocal Retinal Dysplasia

Since 1998 Golden Retrievers have been certified for this inherited condition because of the increased number of the breed seen with the condition while it was being investigated by the KC/BVA Eye Panellists on Schedule 3 for 6 years.

Definition: A retina with lesions (known as folds) and rosettes resulting from defective development. These defects have to be detected by an opthalmoscope; they are not visible to the naked eye. A more severe manifestation of the condition consists of an irregularly shaped dysplastic area known as 'geographic'. A term derived from its similarity in appearance to a map. This is usually associated with partial retinal detachments. Partial retinal detachments can reattach but multiple folds would occur at the original site of detachment. The worst scenario would be 'total' retinal detachment. In the English Springer Spaniel, the defects are known to take place prior to birth. Defects may result in a small quota of dogs being severely visually impaired, but not all. To date, no Golden Retriever has been presented with blindness as a result of MRD but it has been known in the English Springer Spaniel. The condition is not painful.

Causes: Congenital (inherited). The gene identified as being responsible for the condition is a simple autosomal recessive gene.

Comment: Most Golden owners have been concerned at the introduction to the BVA Eye Scheme of MRD as an additional certifiable condition. This is because of the lack of available evidence within the breed of its hereditary nature. There are other aspects: for instance, the fact that a few or numerous folds have been identified in their young dogs' eyes but, at subsequent eye examinations, there has been little or no evidence of the folds. The Eye

Panellists have explained this as being due to pigment changes in the eye as the dog ages. It is hoped that further research into this condition will eventually determine if this an hereditary disease that will need to be screened for in the future.

Action: Breeders - have litters screened for the condition at 4–6 weeks. Select from those free of the condition but be aware that any siblings within the litter with that condition may indicate a problem. There is, however, no guarantee that those litter screened clear will remain clear for life. Also, as for Cataract.

Treatment: None.

Nephritis

Definition: Inflammation of the kidneys.

Symptoms: Excessive drinking and passing of urine; rapid loss of condition; fishy-smelling breath; if untreated, vomiting, mainly during the morning; in advanced cases vomiting becomes more persistent especially after drinking water; mouth ulcers; loss of appetite. Finally the dog is unable to sustain himself.

Causes: Certain bacteria including Leptospira Canicola (see Leptospirosis). Idiopathic (cause unknown), chills, poisons such as paraffin and petrol.

Action: Veterinary consultation is urgently needed; the earlier the treatment, the better the chances of recovery. Kidney damage is likely to be irreparable so the object of treatment is to arrest further damage.

Treatment: Urine and blood samples will be tested to determine the medication required. If infection is the likely cause, antibiotics, injections and pills will be prescribed. Water intake should not be restricted. Feed a low protein diet such as scrambled eggs and white meats.

Osteochondritis Dissecans (OCD)

Definition: Faulty joint bone growth affecting elbows, hocks, shoulders and stifles. It occurs mainly in the elbow joint (elbow dysplasia) but is also found in the shoulder in Golden Retrievers. Elbow lameness can affect different parts of the joint. Abnormalities are called primary lesions, the most common of which is OCD.

Symptoms: For elbow dysplasia, clinical signs usually appear at 4–8 months, more often in dogs than bitches, and tend to be bilateral. Intermittent lameness caused by pain, some of which is the result of surrounding soft tissues becoming inflamed. Joint thickening; stiffness after rest; lameness may worsen after exercise; can result in rapid irreversible secondary osteoarthritis. Pain is also shown on extension of a joint by a veterinary surgeon.

It is believed that there are also many sub-clinically affected dogs that do not limp but have elbow arthritis or are carriers of the genes.

Causes: Multifactorial causes are not yet proven but are believed to have a recessive polygenic genetic make-up connection and an involvement with environmental factors in breeds with rapid growth rates, such as Goldens. Factors include: nutrition; over-feeding and/or over-supplementation, particularly calcium, phosphorus and vitamin D; excessive exercise. Hormone imbalance has also been suggested. Control of these factors is not believed to prevent the condition.

Action/treatment: A veterinary consultation will be necessary as a correct diagnosis can be difficult. Treatment is likely to involve X-rays, anti-inflammatory drugs and, in most confirmed cases, the surgical removal of floating cartilage from the joint. Full recovery is not possible as the condition is irreversible, but good recovery is possible with no sign of lameness in about 60% of cases.

Alternatively conservative management may be tried which involves diet and exercise control, pain killers and drugs. This may help the lameness but will not cure the condition. In most cases, the longer the surgery is delayed the greater the risk of deterioration as the dog ages. A dog with this condition should never be allowed to become overweight. An overweight dog should be placed on a strict diet and his optimum weight should be retained during his lifetime to ensure the wear and tear on joints is kept to a minimum.

A dog may be heavily bandaged after the operation and need to be restricted and rested for a few weeks as advised by the vet. Limited, controlled lead exercise will need to be strictly enforced to begin with, once the bandaging is removed, and gradually increased from about six weeks. Controlled lead swimming in specially-designed pools can be useful to build muscle in the later stages. For the first session, only a few minutes swim is necessary as the dog will tire quickly, shown by his back sinking below the surface of the water. The time can be increased but gradually per session or every other session. The dog needs to wear a collar to which a short pole is clipped to control his entry, turns and exit. This may be provided by the kennel owners.

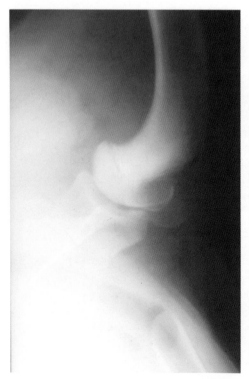

Shoulder osteochondritis dissecans: note the large saucer-shaped lesion of the caudal humeral head.

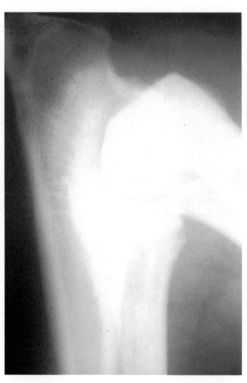

Fully flexed lateral radiograph of elbow with severe arthrosis secondary to elbow dysplasia.

Swimming sessions can be 2–4 times weekly for 3–4 weeks or until the mobility improves. A dog must be removed from the water immediately he tires, even if the lengths target has not been achieved. The pool may contain chlorine, so the dog should be rinsed with clean water after a session and, if possible, bathed a few times between the sessions as chlorine dulls the coat. Dry the dog thoroughly after each session, especially the ears to prevent ear infections, and the tail to prevent wet tail. Hydrotherapy pools without chlorine are now widely available.

These forms of exercise can be very effective in muscle building, are much kinder to joints than roadwork and can be used after most bone and tissue injuries. Vets do not suggest this treatment automatically as usually they do not know of suitable facilities and, of course, road work costs nothing. You may have to make your own enquiries and check with your vet that it is appropriate for your dog's condition and when it is safe to begin.

OCD cases making a good recovery take up to four months before complete soundness returns.

The breeder should be informed. Affected dogs should not be bred from and matings that produce cases should not be repeated.

Comment: This is a recognised disease affecting dogs globally. An International Elbow Working Group is already operating in Australia, New Zealand, Norway, Sweden, Switzerland and the United States of America to screen dogs and grade abnormalities so that breeders can select the dogs with the best elbows, as sub-clinical cases are very common, or there is late onset. In Sweden, 10-year studies (1981–1991) of the Bernese Mountain Dog and Rottweilers that have used screening have already seen a 15% and 10% decrease in incidence respectively. However, due to the nature of OCD, it is unlikely to be totally eradicated.

Screening for OCD became available in the United Kingdom in 1998 under a KC/BVA scheme. As for hip dysplasia, dogs must be at least 12 months of age to be screened. A similar procedure is followed except that three X-rays are carried out on each elbow: an extended lateral (side on) view; a flexed lateral (side on) view; and a cranio-caudal (front to back of joint) view. A grade for each elbow is calculated from the presence of the primary lesions such as OCD and secondary lesions. The grades are: 0 for normal; 1 for mild elbow dysplasia (ED); 2 for moderate ED or a primary lesion; and 3 for severe ED. The dog will be graded according to the higher of the individually graded elbows; they are not added together like the hip score.

Otitis

Definition: Inflammation of the ear.

(a) Otitis externa can affect the external ear canal.

(b) Otitis interna as a result of (a) can affect the inner ear canal.

(c) Otitis media can affect the middle ear canal as a result of (a) or from an infection via the eustachian tube.

Symptoms: Inflammation in either the ear canal or flap indicated by redness, swelling and heat. Odourous smell; dark waxy deposit in the ear; repeated scratching, head shaking or rubbing on the ground due to irritation. Head held at an angle if only one ear is affected with the uncomfortable one lower. Pain if condition is left untreated or goes unnoticed.

Causes: For (a) possibly:

(1). Ear mites (see Ear Mites).

(2). Foreign body such as grass seed (especially common in summer months).

(3). Allergy and/or skin disease.
(4). Bacterial infection.
(5). Fungus/yeast infection.
(6). External ear and flap structure.

Action/treatment: Prompt veterinary consultation is advisable for a correct diagnosis and treatment. Do not use any medication unless it has been prescribed for the dog's specific condition by a vet. Delay may result in greater discomfort for the dog and a straightforward ailment becoming more complex and costly to treat.

If you suspect that an object has entered the ear canal, make no attempt to remove it. This should only be done by a vet.

It is easier to prevent ear disease by:

- Keeping the ears ventilated by trimming the hair on the inside of the ear flap and below the entrance. Take care that no cut hair falls into the ear, causing further irritation.
- Cleaning the outer ear parts with an ear cleaner, using dampened cottonwool. Use only your fingers, no other object. Use only ear cleaners obtained from the vet.
- Combing the hair on and around the ear once a week to prevent knots.
- Inspecting the ears once a week so that you are aware of changes.
- Inspecting the ears after countryside walks for burrs and loose grass seeds.
- Checking other animals, especially cats, for ear mite problems and treating if necessary.

Pancreatic Deficiency

Definition: Digestive enzyme deficiency in the juice produced by the pancreas.

Symptoms: Persistently unformed (sloppy) white faeces, not necessarily diarrhoea. Onset often by nine months of age. Possible indigestion and leanness. Appetite usually remains normal.

Cause: Malfunction of the glandular part of the pancreas. The pancreas is situated near the beginning of the small intestine.

Action: The vet needs to be consulted and given a sample of the dog's faeces to test.

Treatment: Corrective medication to replace the enzymes synthetically as soon as the condition is diagnosed.

Parasites (External – Ectoparasites)

Definition: Parasites that live on the skin, including fleas, lice, harvest mites, mange mites and ticks.

Fleas: Mainly the cat/dog species, but human and hedgehog fleas are also possible. Golden Retrievers, with their soft mouths, are able to pick up hedgehogs and take great joy in presenting them, but suffer the consequences of acquiring more than the hedgehog.

Fleas are thin, wingless, reddish brown in colour, about 1–2mm long, move rapidly through the coat and jump off. They can be located anywhere on the dog but are found mainly around the neck, face, ears, along the spine and tail base. They can act as an intermediate host of the tape worm. In recent years they have become a greater problem, due probably to the increase in pets, central heating, and fitted carpets which harbour the larvae and pupae. Whilst a few may be found on the dog, over 95% will be located on furnishings as well as outdoors.

Symptoms: Scratching and nibbling flea-bite-irritated areas. Sores which may become infected if untreated. Flea droppings look like tiny specks of black dirt but, when placed on wet kitchen roll, release the blood they contain. Allergic dogs will develop a severe allergic dermatitis.

Action/treatment: Immediately your dog starts persistently scratching and nibbling, check for parasites. Wash the dog's bedding and vacuum thoroughly.

Insecticidal baths, powders and sprays are easily obtainable to treat both the dog and his environment, and need to be used at 7–14 day intervals to break the flea life cycle and prevent re-infestation. It may also be advisable to treat the vacuum cleaner. However, concern has been expressed about the toxicity of products containing organo-phosphorus substances; whilst being effective against fleas and other external parasites, they are known to affect some dogs badly. Some products instruct that puppies under one month should not be treated, so the manufacturer's instructions need to be followed very carefully. Flea collars may also have risks for dogs that have a flea allergy, so should be used with care.

A radical new treatment aimed at stopping the problem at source is available in the form of a tablet for dogs and a liquid for cats called Program, administered once a month. It can be used at any time of the year and at any age, and is claimed to be safe for in-whelp bitches as the tablet acts only against the flea. It prevents the flea life-cycle by sterilising the fleas. The active substance is stored in the body fat and released slowly during the month into the blood stream. Treatment can start at any time, or two months prior to the main flea population explosion which takes place in the summer months. Initially the environment will also need to be treated but, once the life-cycle is halted, re-infestation should not be of further concern.

This treatment is only available from your vet. It begins to work within 48 hours but may take about 10 days to halt the life-cycle completely. All household pets should be treated.

If any pet is ill, you can delay giving the tablet for a few days until he is better or you can give with other medication. If you are concerned for any reason, consult your vet.

Non-Organophosphorus products such as Front Line, Spot On and Advantage Spot are very effective. Front Line is also available as a spray.

Comment: I have not had reason to try these treatments, but have known some owners who have tried Program and found it to be very effective.

Harvest mites: These minute, orange larval mites are only just visible. They occur in clusters close to the skin but are mostly found between toes and in ear pockets. They tend to be active from July to October, hence the name. Field mice are their main host.

Symptoms: Irritation, persistent feet licking.

Action/treatment: Immediately your dog starts persistent feet licking, check for parasites and consult your vet for a suitable, available, parasiticide treatment. Some of the effective treatments that once existed are no longer available due to European legislation.

Lice: Lice are very small, fat, wingless, light brown in colour, move very slowly on the skin and lay eggs (nits) that stick to the hair. They are commonly located in the hot parts of the dog – under armpits, inside the thighs and around the neck and ears. They are transmitted by close contact with animals. Their life-cycle is three weeks.

Symptoms: Scratching and nibbling; irritation; in young puppies a severe infestation may cause anaemia.

Action: Immediately your dog starts persistent scratching and nibbling, check for parasites. Wash the dog's bedding. It may be advisable to clean and treat the environment but, as lice cannot exist off a host for more than a few days, the environment is less likely to present a problem than with fleas.

Treatment: Use an insecticidal bath, powder or spray as directed by the manufacturers. Usually treatment will need to be repeated a fortnight later to stop the life cycle.

Mange mites: There are four varieties: three are given below and otodectic mange is dealt with separately. All have a life cycle on their host and do not live long off the host. Adults lay eggs which hatch into larvae within seven days. These mature into nymphs then adult mites.

1. Cheyletiella are minute mites just visible to the naked eye that live on hair and visit the skin to feed with a 5-week cycle. Rabbits and cats can carry this mite as well.

Symptoms: Few signs are seen in dogs but skin scaling (scurf) can be seen along the dog's back if he is heavily infested.

Action/treatment: Insecticidal sprays and treatments are available from the vet. The mite has a long life cycle so treatments may need to be repeated. Ask your vet for advice.

2. Demodectic/follicular mites are of microscopic size and live on hair follicles. Their life cycle is unknown. They can be found on most dogs and in low numbers cause no problems, so there may be an hereditary susceptibility or a link to immune system defects. It is believed that the dam may transmit the mite to her offspring when they are suckling. For unknown reasons the mites may multiply in young dogs, but with no itching.

Symptoms: Severe dermatitis. Hair loss which can start around eyes, nose, feet and legs. Can be localised, then may erupt suddenly all over the body. Lesions are tufted and reddened with pustules at the bottom of the tufts. There is a typical odour. Secondary bacterial infection may occur due to staphyloccocus which the mite takes into the skin. It is this bacteria that causes the lesions.

Action/treatment: Seek veterinary diagnosis without delay as, if it erupts generally, it will be more difficult to treat and control although medications are improving. The dog may need clipping all over and diagnosis is likely to involve a skin scraping. If the disease becomes widespread, euthanasia may be the only option.

3. Sarcoptic mange (scabies): A highly-contagious, invisible mite that burrows into the surface layer of the skin (the epidermis) to lay eggs, which hatch continually. Found mainly on the underside of the body, especially armpits and the inner thighs and ears, head, neck, elbows and stifles. Can occur at any age. Transmission can be from dog to dog; foxes have also been blamed for many recent outbreaks.

Symptoms: Intense irritation; persistent, frantic scratching; reddening of skin with minute red pimples; hair loss. If untreated, lesions will spread over the whole body, which will lead to a loss of condition and a 'doggy' odour. The acute irritation will result in almost permanent scratching and the dog will be unable to sleep.

Action: The dog is highly contagious, so isolate him from other animals. Seek veterinary attention as soon as possible. This will involve a skin scraping and microscopic investigation. It is advisable to destroy and replace bedding.

Treatment: Use an insecticide spray in all places inhabited by an infected dog. Obtain the most up-to-date treatment available from your vet. Treatments are likely to be needed several times at weekly intervals to prevent newly-hatching youngsters becoming sexually mature. It may be advisable to treat other dogs living in the same environment.

NB Hygiene is very important when handling dogs with mange, particularly in cases of cheyletiella and sarcoptic mange as the mites are transmissible to human skin, resulting in an irritating rash or spots. However, they rarely affect humans.

Ticks are small, light grey or bluish-black parasites that burrow their heads into the skin (the epidermis) to suck blood from their host. After a feed, their body swells to the size of a pea and they look like a blister with the head remaining firmly buried. They are usually detected when the dog is being handled or groomed. Transmission takes place when dogs are exercised in areas inhabited by natural hosts such as sheep. The ticks leave their hosts and lay eggs; the hatched larvae climb up grass where the chance encounter with a dog occurs. Frequently ticks are found from March to October. Other forms are deer and hedgehog ticks.

Symptoms: Usually none, if only one or two ticks have attached themselves. If infected with larvae, some dogs may show signs of irritation. The presence of many ticks can cause the dog's resistance to disease to be reduced.

Action: Deny dogs access or exercise in areas where natural hosts are known to have been to prevent tick infestation or re-infestation.

Treatment: It is important to remove the whole tick, including its head, otherwise a local skin infection may result. Soak some cottonwool in either methylated, surgical spirit or ether, and smother the parasite for approximately five minutes. Then use tweezers to pull the whole tick off the dog gently. A pet insecticidal spray can be obtained if you prefer. All you need to do is spray the tick and wait for it to drop off. If you have any concerns or there is a heavy infestation consult your vet.

Comment: Ticks can be transmitted from pets to humans.

Parasites (Internal – Endoparasites)

Definition: Parasites that live in the body, including hookworms, lungworms, roundworms, tapeworms, and whipworms. Transmission takes place when hatched larvae are eaten. The dog may eat infested grass, some are ingested when the dog cleans his coat and paws, or the parasites are brought into the home on footwear. A dam can infect her puppies when she cleans them. Some are transmitted from the dam to the foetuses prior to the birth (see roundworms).

Hookworms are about 12mm (0.5in) long, round and thick, and live in the small intestine.

Symptoms: Usually none, but there may be diarrhoea and possibly anaemia as the adult hookworm feeds on blood. If larvae invade the skin, dermatitis may occur between toes.

Action: Clean up faeces, disinfect and wash areas where your dog passes faeces regularly. If possible, prevent the dog eating grass. Implement a regular worming programme.

Treatment: Obtain an all-round worming product that covers this parasite from your vet.

Lungworms are about 2mm ($1/8$in) long and are located in nodules in the bronchea and trachea. Transmission of this endoparasite is not fully understood but it mainly affects youngsters and groups of dogs housed together.

Symptoms: Infection, but it may not be obvious. In severe cases, there is a harsh cough, especially after exercise, and possible weight loss.
Treatment: Problematical. Surgery to remove the nodules may be the only option.

Roundworms: (a) *Toxocara canis* and (b) *Toxascaris leonina*, which also includes hook and whip worms. See below.

Tapeworms There are several types which generally show few signs or problems for dogs and humans. The most common in dogs, which can occur at any age, is dipylidium caninum. This is a segmented tapeworm, which can be anything up to 500mm (20in) in length. It embeds its head into the intestinal wall. Each segment is about 12mm (0.5in) and contains maturing eggs. Sight of a whole worm in faeces is rare; instead segments with ripe eggs are passed which, when dry, look like rice grains.

The life cycle of the tapeworm is interlinked between fleas and dogs. Flea larvae eat the eggs passed by dogs. The eggs mature in the flea as the flea matures, resulting in adult fleas being infectious to dogs. The cycle is completed when a dog swallows an infected flea and the worm larvae is released into the intestine where it matures into a worm to begin the process again.
Symptoms: Poor growth in puppies and, in severe cases, diarrhoea.
Action/treatment: As for hookworms and fleas. Also check for signs of segments and eggs in the dog's bedding and around the anus hair.

Toxocara canis are anything up to 180mm (7in) long, white and round with pointed tips. They can be transmitted as follows:
- Migration of larvae (immature worms) across the uterus to foetuses, so that puppies at birth are always infected.
- Transfer of worm larvae to the puppies via the bitch's milk.
- Re-infection of the nursing bitch whilst cleaning her puppies.
- A chance encounter by the dog eating anything containing roundworm larvae, such as earthworms, birds or soil. Often several worms are passed together like a tangled string, but one seldom sees the worms with modern-day worm preparations as they are dissolved in the motions. Occasionally some mucus might be seen.

Symptoms: Puppies that ingest toxocara eggs may have respiratory problems and possibly pneumonia as the larvae develop and pass through the lungs. If the larvae end up in the stomach and intestines, the dog will suffer from: abdominal pain, diarrhoea, pot-belly, staring coat (dry, coarse, thin and spiky), generally poor appearance, stunted growth, and blockage if heavily infested. The dog may whine.

The health risk is far greater for a puppy, and a heavy infestation can be life threatening. Older dogs are unlikely to show symptoms or produce many worm eggs as, over five weeks of age, any infection migrates to muscles and lies dormant, and does not affect the intestines. No wormer has yet been found to deal with the dormant larvae, so the cycle begins when a mated bitch reaches her seventh week of gestation when the dormant larvae come to life and cross to the womb.
Action: Keep the dam and puppies groomed and as clean as possible after birth until they depart for the new homes.

Treatment: Follow the worming procedure set out in Chapters 3 and 11.

Comment: There is a slight risk to humans, especially children, if they swallow eggs of this endoparasite by touching something in the environment, the dog's coat or bedding where eggs may be present. They are too small to see but, if consumed, they hatch into larvae in the gut and then migrate around the body. Most lodge in tissue resulting in no difficulties. It is only if larvae settle in the retinal tissue that sight problems may occur. This is a rarity, but underlines the importance of regular worming and observing good hygiene.

Treading in fresh faeces, albeit unpleasant, is not a health risk as it takes some time for eggs to hatch and mature outside the host and become infectious. However, they can remain infective in the environment for a number of years,

Toxocaris leonina are anything up to 100mm (4in) in length and very like *canis* in appearance. Their life cycle begins with infective eggs being eaten accidentally and hatching in the stomach. Larvae developing in the stomach wall and intestine later pass eggs back into the environment in faeces.

Action/treatment: As for hookworms.

Whipworms are up to 75mm (3in) in length. They are thinner at the front and thicker at the rear. Found in the caecum in the digestive tract. Transmission is by ingestion of larvae.

Symptoms: Usually none but there may be intermittent diarrhoea with dark faeces, possible loss of condition and occasional vomiting.

Action: As for hookworms, but prevention and treatment is difficult as eggs can remain dormant in the environment for several years. It may also be necessary for a faeces sample to be tested to confirm the presence of this worm type as those passed may be quite small.

Parvovirus (CPV, Canine Parvovirus)

Definition/cause: Virus infection in two forms which became recognised in 1978.

Canine Parvovirus Myocarditis occurs where a dam of a litter has not been inoculated or, because she had not become infected with the disease, has no antibodies to pass on to her puppies. If a puppy is then exposed to the virus, the result is usually death due to heart muscle weakness or destruction by the virus. Usually the whole litter is affected and deaths occur from 4–10 weeks as soon as the puppies start to get up on their legs. Such occurrences are now rare, as breeding bitches have either been inoculated or exposed to the infection.

Intestinal form of CPV can affect dogs from 4 weeks to old age, particularly youngsters, and can be fatal.

Symptoms: A rapid onset with varying degrees of severity; abdominal pain; fever; depression; severe vomiting; profuse, bloody diarrhoea; dehydration; refusal to eat and drink; recovered young puppies may be bald for up to 12 months, and have a poor growth rate.

Action: Isolate the infected dog and consult your vet urgently by telephone, to avoid meeting other dogs at the surgery. This virus is highly contagious and can be transmitted on clothing and shoes, so everyone living with an infected dog must avoid contact with other dogs.

Disinfect the premises thoroughly and regularly with Parvo-Viricide available from Animal Health Company Ltd as the organism is very difficult to eradicate from the dog's environment for several months after infection has passed.

Do not delay having your puppy's inoculations and adults booster carried out. If your dog dies of this disease, it is advisable not to get a new pet for at least six months.

Treatment: May involve rehydration, medication and lengthy hospitalisation. In severe cases, where the intestine cell lining has been destroyed, dogs are unlikely to recover as they will be unable to absorb fluids and goodness from food.

Poisons

Like many things associated with dog ownership, preventing access to poisons is far more effective and kinder to the dog than dealing with the consequences, which may be expensive as well as result in a very ill dog or the loss of a loved one.

It is impossible not to have plants, trees, shrubs and substances around the home and garden that are poisonous to dogs, such as disinfectants, medicines, anti-freeze and slug pellets. Dogs, and especially puppies in their chewing stage, should be denied access to places likely to contain such poisons, or the poisons should be stored elsewhere. Take care where you know such substances have been used at home, which should never be where dog food is stored or prepared, and off your premises, such as sprayed areas of crops.

If exposure is suspected, wash the dog's paws before he can lick them and ingest any poisons, plus his coat if necessary.

If you suspect that your dog has eaten something poisonous, obtain veterinary advice without delay. Take information on the substance you believe is involved and, if the dog has been sick, a sample of the vomit. This will help the vet to make a correct diagnosis and administer the appropriate antidote. Some products may list the appropriate antidote.

Emergency: The dog should be made to vomit only if the poison is known to have been ingested in the last two hours.

Vomiting can be induced by the following methods:

(a) Administer a small lump of washing soda crystals – about 1 large dessertspoonful. The results should be seen in under five minutes. Once the dog's stomach and bowels are flushed out, you should then proceed to the vet without further delay.

(b) A strong saline solution.

Do not induce vomiting if acids, alkalis, caustic soda, chlorine bleach, drain cleaners, dishwasher salts, oven cleaners, paint thinners/removers, petroleum products, polishes, toilet cleaners, washing detergents and wood preservatives are consumed.

If the coat comes into contact with anything other than petroleum products and paint, wash the area involved with warm water for five minutes and then with a baby shampoo. It would be advisable to wear protective gloves.

Progressive Retinal Atrophy (PRA)

Definition: Progressive destruction and loss of retinal tissue (the light-sensitive tissue at the rear of the eye). There are two types: (a) Central and (b) Generalised. Golden Retrievers are certified for both: (a) since the onset of the KC/BVA Eye Scheme and (b) since 1998.

Central PRA or Retinal Pigment Epithelial Dystrophy (RPED) is a bilateral (affecting both eyes) disease of the retinal pigment, which can be detected from 12 months onwards.

Clinical symptoms: At onset there may be difficulties of working/seeing in bright light.

Advanced cases may have greater difficulties. Central visual defect. Peripheral vision is usually retained. Total blindness or secondary cataract formation is unlikely.

Causes: Probable combination of a Vitamin E deficiency and a metabolic defect of genetic origin which causes the liver to produce insufficient transport factor to move Vitamin E round the system.

Action: As for Cataract.

Treatment: Vitamin E supplementation will prevent further deterioration but cannot repair the damage.

Comment: In 1995, the BVA reported that the incidence of cases had fallen from 14% to less than 0.5% over the preceding 20 years.

Generalised PRA is either rod/cone dysplasia or rod/cone degeneration. The signs of both are similar. In rod/cone dysplasia, the photo receptors are abnormally formed to begin with and there is a degeneration before maturity which can be detected at an early age. Rod/cone degeneration affects the photo receptors after reaching maturity and is detected at a later age.

Clinical symptoms: Loss of night vision. As the condition progresses, there is a total loss of sight. Poor pupillary light reflex with dilated pupils. Secondary cataract forms later and progresses to a total cataract. Not congenitally present, as in Irish Setters.

Causes: Inherited. In breeds investigated to date, the mode of inheritance appears to be a simple autosomal recessive gene.

Action: As for cataract.

Treatment: None available.

Ringworm

Definition: Fungal skin infection.

Cause: Fungi that lives on the skin's surface or in hairs near a lesion, which can occur anywhere on the dog. May originally be due to poor management of the dog, and overcrowding. Transmission can spread rapidly from dog to dog and, whilst it is not life threatening, it is contagious to cats and humans. It also appears as a ring of small red spots or reddened skin on humans.

Symptoms: Scratching or nibbling an infected area of the skin begins as a red raised lump. A rounded patch of crusty, scaly skin develops. Hair loss around the lesion. Reddened area enlarges to form a ring, hence its name. Will spread if untreated.

Action: If you have other cats or dogs, isolate the infected animal straight away until signs of the infection have gone. Burn the dog's bedding. Disinfect the dog's living quarters twice a week, until the infection is clear, with Parvo-Viricide. Prevent children from handling the infected dog. Ringworm may take several weeks to clear from the skin.

Treatment: A course of tablets to be given orally from the vet. Humans contacting ringworm need to visit their doctor to obtain the appropriate medication.

Shock

Causes: Accidents, fights, trauma.

Symptoms: In minor cases, the dog may appear dazed. Other symptoms are faint or accelerated pulse rate; rapid breathing; weakness; cold pads and anaemic or blue gums.

Action/treatment: Keep the dog warm and quiet except in cases of heat stroke (see before), and reassure him until he returns to normal. Do not give anything by mouth until you are sure there are no complications; then you may decide to aid recovery with a homeopathic remedy such as Arnica. In severe cases, follow the same procedure but give nothing by mouth and consult your vet urgently, as it is a possibly life-threatening condition due to body circulation failure. The causes may vary from torsion to poison and it may not occur until several hours after an incident. If other injuries are involved, stem the flow of any bleeding and then deal with the shock before anything else.

Interim action: In order to sustain the body's vital functions it may also be necessary to use artificial resuscitation (mouth to nose) and heart massage but only if the dog is unconscious. See Chapter 4: Adult Care – dealing with emergencies

Slipped Disc

Definition: Dislocation of cushioning discs situated between spinal vertebrae.

Symptoms: Inflammation. Possibly intense pain, or no pain but loss of feeling and mobility below the condition. Weakness, particularly in the hind quarters, and possible paralysis. Possibly a loss of urinary control.

Causes: Accidents and injuries.

Action: Keep the dog as still as possible and transport him to the vet urgently, on a board to prevent further discomfort.

Treatment: X-rays and perhaps surgery. Anti-inflammatory injections and/or tablets. Confinement and rest, to be followed by gentle, controlled lead exercise until recovery is made, perhaps using a harness if advised by the vet.

Comment: I had a Golden aged 12 years that dislocated a disc near his shoulder blades. The symptoms took over two weeks after the injury to appear. They were: difficulties in rising from or laying down on the ground and intense pain due to inflammation. The dog was also distressed. A full recovery was made with medication and rest followed by gentle exercise.

Spondylitis

Definition/causes: Inflammation of the spinal joints and vertebrae.

Symptoms: Rigidity of the back, immobility. Severe cases may result in Spondylosis (extra bone growth around the vertebrae, causing them to fuse).

Treatment: See Arthritis.

Comment: I do not know the percentage of dogs affected by this condition, but have heard of a number of Goldens affected by the condition as they age.

Sprains/Strains

Definition: Sprain - overstretched or torn ligament or tendon; mainly hocks, shoulders, stifles and wrists.

Strain - overstretched or torn muscle.

Symptoms: Sprain - discomfort when touched, limb immobility or limping and swelling. Strain - abrupt pain whilst moving, loss of power and swelling.

Comment: I have heard of an increasing number of Golden Retrievers that are suffering torn cruciate ligaments in their stifle joints but am not certain if this has any implications for the breed at present. Partial ruptures need to be dealt with to try to prevent the onset of arthritis as well as torn ligaments which will need surgical repair. As the condition can be bilateral, extreme care needs to be taken after the dog has had surgery. Initially, the dog needs to be very restricted. Exercise can be increased very gradually under veterinary advice. Therapeutic swimming can be useful to strengthen the affected limb's muscles in the latter stages (see OCD).

Action/treatment: Seek veterinary advice without delay to ascertain the seriousness of the injury. In major cases, treatment is likely to be as for slipped discs.

For a minor sprain, apply a cold compress to help with pain and swelling. An easy way to do this (for low limb sprains), if your dog will let you, is to fill a bucket with cold water and gently place the affected limb into the bucket for a few minutes several times a day (outside!). You may need to take the weight or support the dog whilst placing the limb in and out of the bucket.

Stings

Symptoms: Mainly minor swelling at the site of the sting. A little temporary pain (a few hours at the most). Some dogs may react more, especially if they have an allergic reaction and swellings may occur apart from at the sting site. Youngsters are more likely to chase bees and wasps and get stung around the head, mouth (out or inside) or even in the throat. This may lead to respiratory problems when the sting swells.

Action: Check for a sting and remove with tweezers (usually only bees leave their sting). If you suspect the insect has been swallowed, observe the dog for at least one hour to ensure any internal swellings do not interfere with the respiratory system. If they do, or swelling can be seen by the nostrils, nose, back of mouth or throat, contact the vet immediately for advice.

Treatment: Apply meat tenderiser to the sting – it is very effective. Anti-histamine (for animals) if you have any, but phone the vet and ask for details of the quantity to administer according to the dog's weight. If you have a dog that is prone to over-react or is allergic, it would be wise to keep a supply of anti-histamine tablets for such occasions.

For bee stings, mix a teaspoonful of either bicarbonate of soda or washing soda with a little water into a paste and apply with cottonwool. For wasps, apply either vinegar or lemon juice with cottonwool.

Stroke

Cerebral Haemorrhage and CVA (Cerebro Vascular Accident).

Definition/cause: 'Stroke' is a very difficult term to define in dogs. It encompasses three possible sets of diseases:

(a) Hypertensive Cerebral Haemorrhage.
(b) Idiopathic Vestibulitis.
(c) Other brain diseases.

All three can cause the symptoms described. The most common is (b), which is not a brain problem at all but an inflammation of the inner ear. Other main causes are old age or old age combined with sudden exposure to very cold temperatures.

Symptoms: Head held on one side; dilated pupils; disorientation; circling; fright and distress; involuntary emptying of bladder and bowels; vomiting; lack of acknowledgement of owner;

abrupt blindness; loss of use of one or more limbs or complete paralysis. Some or all the symptoms may occur quickly without warning from which there may be a gradual recovery.
Action: If possible, confine the dog to avoid him falling and hurting himself; keep him warm; stay with the dog to reassure him and prevent any further confusion whilst someone seeks prompt veterinary assistance for a correct diagnosis.
Treatment: Depends on severity of symptoms and how frequently other haemorrhages occur. Intensive nursing, that is hand feeding, physiotherapy, and so on. Medication to help blood circulation, vitamins, steroids. If haemorrhaging occurs every few hours and the symptoms are severe, euthanasia maybe indicated.

Tetanus

Definition/cause: Bacterial infection leading to amassing of toxins in the blood (rarely seen in dogs). Usually enters through an open wound or injury.
Symptoms: Initially there may be a general, non-specific lack of wellbeing. Eyes may flash upwards if the dog is tapped gently on the head. This can assist an early diagnosis. Gradual immobility of muscles, stiffness leading to rigidity and spasms. Face and head are usually affected first and can progress rapidly throughout the body if not detected and treated as an emergency. Lock-jaw, that is, the dog is unable to use or open his jaw effectively to eat and drink. If it affects other vital organs, tetanus can be fatal.
Action: This is an emergency – seek veterinary attention for correct diagnosis.
Treatment: Medication to combat infection. If lock-jaw occurs, watering and feeding assistance will be required until the dog makes a recovery and especially until the muscle rigidity of the jaw lessens.
Comment: If the infection progresses as far as the bladder and bowels, rendering the dog unable to pass urine and faeces, nursing and recovery may be impossible; either the dog will die or euthanasia may be advised.

In the tetanus case encountered in our kennel in the late 1970s, we were able to open the dog's mouth enough to syringe in water in small doses very regularly to prevent dehydration and he was just able to suck and swallow moistened chopped boiled eggs. Liquidised food may have also been used. The onset had taken 1–2 weeks and even the vet was unable to diagnose what was wrong with the dog until the signs began to show, despite three previous visits. The lock-jaw symptom lasted at least 7, maybe 10 days.

A full recovery was made; weight lost was soon replaced, but it took about two months before the muscle stiffness completely subsided. The dog lived to be almost 11 years. He did subsequently have a problem with his pancreas and required a special diet but it is not known if this was a consequence of tetanus.

Ulcers

Definition/symptoms: Abnormal localised break in the surface of a membrane organ or tissue often accompanied by an odorous smell. Seen mainly on upper gums or inner lips, leading to excessive salivation and loss of appetite.
Causes: Bad teeth, infected wound, kidney problems (nephritis), leptospirosis, Vitamin B deficiency.

Action/treatment: A visit to the vet will be required for the cause to be identified. Bad teeth will need to be descaled under anaesthetic or removed if the decay is very serious. Veterinary advice should be given on future prevention, including dental care. Wounds may need to be cauterised. Vitamin deficiency or kidney problems will require corrective medication.

A Golden recovering from tetanus. The head and facial muscles are still taut,
but do eventually return to normal.

Unconsciousness/Coma

Definition: Asleep and unaware of surroundings.

Other symptoms: Low or increased heart rate (shock). Anaemic or blue gums (severe shock).

Causes: Choking or concussion. Diabetes. Disease or condition with breathing difficulties. Electrocution. Fainting. Heart failure. Heat stroke. Inhalation of irritants such as carbon monoxide poisoning. Kidney disease (see Nephritis). Loss of blood. Near drowning. Old age. Poisoning. Serious illness. Shock.

Action: Check for signs of consciousness by:

(a) Calling the dog's name to see if there is any response.
(b) Extend a limb to see if the dog pulls it back.
(c) Pinch the skin between the foot pads and, at the same time, check if the eyelids blink.
(d) Feel for a heart beat.
(e) Check for abnormal gum colour which will indicate if there is a circulation problem.

Treatment: Veterinary assistance will need to be sought urgently for most of these causes. If the gums are an abnormal colour, cardiac massage will be required but must only be given if the dog is unconscious. (See Chapter 4 for method.)

Von Willebrands Disease

Definition: Bleeding disorder affecting both males and females.

Symptoms: (a) In severe cases, spontaneous bleeding such as nose bleeds may take place. Seasons may be prolonged. Bleeding may be lengthier when a bitch is about to give birth to a litter. Gastro-intestinal tract bleeding. Easy bruising.
(b) In some cases inadequate healing with a wide scar.
(c) In most cases the disorder is often only detected after a dog has had surgery or has encountered trauma. Bleeding incidents may lessen in severity as the dog ages.

Cause: Inherited platelet and adhesion defect (deficiency of the Von Willebrand factor). Hypothyroidism can aggravate the condition. The gene involved in most breeds is a dominate with incomplete or partial penetrance.

Comment: In 1988 Golden Retrievers were identified as one of seven breeds in the United Kingdom known to be affected by the condition, and one of 57 breeds in America.

Action: Diagnosis of the disease can be made by a vet measuring the Von Willebrand factor antigen in a blood sample using an immunological method. Owners of affected dogs should inform the breeder as it is a known inherited condition. America has been successful in reducing the number of affected dogs by screening breeding stock and taking the results into consideration when planning litters.

CHAPTER SEVEN

Remedies

Homeopathic Remedies

Homeopathy was evolved over 200 years ago on the basis that 'like may be cured with like'. It is a natural and safe way to deal with pet ailments. Treatments stimulate the body's own powers to self-heal and regulate, resulting in better health. The greater the dilution, the more powerful the remedy. (On a cautionary note, although on the whole homeopathic remedies are very safe, if the remedy is not accurately matched to the symptoms of the patient it is possible to induce side effects. This is more likely to happen with a wrongly chosen remedy if it is given over a long period of time or in very sensitive patients. The more powerful, the longer acting the remedy is and the more chance of side effects if the remedy is not well chosen.)

It has had good results in both the short and long term for chronic conditions which have failed to respond to other forms of medication. Many sceptics say that homeopathic treatments only work psychologically in humans but this argument fails when acknowledging its success in the animal kingdom.

Homeopathy is suitable for home treatment for first aid, minor ailments and initial treatment. Homeopathy is not a substitute where veterinary attention and treatment are required. If you are not sure what your dog's problem is, whatever its seriousness, you should always consult your vet or a homeopathic vet for a correct diagnosis rather than trying out treatments by a process of elimination. Also, if the symptoms worsen at any time or the animal has not improved after 4-5 days, the owner should seek veterinary help. It is advisable to seek a referral from your local vet whether or not the dog is under his treatment. If the homeopathic consultation is a means of seeking a second opinion for a complaint, the homeopathic vet will require the dog's veterinary history and results of any tests carried out in advance of the consultation.

More than one remedy may be identified to use for long term or recurrent conditions. Differences between pets may mean that one remedy may prove more beneficial to one dog than another suffering from the same complaint. In such circumstances, an alternative remedy can be tried on the dog to see if it has a more lasting effect.

All treatments should be given in tablet form unless stated. External treatments such as mother tinctures (Ø) should be diluted by 1 drop to a minimum of 10 drops of water.

Homeopathic tablets should be administered between meals, preferably without food or being touched. Tablets (which should *not* be swallowed whole) can be administered by crushing and placing in a spoon with a little water. Tip onto the back of the dog's tongue, rub the throat and probably the dog will swallow it easily. Alternatively, a tablet can be given crushed with a small amount of food, or crushed between two clean teaspoons into a powder, to be placed on the dog's tongue. Handle the remedy as little as possible and ensure your hands are dry and clean.

An adult dog may be given the same homeopathic dose as a puppy.

I have used some, but not all, of the remedies and some to great effect. My bitches tend to object to pill taking but my males think it is fun and come to me for tablets even when they are not on any treatment but see me giving pills to another dog.

Remedies should be stored in the containers in which they were supplied, in a cool dry place away from strong smells and sunlight, and then they should last almost indefinitely.

Dosage

Homeopathic remedies are safe for puppies; doses remain the same regardless of your dog's age, size or weight. Whilst it is not possible to overdose your dog, caution should still be taken to keep to the dosage recommendations. Remedies can be combined or used with conventional medication prescribed by non-homeopathic vets and, in fact, some vets are now recommending their use alongside conventional treatments.

Most treatments are available from major chemist shops. The potency to be used, unless prescribed otherwise by a qualified homeopathic veterinary surgeon, is 6c (6 times by a factor of 100).

The treatment can be reduced or stopped as soon as you see a positive improvement in your dog. If no improvement is seen within 2–3 weeks, an alternative or combined remedy may be necessary. A list of vets who have the homeopathic qualification, together with a list of books for further reading, is available from Mr C E I Day who is the Hon. Secretary of the British Association of Homeopathic Veterinary Surgeons, provided a stamped addressed envelope is enclosed (see Appendix 1).

The following list refers to some conditions which may respond to homeopathic treatment. However, homeopathy is a complex subject and these remedies should only be used in the first aid of non-life threatening conditions. A veterinary surgeon should first confirm that the condition is not life-threatening.

Conditions	Treatments which may be used
Abscess (chronic)	Silicea will help pus to form so abscess can ripen.
Abscess (in the mouth)	Mercurius Solubilis (Merc Sol).
Aggression	Belladonna.
Allergic reactions	Sulphur.
Appetite loss	Arsenicum Album (Arsen Alb) promotes a general feeling of well being).
	Nux Vomica (Nux Vom), used particularly when constipation accompanies the loss of appetite.
Apprehension	Scutellaria Lateriflora (Scutellaria) (see excitability).
Arthritis (worse with movement)	Bryonia Alba (Bryonia). It affects joints, ligaments, tendons, fibrous tissues and membranes which secrete fluids.
Arthritis (better with movement)	Rhus Toxicodendron (Rhus Tox). Rheumatic remedy to relieve physical stiffness.
Arthritis (where bone is affected)	Calcarea Fluorica (Calc Fluor).
Barking (when owner is away)	Pulsatilla Nigricans (Pulsatilla).

Bereavement (loss of litter or companion dog or otherwise)	Ignatia Amara (Ignatia), for emotional upset.
Bites, wounds and cuts	Hypericum and Hypercal tincture solution externally or ointment.
- small wounds, such as ear tips	Arnica Montana (Arnica).
Bleeding (with shock)	Aconitum Napellus (Aconite).
Bruising	Arnica Montana (Arnica) for internal and external bruising before/after surgery, helps tissue to heal.
Burns (minor cases)	Burn ointment/Cantharis vesticatoria (Cantharis).
Canker	Sulphur.
Colic (if accompanied by flatulence)	Argentum Nitricum (Argent Nit).
Colic (acute)	Nux Vomica (Nux Vom).
Conjunctivitis (straight forward)	Argentum Nitricum (Argent Nit).
(if due to car window draughts)	Euphrasia Officinalis (Euphrasia).
Constipation (straight forward)	Carbo Vegetabilis (Carbo Veg).
Constipation due to overeating	Pulsatilla Nigrans (Pulsatilla) or Nux Vomica (Nux Vom) and liquid paraffin.
Convalescence	Kali Phosphoricum (Kali Phos). Very good for operation recuperation.
Cough (spasmodic)	Arsenicum Album (Arsen Alb) or Cuprum Metallicum (Cuprum Met).
Cough (dry/harsh)	Phosphorus.
Cystitis	Cantharis Vesicatoria (Cantharis) or Sulphur. If accompanied by excessive drinking or traces of blood in the urine, see a vet immediately.
Dandruff	Sulphur or Arsenicum Album (Arsen Alb).
Dental extractions	Arnica Montana (Arnica). It helps lessen the effect of trauma and bleeding and may help to increase resistance to bacterial infection because it stimulates white blood cells which combat bacteria.
Digestive upsets	Nux Vomica (Nux Vom).
Dull/dry and scaly coat	Arsenicum Album (Arsen Alb).
Ear haematoma	Hamamelis Virginica (Hamamelis).
Eczema (dry)	Sulphur is used for skin ailments.
Eczema (wet)	Graphites is used for skin ailments with wet sticky discharge or Calendula Tincture or Cream.
Excitability (highly strung)	Scutelleria Lateriflora (Scutelleria) as it is a nervous sedative.
False pregnancy	Pulsatilla Nigrans (Pulsatilla). It is associated with the female of the species, especially used for inflammation of the reproductive system.
Fear	Arsenicum Album (Arsen Alb).
due to sudden noise (eg thunder)	Phosphorus.

noise hypersensitivity	Kalium Phosphoricum (Kali Phos).
timidity	Gelsemium Semperivens (Gelsemium).
Fever	Belladonna, which is mainly a fever remedy.
Flea allergy	Sulphur.
Foreign body (splinter, grass seed, thorn)	Silicea.
Hair loss	Graphites and Arsenicum Album (Arsen Alb).
Heat stroke	Belladonna.
Homesickness	Ignatia Amara (Ignatia) which is often used for emotional upset.
Incontinence (not due to age)	Calcarea Phosphorica (Calc Phos).
Infections	Silicea.
Injury (after)	Arnica Montana (Arnica) helps tissue healing.
Insect stings	Sulphur – bathe with Pyrethrum liquid.
bees and wasps	Apis Mellifica (Apis Mel).
Insomnia in the older dog	Arsenicum Album (Arsen Alb).
Jaundice	Mercuris Solubilis (Merc Sol).
Knocks	Arnica Montana (Arnica).
Litter loss	Ignatia Amara (Ignatia).
Mastitis	Bryonia Alba (Bryonia) where glands feel hard and Pulsatilla Nigrans (Pulsatilla).
Milk – lack of	Pulsatilla Nigrans (Pulsatilla).
Neutering (after)	Arnica Montana (Arnica).
Pain (sudden/muscular)	Chamomilla.
Pining	Ignatia Amara (Ignatia), particularly useful for dogs in kennels.
Rescued/rehomed dogs	Ignatia Amara (Ignatia).
Restlessness	Arsenicum Album (Arsen Alb) or Aconite Napellus (Aconite).
Rheumatism	Bryonia Alba (Bryonia) and Rhus Toxicodendron (Rhus Tox).
chronic	Sulphur.
Show fright	Gelsemium Semperivens (Gelsemium).
Skin irritations – itchy and red	Sulphur.
Sprains and strains	Rhus Toxicodendron (Rhus Tox).
Stress	Kalium Phosphoricum (Kali Phos).
Teething and teething convulsions	Chamomilla Granules.
Toothache	Belladonna.
Travel sickness – panting,	Cocculus. Use 1 tablet one hour before a journey, followed by another tablet half an hour later. You may need to give a third tablet for long journeys. If you have a long break before a return journey, give a repeat dosage before you return.
Whelping remedy after giving birth	Arnica Montana (Arnica).

Some Other Remedies

An increasing number of alternative medical treatments such as acupuncture, magnetic collars, physiotherapy, lasers and natural and produced remedies for treating dogs are becoming available. I have made reference to a few within the text as appropriate. Some are also 'every day' type of products, such as honey and can be used in conjunction with one another.

Acupuncture

This involves the use of needles at certain points of the anatomy to promote self-healing, particularly when used for an injury, but can be used for other purposes.

Aloe Vera

All products are claimed to be non-toxic and totally safe with no side effects. In general they aim to reduce inflammation, relieve pain and accelerate healing. Conditions which can be treated are: arthritis; abscesses; bites, cuts and burns; cancer; cystitis/uterine infections; diarrhoea; ear infections; eye infections and injuries; injuries; joint swellings; parasites (external) including fleas, mange and mites; parvovirus; respiratory problems; ringworm; skin infections; sprains and strains; throat infections; tooth/gum problems; wounds.

Bach Flower Rescue Remedy

Available from most chemists/health food shops and is useful for treating shock and trauma. I have known this to be used with dogs that have had difficulties in handling certain situations, for example at shows. It is not a preventative treatment but should be given following a problem. Has also been used to revive new-born puppies.

Bicarbonate of Soda

Has many uses such as teeth cleaner, an antidote for acid poisoning, and heat stroke (one third of a teaspoon in the dog's food).

Cider Vinegar

Can help to improve coat condition and appetite. Add 1 teaspoonful to food 2 or 3 times per week. Can also be used as a disinfectant.

Cornflour

Will help burns if made into a paste with water and left to dry until it comes off.

Garlic

Useful for improving blood circulation and as a cleansing agent against infections and internal parasites.

Glucose

To replace/top up energy levels, for example post whelping and to aid recovery from illness. Dissolve in water or milk.

Honey

This has many properties. It is claimed to have healing and antiseptic powers. Useful for aiding recovery and post whelping. Dissolve in warm milk or a gruel.

Live Yoghurt

Following a bout of diarrhoea, live yoghurt balances the disturbed bacterial flora in the bowel. Can be given on its own before re-introducing food and, subsequently, with rice.

Magnetic Collars

I do not profess to know how these work but, having heard many excellent reports on them, I tried one on several of my ageing Goldens and found them all to have a new lease of life. It also helped immensely in returning one of them to almost 100% soundness after a bad ligament strain 9 months previously.

Oils

For internal use, fish oils (from tinned fish, such as sardines), and cod liver oil. They are useful for improving coat and arthritic joints. Give no more than 1 teaspoonful per day on food. Sunflower oil is also useful for improving the coat condition.

Externally, use almond or coconut oil. Useful for improving coat condition and for bringing up texture and gloss. Work a little into the coat and brush with a polisher, hand glove or bristle brush. Remember, all traces need to be removed before a show. Do not apply too much, as the dog and his companions may want to lick it off!

Parsley

Chopped parsley is useful for cystitis. I tried a dessertspoonful with a little food administered in two separate doses, ten hours apart, when a bitch had a problem before a season. Within twelve hours of the first dose, the problem had completely disappeared.

Tridex System

This is a specific method of combinations of formulations based on the homeopathic system of medicine, that is, natural remedies rather than drugs. They were developed and have been marketed for over 40 years following the study of 2,000 homeopathic substances. Remedies are available for most conditions, from appetite problems to whelping aid, including one for fading puppy syndrome.

Veterinary Herbal Medicines and Dietary Supplements

Medicines are recommended for the treatment of specific conditions. They carry a Product Licence Number which means they have been checked by the Government's Veterinary Medicine Directorate for safety, efficacy and purity, and have proved to be effective for the treatment of the conditions for which they have been recommended.

Supplements include minerals and vitamins and are added to the dog's diet. The following are examples from the Dorwest range. Other brands are available from health food shops and chemists.

Herbal medicines	**Used for**
Damiana and Kola Tablets	Improving alertness and stamina, including stud dogs.
	Depression which may occur after an injury or illness.
Garlic Tablets	Improving general health.
	Treating coughs and upper respiratory problems.
Garlic and Fenugreek Tablets	For coughs, dermatitis, eczema, infections.
	Also for improving infection resistance, if administered daily.
	Interdigital cysts.
	Arthritis and rheumatism, if used with Mixed Vegetable Tablets.
Kelp Seaweed Tablets	Coat growth improvement. Obesity and pigmentation improvement. (Do not use this in the hotter months as Goldens are prone to skin problems as a result of blood overheating.)
Malted Kelp Tablets	Stimulating poor appetite*.
	Coat growth improvement.
	Pigmentation improvement.
Mixed Vegetable Tablets	Symptomatic relief of rheumatism and rheumatoid arthritis.
	Bladder disorders, such as incontinence.
	Kidney disorders.
	Skin disorders when used with Garlic and Fenugreek.
Natural Herbal Tablets	Constipation – use as a laxative.
Raspberry Leaf Tablets	Easing whelping. Prevent or reduce effects of phantom pregnancy (also try Garlic and Fenugreek and Scullcap and Valerian tablets).
Scullcap and Valerian Tablets	Calming and relaxing dogs that suffer from anxiety, excitability or nervousness without causing drowsiness (including shyness and showing difficulties).
	Nervous travellers.
	Epilepsy (use under veterinary supervision with orthodox anti-convulsant drugs).

Natural supplements	**Used for**
Cod Liver Oil Capsules	A source of Vitamins A and D. See Oils overleaf.
Digestive Supplement Tablets	Settling the stomach, aiding digestion and relieving flatulence.
Elderberry and Nettle Extract (liquid)	Pigmentation and improvement in coat condition.

Evening Primrose Oil Capsules	Provide a source of Vitamin E. Coat growth improvement. Skin condition maintenance. Assisting hormone imbalance correction.
Garlic Juice	Cleaning inflamed anal glands, pads, feet, ears, sores and minor abrasions.
Keeper's Mix	Major body organs tonic providing health and vitality.
Kelp Seaweed Powder	Providing all the necessary minerals and trace elements. Pigmentation improvement. Coat growth improvement.
Parsley and Watercress	Preventing blood overheating*.
Wheatgerm Oil Capsules	Providing a natural source of Vitamin E for females and males prior to mating* and to bitches for 3 weeks after mating. Skin maintenance. Coat maintenance. Nervous system maintenance.

*I have used the products for the purpose identified and have been pleased with the results.

Vitamin C (Ascorbic Acid)

Vitamin C is essential for the formation of bone and cartilage and helps to prevent the tearing of soft tissue and other conditions. Dogs can produce their own vitamin C and some diets contain it, but most dogs benefit from supplementation as vitamin C cannot be stored and it is generally believed that diets do not include sufficient quantity. You are not supposed to be able to overdose on Vitamin C.

A study in America has indicated that some success has been achieved in preventing the onset of hip dysplasia symptoms by administering large doses of Vitamin C to a mated bitch, smaller doses to the puppies after birth and then higher doses until they reach maturity. I have tried this with 2 litters and the bitches I kept have had lower hip scores than either sire or dam. Is this a coincidence I wonder (they also had a lower protein diet)?

Dosage used per day

For mated bitch - from day 1 to when puppies are 4 weeks old: one tablet am and one tablet pm, 200mg strength.
Puppies - from 4 to 6 weeks: quarter of a tablet, 200mg strength.
   at 7 weeks: half a tablet, 200mg strength.
   from 8-12 weeks: one tablet, 200mg strength.
   from 3-12 months: one tablet am and one tablet pm, 200mg strength.
   from 12-18 months: one tablet, 200mg strength.

Finally, I would stress again that homeopathic remedies should only be used in the first aid of non-life threatening conditions and that veterinary help must be sought if symptoms do not improve after 4-5 days.

CHAPTER EIGHT

Showing Goldens

Introduction

Dog showing should be fun and rewarding for both you and your dog, but at no time in the process should you compromise the health and well-being of any dog.

Over the years it has been interesting to observe the coming and going of show exhibitors in the breed. Those who continue for many years love the breed for what it is and rarely have enjoyed early success. Some people who participate in the hobby only want to win at any price but, due to the enormous popularity of the breed and large entries, this is difficult to achieve and they either move to numerically smaller breeds or discontinue showing altogether.

If you decide you want to show a Golden Retriever, you must be prepared for the larger class entries compared to many other breeds, particularly at Championship Shows. However, winning a class with 30 or more entries at a Championship Show gives immense pleasure and prestige.

Many people start by showing their pet Golden because someone has praised the dog's conformation. If you are uncertain whether your pet has sufficient qualities to compete, either seek the opinion of one or two established show breeders who judge (most are very happy to be approached), or enter some shows to find out the opinion of an appointed judge. I recommend the first suggestion. It is less costly and time consuming and, without assistance, a beginner may enter the wrong class, and/or exhibit an unprepared and unschooled dog which may reflect in the judge's results, irrespective of whether the dog is good enough to be

Example of handling techniques – natural and 'topping and tailing', taken at the ECGRC Championship Show 1996. This is the dog line up for the CC challenge.

shown. The show breeders may also be able to say at what level the dog could be expected to compete successfully and whether they can help with ringcraft, trimming, and so on.

Alternatively you may decide to buy from a breeder who has puppies with show potential. I would emphasise the word 'potential', as it is impossible for any breeder to give a guarantee as to precisely how a puppy will develop and much will depend on care and rearing once he has left the breeder. You may have to wait, sometimes months or years, for the right breeding combination or to have first or second choice of puppy. Ask the breeder (and anyone else who helped you select the puppy) to check him as he approaches 6 months to evaluate his prospects before you begin to send off show entries or attend your first show. They may also help with the choice of shows and judges. More information on the best procedure is given in Chapter 2.

Training Equipment

The only piece of equipment needed to begin with is a show lead. Many varieties are available made from nylon, rope, fine chain or leather with either a fixable collar size or unfixed (slip lead).

My recommendation is to use a nylon or fine rope slip lead. They are strong and machine washable. I have known fine show leather leads to break because owners have underestimated their dog's strength. Fine chain slip leads can be used for the more difficult dogs as the sound of the chain helps to keep them in check, or for those dogs that predict corner turns on the move, but generally I find them unnecessary for Goldens and they can cut the hair around the neck. The other difficulty is finding one which is large enough to loosen around the neck and front when the dog is being stood for the judge. It may be necessary initially to use a smaller lead for a very young puppy.

Lead colour is very much up to the individual. Some exhibitors prefer to have a colour that matches the coat so as not to distract from the lines of the dog when it is being assessed, whilst others use bold, contrasting colours.

Ring Training

Many people believe that ring training means only teaching your dog how to stand and move for a judge's assessment. In fact, it is a specialised extension of basic training and is easily achieved if the groundwork such as early socialisation, heelwork and moving in a straight line has been completed.

Training can begin when you acquire your puppy at 7–9 weeks but, initially, only ask him to do any one thing for a few seconds because his concentration span will be short. Training should always be pleasurable so that the puppy develops a rapport with you, associates showing with fun and grows in confidence. Keep commands simple and clear, preferably using single words not a sentence or string of words, and only train if you are in a good frame of mind. If the dog senses that you are harassed, things may go wrong and it may take a long time to correct a bad training session. Remember, the dog is a puppy up to 12 months and many Goldens do not begin to mature mentally until they are two years or over, so be realistic in your expectations.

Until the the puppy is 12–14 weeks old, any training will have to be on home territory until the vaccinations are completed and the vet gives you the all-clear to go out. In these early weeks, you should car-train your puppy, and lead-train him to heel. I strongly advise anyone who wishes to show a dog not to teach him to sit until he is 8–9 months old. This normally prevents the dog from sitting every time you come to a halt in the show ring. Instead, teach him to stand, using the command 'stand' or any other word. It is not imperative that young

Topping and tailing.
Handler and breeder Ann Woodcock with Mr J Brownlie's Sh Ch Stanroph Soldier Boy.

puppies stand perfectly still. If this is ingrained into them too early they are likely to become very flat and dull in personality.

I find it very effective to ask a puppy to stand without touching him and encourage him to wag his tail for about 5–10 seconds once every few days for one of his meals. As he progresses to 6 months old, the time can be increased by a few seconds and practised once a day. The pup should receive praise as well as his meal. Alternatively, you can use a little bait, such as cheese or dog treats, to do the same between meals but sessions should be brief and no more than three times per week if you want to retain the puppy's interest and co-operation.

You will also have to decide how you wish to show your Golden: freely, by standing in front of him with or without show bait, or by standing along his off-show side and holding his head in your right hand and his tail in your left hand (topping and tailing, as shown in the photo above). You can also use bait with this method to encourage him to look forward and stretch his neck out. Care should be taken not to overstretch him, raise his head too high or unbalance him. Showing freely also has one drawback. Many dogs push their neck back into their shoulders, giving the appearance of a short neck, whether or not this is true. Both methods may require you to place the dog's legs in the correct show stance. The method chosen should be the one which makes your dog look best and with which you and the dog are most comfortable.

It is a great help to practise in front of a window or mirror to see the dog's reflection. You will then be able to see the judge's view and know whether your dog looks right. I also use this aid for adult dogs who need some re-training or a quick practice.

Some dogs do not like their tail being held. If this is the case but you wish to stand alongside the dog, then just hold his head.

The dog's conformation and bite have to be assessed by the judge so it is essential that he does not mind being handled. Lots of physical contact with your young puppy should mean that he does not object to this as he grows up. Grooming a puppy frequently also helps. To begin with, ask people familiar to the pup to run their hands over him. Gradually, the pup should get used to people he is less familiar with, such as the ringcraft class trainers.

When the puppy is teething, his gums may be sore so do not overhandle his mouth. I ask ringcraft trainers not to check the mouth until a puppy has finished teething.

From about 3 months onwards, once the vaccinations are completed, you can begin to socialise your puppy away from home. This is important for the show dog as well as for pets, because he will encounter all sorts of things at shows such as strangers, children, halls, trolleys, cages, benching, flapping marquees, ring ropes and refuse sacks, clapping, chairs being dragged along the ground, matting being laid out, strange surfaces including ribbed rubber matting, traffic and, of course, other dogs. The list is endless.

Ringcraft training classes provide suitable opportunities for your dog to get used to strangers, other dogs and many of the things that he will encounter in the show world, as well as teach you and your dog show techniques. Classes are run by dog show societies around the country. To find your local club, ask your vet, other dog breeders or The Kennel Club for a list of clubs in your area. You will probably find a class within a half hour journey.

Sometimes breed clubs run classes but it would be advisable to attend all-breed ringcraft classes to ensure your puppy is socialised with other breeds and is familiar with breeds other than Goldens.

Once you have located a class I would advise you to go along first to watch the trainers and other handlers at work before you take your puppy, to make sure you are happy with the methods, hall, atmosphere and so on.

For the puppy's first two visits, let him socialise with the other dogs and people and sit and watch the proceedings for 30–60 minutes at the most. On the second visit I may allow the pup to run up and down the hall or the matting, but I never ask anything further of him until I know he seems relaxed with his surroundings. This activity will tire him immensely as there is so much to take in and learn. Only permit your Golden to mix with the other dogs of good temperament. A bad experience at class could affect the dog adversely for life.

On the third visit I would allow a puppy to be stood and moved once or twice so that he is not over-taxed.

From the fourth visit onwards, when the puppy is about 4 months old, he should be able to cope with the class training more easily, but an hour is still the most he should have. If your puppy performs the required routine correctly, give him lots of praise and do not continue until he is too tired to concentrate and then performs badly. It is always best to end any training on a good note. If a training session has not gone well, carry out the simplest exercise the dog can do, so that he can be praised and go home with happy memories.

The trainers should be able to let you know if you are moving your dog at the correct speed. The needs of each dog will be slightly different. It is also important to get your puppy to move in a straight line. Heelwork alongside a straight fence or hedge can help this. Generally, judges only require exhibitors to move around the ring collectively, and in a triangle and up and down individually.

One ringcraft class a week should suffice, or two if you have a very difficult puppy to train, but certainly no more. Once the dog is old enough to show or is entered for his first show, I cease class training for three reasons. First, the show can provide all the training opportunities you need from then on. Second, you need to prevent your dog becoming too bored. A healthy Golden can be shown for up to 12 years, so it is inadvisable to overshow or overtrain a youngster if you want him to last in the ring. An overshown Golden rarely wants to show much beyond the age of 3–5 years. Third, the real showing atmosphere does not exist at classes and the dog may sense this and your mood change. However, this does not mean that you should not participate in the class's internal/external matches or attend occasionally. Also, if a dog has a major ringcraft problem, it will be necessary to return for a few sessions to try to overcome the difficulty. It is obviously easier for a handler to correct a mistake at a class when the dog and handler are not under the same pressure as they would be in the show ring.

Handling Tips

- When handling, at all times watch where the judge is in relation to your dog, so as not to obscure your dog. Always keep the dog between you and the judge so that he has an uninterrupted view of your dog.
- Make sure your dog can move on your left and right sides for two reasons:
  - (a) the judge may require to see the dog's movement from the side, especially if the ring is narrow;
  - (b) the judge may want to see two dogs moving together side by side in order to select the one with the best movement.
- Know your dog's age in case you are asked by the judge.
- Develop a set of simple word commands for the training. Use one-word commands, for example: heel, side, turn, close, back, left, right, stand, show, no, leave, ready or ready-steady-go (or an equivalent key word).
- All through his show career use the dog's name and lots of praise when he does something right and, being a Golden, his will to please should remain.
- Use bait if necessary – liver or livercake with garlic.
- Use toys if necessary (discretely when in the ring).
- Try to give the dog a 3-month break from the ring every year to help him to retain his enthusiasm. Coat changes usually provide the ideal opportunity for this. Record how long your dog takes over his coat change and, if it is the same each time, you will save yourself a lot of wasted entry fees.
- Use a friend to move your dog to determine the correct speed or ask him to video you moving your dog. A video can also help you decide how best to stand your dog.
- If the dog paces, move a little faster, especially when leaving the judge, to get the dog into a trot.
- If a judge requests you to move in a triangle, make certain it *is* a triangle, not a loop, and try to make it as smooth as possible.
- Relieve the dog's or your ring tensions by laughing or by some other effective means!
- Teach your dog to relax – 'down' exercises are very useful for this, especially when the dog is on his side. Increase the time from seconds to minutes. Practise at home, remembering to always release and praise the dog before moving on to something else. Then practise on walks and at shows.
- This exercise can also be used if your dog is wary of judges approaching. Once you are happy with the dog doing the 'down' exercise, ask people who know the dog to approach him whilst he remains in the down/stay beside you, on a lead if necessary. Avoid eye contact but use the dog's name and, if the dog remains relaxed, he can be rewarded with a treat. Progress to strangers doing the same, but only if no stress is shown. If the dog appears worried, revert to people he trusts and build up slowly again.
- You may need to consider altering the dog's diet if you think it might be affecting his behaviour. Foods including colouring, sugars such as glucose, lactose, and molasses (often found in many biscuit brands) can cause problems.
- If jumping up at the handler is a problem, lift your knee up to discourage the dog from doing this or rattle stones in a tin when practising, but not in the ring.
- If barking is a serious problem, a water pistol may help when practising but, again, is not to be used in the show ring.

- Homeopathy may help, but you need to discuss your problem with an expert who can assess the correct treatment required, unless it is one of the conditions listed in Chapter 7.
- Use exemption shows to see if you have resolved any problems as they are fun and should be less stressful for your dog and yourself.
- If your dog is not giving of his best, try distancing yourself from him the day before the show. For example, if he is allowed in the bedroom to sleep with you, then do not permit this the night before the show.
- I do not believe in starving the dog on show day, as travelling and showing can take a lot out of him. I feed all mine breakfast on the day of the show. Some exhibitors also take their dog's dinner with them in case they are late home or have a long journey.
- Use kerb edges, or small objects that you can place under the dog, to teach him to stand still. The object should be large enough for the dog to feel under the brisket. In the ring you can use your fingers under the brisket and, hopefully, the dog will think the object is there.
- Line your dog (not yourself) up with the judge when moving him.
- Do not over-react to a bitch acting out of character in or out of the ring anything up to 6 weeks prior to seasons. This can be difficult to predict if she has not had her first season. It does not affect all bitches and sometimes only occurs prior to the first season.
- Important: your attire and footwear should also be appropriate for showing and moving the dog. Dark colours set off Goldens well but beware, they may also show off your dog's lack of coat or hair loss!

Livercake recipe (can be discretely used as bait in the ring)
225g (8oz) liver
1 packet of pizza mix (wholemeal preferably) or dough mix
2 tblsp of sunflower or olive oil
water to mix
garlic (optional)
1. Boil the liver in water until cooked and soft.
2. Reduce the liver as finely as possible.
3. Add the pizza or dough mix and oil (follow the instructions on the packet, if any).
4. Add water to mix (the liver stock can be used).
5. Add a little garlic if required.
6. Roll out on flat board/surface.
7. Cut into strips.
8. Bake in oven 190°C/375°F until cooked.
   Cooking time will vary slightly depending on the type of oven and whether you want the livercake soft or crisp. It will freeze, so you can make greater quantities if required.

Dog Shows
There are currently five types of Kennel Club licensed shows.
A **Championship Show** is open to all exhibitors (Crufts is an exception to this rule as a qualification for entry is required).
An **Open Show** is open to all exhibitors.
Limited Shows and **Matches** are limited to the organising show society's members but exclude dogs which have won a CC or an award that counts towards the title of Champion.
Exemption Shows are for both registered and unregistered dogs. A dog that has won a CC, an award that counts towards the Champion title, a Reserve CC or a Junior Warrant is

ineligible for entry in the pedigree classes. A similar ruling applies to obedience classes, when they are scheduled, at such shows.

The best way of finding out about most shows is to order one of the weekly dog journals such as *Dog World* or *Our Dogs* and apply for schedules. They do not usually include details of Matches but societies inform their membership of these during the course of the year. Some Exemption Shows also advertise in these papers.

Show Entries

The schedule for each society's show sets out the rules and regulations, together with the class definitions for that show. A full list of classifications follows for reference. It is best to familiarise yourself with the classifications before entering and attending the show.

Most societies offer breed classes for Goldens due to their popularity. Class definitions vary slightly depending on the level of show, so it is advisable to keep a record of your dog's wins to ensure you comply with the rules of eligibility. It may take a little while to acquaint yourself with them fully.

Places are awarded down to at least 4th place (reserve) in every show and sometimes 5th (very highly commended), 6th (highly commended), and 7th (commended). In breed classes, a Best of Breed and a Best Puppy are always awarded, and at Championship Shows the best of each sex is awarded the Challenge Certificate. From these two dogs the Best of Breed and the Best Opposite Sex are then determined.

At most Championship Shows, the large entries for our breed mean that the dogs are split into sexes and a separate judge is appointed for each. If they cannot decide jointly which dog to declare Best of Breed, then the appointed referee is called on to make the decision.

Many different special awards and trophies are offered at shows, details of which should be given in the schedule.

Numerous Kennel Club regulations govern events held under its jurisdiction, including shows. Some of these rules may be incorporated into the society's show rules, but not all. A few of the important rules are:

1. A dog must be Kennel Club registered. If you are still awaiting Kennel Club confirmation of the dog's name, enter the dog under the first name requested and add afterwards NAF (Name Applied For). The same applies to the dog's transfer; TAF (Transfer Applied For) should be added after the dog's name.
2. No puppy under 6 calendar months of age on the first day of any show is eligible to compete.
3. Posted entries must have a post office date postmark of the closing date or earlier.
4. Lost entries have to be substantiated to The Kennel Club after the show. The only evidence accepted by The Kennel Club is recorded delivery, registered post, a certificate of posting or special delivery. Without such proof, any prizes won will be forfeited at a later date.
5. Only dogs entered at the show are permitted within the jurisdiction of the dog show. If it is necessary to take a dog which is not for exhibition, he can be entered 'Not for Competition', as long as he is aged 6 months or over.
6. The mating of dogs within the jurisdiction of the dog show is prohibited.
7. Exhibit owners/handlers are required to clean up any of their dog's faeces or grooming waste within the show precincts.
8. No dogs suffering from, or exposed to, any disease during 21 days prior to any show should be exhibited. Each entry form requires the owner to sign a declaration to this effect. Anyone infringing this rule will be fined or disciplined by The Kennel Club.

9. The attraction of exhibits from outside the ring is prohibited.
10. It is no longer permitted to enter a dog under a judge who bred the dog. However, if after the close of entries a judge has to be replaced and the replacement judge is the breeder of your dog or they have handled/boarded the dog in the preceding 12 months, it is still permissible for you to show your dog under them.

Definitions of Classes

*   at Championship and Open Shows only
**   at Limited, Sanction and Primary Shows only

Where there is no qualification, the definition applies to all types of shows. In estimating the number of awards won, all wins up to and including the seventh day before the date of closing of entries shall be counted when entering for any class. Wins in Variety Classes do not count for entry in breed classes, but when entering Variety Classes, wins in both Breed and Variety Classes must be counted.

Minor Puppy: For dogs of 6 and not exceeding 9 calendar months of age on the first day of the show.

Puppy: For dogs of 6 and not exceeding 12 calendar months of age on the first day of the show.

Junior: For dogs of 6 and not exceeding 18 calendar months of age on the first day of the show.

Special Yearling: For dogs of 6 and not exceeding 24 calendar months of age on the first day of the show.

Beginners: *For owner, handler or exhibit not having won a first prize at a Championship or Open Show.
**For owner, handler or exhibit not having won a first prize at any show.

Maiden: *For dogs which have not won a Challenge Certificate or a First Prize at an Open or Championship Show (Minor Puppy, Special Minor Puppy, Puppy and Special Puppy classes excepted, whether restricted or not).
**For dogs which have not won a First Prize at any show (Minor Puppy, Special Minor Puppy, Puppy and Special Puppy classes excepted, whether restricted or not).

Novice: *For dogs which have not won a Challenge Certificate or three or more First Prizes at Open or Championship Shows (Minor Puppy, Special Minor Puppy, Puppy and Special Puppy classes excepted, whether restricted or not).
**For dogs which have not won three or more First Prizes at any show (Minor Puppy, Special Minor Puppy, Puppy and Special Puppy classes excepted, whether restricted or not).

Tyro: *For dogs which have not won a Challenge Certificate or five or more First Prizes at Open and Championship Shows (Minor Puppy, Special Minor Puppy, Puppy and Special Puppy classes excepted, whether restricted or not).
**For dogs which have not won five or more First Prizes at any Show (Minor Puppy, Special Minor Puppy, Puppy and Special Puppy classes excepted, whether restricted or not).

Debutant: *For dogs which have not won a Challenge Certificate or a First Prize at a Championship Show (Minor Puppy, Special Minor Puppy, Puppy and Special Puppy classes excepted, whether restricted or not).

**For dogs which have not won a First Prize at an Open or Championship Show (Minor Puppy, Special Minor Puppy, Puppy and Special Puppy classes excepted, whether restricted or not).

Undergraduate: *For dogs which have not won a Challenge Certificate or three or more First Prizes at Championship Shows (Minor Puppy, Special Minor Puppy, Puppy and Special Puppy classes excepted, whether restricted or not).

**For dogs which have not won three or more First Prizes at Open and Championship Shows (Minor Puppy, Special Minor Puppy, Puppy and Special Puppy classes excepted, whether restricted or not).

Graduate: *For dogs which have not won a Challenge Certificate or four or more First Prizes at Championship Shows in Graduate, Post Graduate, Minor Limit, Mid Limit, Limit and Open classes, whether restricted or not.

**For dogs which have not won a Challenge Certificate or four or more First Prizes at Open or Championship Shows in Graduate, Post Graduate, Minor Limit, Mid Limit, Limit and Open classes, whether restricted or not.

Post Graduate: *For dogs which have not won a Challenge Certificate or five or more First Prizes at Championship Shows in Post Graduate, Minor Limit, Mid Limit, Limit and Open classes, whether restricted or not.

**For dogs which have not won five or more First Prizes at Championship and Open Shows in Post Graduate, Minor Limit, Mid Limit, Limit and Open classes, whether restricted or not.

Minor Limit: *For dogs which have not won two Challenge Certificates or three or more First Prizes in all at Championship Shows in Minor Limit, Mid Limit, Limit and Open classes, confined to the breed, whether restricted or not at shows where Challenge Certificates were offered for the breed.

**For dogs which have not won three or more First Prizes in all at Open and Championship Shows in Minor Limit, Mid Limit, Limit and Open classes, confined to the breed, whether restricted or not.

Mid Limit: *For dogs which have not won three Challenge Certificates or five or more First Prizes at Championship Shows in Mid Limit, Limit and Open classes, confined to the breed, whether restricted or not.

**For dogs which have not won three Challenge Certificates or five or more First Prizes in all at Open and Championship Shows in Mid Limit, Limit and Open classes, confined to the breed, whether restricted or not.

Limit: *For dogs which have not won three Challenge Certificates, under three different judges or seven or more First Prizes in all at Championship Shows in Limit and Open classes, confined to the breed, whether restricted or not, at shows where Challenge Certificates were offered for the breed.

Exhibitors relaxing and socialising beside the ring at an outdoor show.

	**For dogs which have not won seven or more First Prizes in all at Open and Championship Shows in Limit and Open classes, confined to the breed, whether restricted or not.
Open:	For all dogs of the breeds for which the class is provided and eligible for entry at the show.
Veteran:	For dogs of not less than seven years of age on the first day of the show.
AVNSC:	For breeds of dog for which no separate breed classes are scheduled.
(Any Variety Not Separately Classified)	
Brace:	For two exhibits (either sex or mixed) of one breed belonging to the same exhibitor, each exhibit having been entered in some class other than Brace or Team.

Tips on Etiquette

- Try to get the best out of your dog, but not at the expense of your fellow exhibitor!
- Give yourself plenty of time to get in the ring for your class.
- Do not push into the line of exhibitors when you enter the ring. Many want to be first or in the first few but any judge worth their salt will find the better specimens wherever you stand. If, in your opinion, the judge cannot do this, you will have to ask whether his opinion is worth having in the future.
- Give yourself and the exhibitors either side of you plenty of space to stand the dogs.

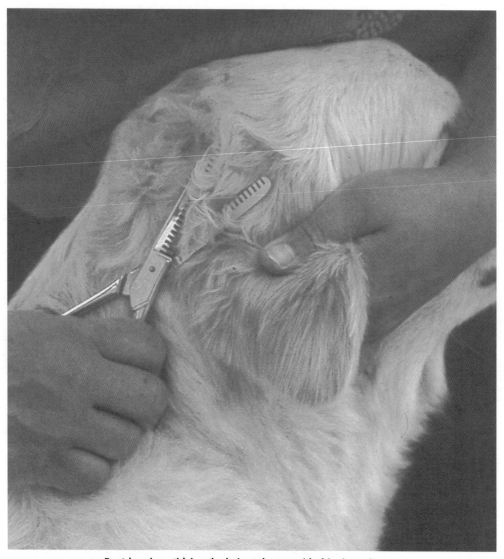

Ear trimming - tidying the hair at the top with thinning scissors.

- Do not let your dog interfere with other dogs in the ring standing or on the move, by keeping him on a short lead. This is also wise at shows/events when you are not competing.
- Watch and remember what the judge wants each dog and handler to do.
- Do not crowd the dog that is being judged or being set up for assessment.
- Set your dog up in readiness for the judge whilst the one in front is moving only if the ring space permits and it is what the judge wants.
- If your dog needs time to settle in a ring, show him nearer the end of the new dogs to be seen.
- Check your number before entering the ring if you need to collect it from the steward or make sure you have the correct number if you have collected it from the bench etc.

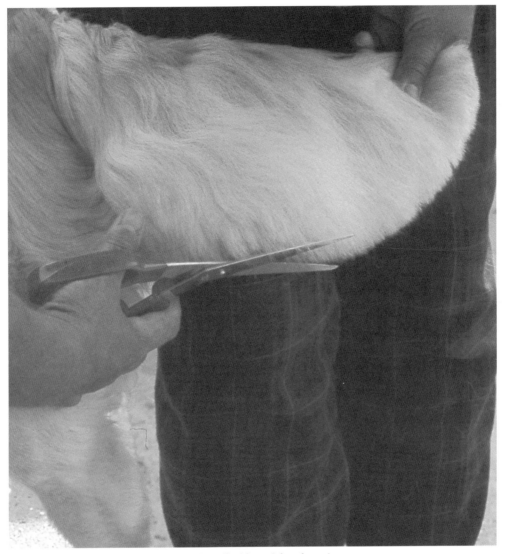

Trimming the tail with straight edge scissors.

- Wear your number so that it is visible to the stewards and ringside observers.
- Follow your judge's and steward's instructions.
- Do not volunteer information about your dog or speak to the judge unless asked a specific question about the dog.
- If you have a class clash with your dogs, inform the stewards; most (!) are very helpful.

Preparing for Exhibition
Equipment

Basic: Comb, wire brush, straight edge scissors, thinning scissors.

Other: Nail clippers, teeth descaler, curry comb, glove brush/polisher, rubber hand glove, man's bristle brush, stripping knives.

Shampoos: Conditioner, insecticidal, hypo-allergenic emollient (detergent-free for normal and dry skin pH7), dry shampoo (for emergencies).

Other: Vitapoint/coconut/almond oil (to condition the coat), baby or olive oil to remove grease or tar, ear cleaner, water spray bottle, towels for drying, chamois leather for drying.

Trimming

Trimming should be invisible and look natural. Do any major trimming a week or two before a show and then just tidy the dog each week whilst he is in coat and showable.

Generally, thinning scissors should only be used underneath the top coat and against the lay of the coat. However, they can also be used to carefully tidy fly-away hair on top coat and feathering. Until you feel confident, practise if you can on a non-show dog or, if this is not possible, do the off-show side first. Using your thinning scissors make just one or two snips at a time until you find out how they cut as new or sharpened scissors can leave severe scissor marks.

Trimming area	Scissor usage
Ears	thinning and straight
Neck	thinning only
Front	thinning only
Feet	thinning and straight
Hocks	thinning and straight
Second thighs	thinning only
Tail	straight only

Presentation Tips for Improving the Show Dog

The purpose of bathing and trimming is to enhance outline, balance, symmetry and virtues – and to hide faults! To make use of the following tips you must know your dog's virtues and faults and then apply the tips accordingly.

Ears

Too large	Keep as neatly trimmed as possible.
Too small	Allow some hair growth but keep neat.
Low set	Do not over-trim hair at top of the ear but keep tidy.

Neck

Too short	Trim out as much as possible, in front, side and behind.
Too long	Keep neat and tidy but allow more growth on chest. Some dogs with a good reach of neck that are overtrimmed can look unbalanced.

Front

Tall on leg	Leave more growth on front where top of leg meets chest.
Short on leg	Trim chest hair back as far as possible where top of leg meets chest, but only above leg each side, not across the chest.
Straightness	Check hair on elbows does not protrude standing or on the move. If it does, thin it out. Likewise, check the front leg feathering. This can be washed and hair dried folding the hair inwards.

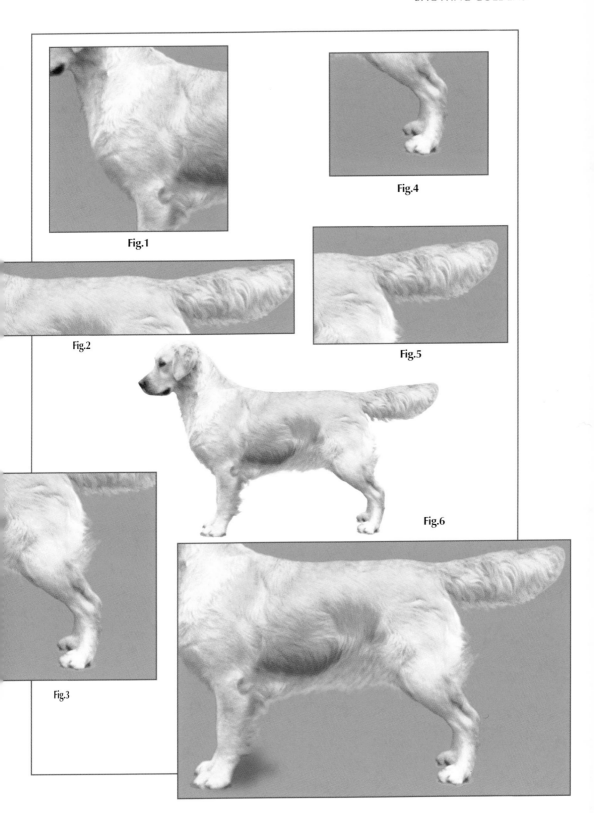

Fig.1

Fig.4

Fig.2

Fig.5

Fig.3

Fig.6

Shoulders (see Figure 1 on page 143)

Lack of layback   Withers are often higher, giving the appearance of lack of neck, shorter back and unlevel topline. Thin hair on top of withers to improve the line of neck into the shoulders.

Good upperarm   Enhance by trimming neck above point of shoulder leaving a gradual line to the point, and thin coat from point to the top of the leg.

Poor upperarm   Do the same as above, leaving as much hair as possible on the point of shoulder to give the appearance of better angulation.

Wide   Thin coat on shoulder sides.

Overloaded   Long term – place the dog on a diet.

Short term – thin coat on shoulder sides and across withers.

Topline/croup and tail set (see Figure 2 on page 143)

Topline on the body should be level and the tail should be set on so it is carried level with the back. If any part dips, dampen the hair on this part shortly before entering the ring. Dry the top coat so that the judge cannot feel any dampness and then brush the wrong way a little.

Sloping croup   In addition to the above, thin the undercoat near top of the hip joints to
and low tail set   make the fault look less severe.

Second thighs (see Figure 3 on page 143)

Too short   Trim out as much as possible and keep neat.

Too long   Keep tidy but leave more hair length visible.

Hocks   As above, but hair should only be cut or thinned to give the appearance of a straight hock.

Stifles

Too angulated   Trim out as much as possible so coat does not exaggerate the angulation.

Insufficient   Keep tidy but have as much hair as possible on the front of the stifles.

angulation   Also, when drying the dog after a bath, comb/brush the hair on the inside of the leg in a forward direction; a hair dryer is very effective.

Feet (see Figure 4 on page 143)

Good or bad   Trim as round as possible and on front feet up the back of the pastern.

Nails too long   Clip them if you can, if not it is better to trim feet so the nail does not show than to expose them and draw attention to their length.

Tail (see Figure 5 on page 143, also photo on page 141)

Too long   Cut into fan from the tip of the tail.

Too short   Cut fan further from tip than usual thumb's length.

Level   Check carried level when moving. Sometimes there is nothing wrong with the tail but the way the coat lies can give the wrong appearance. If this is the case, then try and correct with a bath and hair dryer. If this does not work, thin the offending area of coat on the top of the tail.

Feathering (see Figure 6 on page 143)

Except for the tail, I believe as much as possible should be left untouched but there may be reasons to make a few exceptions.

Front legs	I do not recall any reasons to trim the feathering length on the front legs but if the short hair beside the long feathering is too thick and affects the front's appearance, it could be carefully thinned.
Hind legs	This can grow very long on bitches and spayed and neutered Goldens. If it grows longer than the top of the hock then I believe it affects the dog's balance at the rear, standing and on the move. I would then carefully reduce the length with thinning scissors by twisting the hair tightly before cutting only a little at a time.
	If there is insufficient (because the dog is losing coat or you want to make more of what there is), then dampen and dry a little prior to going into the ring, brush up the wrong way and neaten.
Undercarriage	Length could be reduced a little with thinning scissors if it is too long and affecting the balance of the dog. This may apply more to the small dog.

Thinning the Coat

It should be remembered that if the coat is thinned anywhere on the dog, other than on the front and sides of the neck, hocks and second thighs, the length of time you can show your dog may be reduced, albeit by a few weeks. This is because when the coat starts to blow, there is less in the trimmed areas and coat loss will show up sooner.

Coat Preparation

Coat condition can be improved by diet and regular brushing with a polishing glove or brush to encourage the natural coat oils. Almond or coconut oils can also be brushed into the coat to improve condition. Excessive bathing and swimming, particularly in the sea, can reduce/remove the coat oils, leaving the hair dry and coarse and loosen the undercoat and topcoat more quickly than normal but it can also remove old coat more quickly if you are trying to achieve a faster coat turn round. A bath or fresh water swim can also help to encourage a new coat in a little faster but only if done once or twice.

One of my dogs was usually out of the ring for 5 months, but I managed to show him 2 months earlier by brushing 100 strokes or more all round him each day, and a bitch that was usually out of the ring for 4 months was shown one month earlier by doing the same.

You must also decide where you are going to bath your dog. If you use the shower or bath, the dog may need to get used to this as he will to a hair dryer.

Let your Golden sit or stand on a non-slip surface in the bath. A soaked vet bed has been used here, which also prevents the nails scratching the bath's surface.

Make sure that the dog cannot slip in the shower or bath. I prefer to bath a dog outside but this can only be done in warm weather to prevent the dog becoming chilled. Some breeders have an outside hot water tap plumbed in to assist them with outdoor bathing.

Find out before the dog's first show what a bath does to the coat. Some coats need to settle 2–3 days before, whereas others are all right if done the day/night before or even the morning of the show, if there is time.

Dry the coat thoroughly with a hair dryer or any other means. I always towel-dry the whole dog and then dry the tail area first with the hair dryer. This is because some Goldens get wet/dead/frozen tail and I prefer not to find out if one of them is mine. Shampoo contacting with the anus may cause the condition, so I take care not to allow this to happen. This condition is painful and often takes 12–24 hours to show up, so you can arrive at the show the day after a dog has been bathed and find out he has a problem. In this case, it would be better not to show the dog as he will be uncomfortable, unable to hold his tail level on the move and his movement will be affected. He may also be in pain if the tail is held by yourself or touched by the judge.

I will only bath a dog's feathering if I think that is all that is necessary.

It is possible, if the dog is not very dirty, just to bath his top coat. You can do this by wetting the dog's coat, lightly stroking the coat with the shampoo, **not** rubbing it in, then quickly and thoroughly rinsing it with water.

Whatever you do to the coat, remember that The Kennel Club ruling clearly states that nothing should remain in the coat when the dog is exhibited and only water usuage is permitted at shows. I believe the ruling also includes any interference with a dog's pigmentation.

Showing Equipment
Collar for travelling and benched shows (must be worn in public places by law).

Lead and show lead.

Benching chain for benched shows. This can also be very useful at unbenched shows to temporarily fix the dog to something immovable. Very few Golden owners take cages into the showground and, if it is very hot, it would not be possible to leave a dog in the car. Many societies have strict rules to deal with owners who leave dogs in cars in hot weather. It may be possible to use a corkscrew stake at outdoor shows, if the ground is soft enough, and don't forget to take a strong implement to turn it. (Do not tie your dog to any movable object such as a chair. If he takes fright, he will run off, becoming even more frightened by the chair that will appear to be chasing him. It can be a very bad experience for a dog of any age but especially a youngster.)

Ring clip for exhibit number.

Show bait/small toy You may also require a waist pouch ('bum bag') for the bait if you do not have a suitable pocket.

Towel(s) for emergency cleaning or for the dog to lie on.

Blanket for the dog to lie on, on the ground or the bench. Towels can be used instead.

Brush, comb and any other grooming equipment of your choice. I do all my trimming prior to the show, so I do not take scissors. I believe if you pack them you can be tempted to over fuss the dog by continuing to trim him.

Water spray bottle.

Talcum powder for emergency drying, but it must be brushed out to comply with Kennel Club Rules and Regulations.

Dry shampoo cleaner for emergencies only, such as a car exhaust mark on head or coat.

Show bag equipment.

Show Bag

I try to carry essential items only to keep the weight down, as the distances from some car parks into the shows can be considerable, especially if you have two or more dogs.

In addition to the items referred to above, I also include water, a water bowl, biscuits, other dog food if we are to be away at meal times, and a feeding bowl. Some Goldens refuse to drink water away from home but can be tempted if a little milk is added. Do remember that milk can upset their stomachs if they are not used to it or are given too much.

Other items to remember are the schedule, show/exhibitor passes, car park passes (mainly used for Championship Shows only) and catalogue voucher. Catalogues can be pre-ordered at some shows. Many societies impose a time by which they need to be collected. Ring numbers are not sent beforehand. They are usually given out in the ring at the smaller shows or by a society official on arrival. At benched Championship Shows they are normally placed on the bench.

Some exhibitors take a few medical supplies with them for emergencies, such as 'New Skin' for a cut pad, or an emetic.

On very hot days, I have found it quite useful either to spray a Golden with water or allow him to lie on a wet towel to keep cool, rather than covering him with a wet towel. Wet towels can be used similarly in a car without air conditioning if it is necessary to travel in hot weather.

Challenge Certificate/Bench Title

This is an award which can only be given at a Championship Show by a judge to an unbeaten dog that in their opinion is of outstanding merit and worthy of the title of Champion. Two can be awarded at every show where CCs are on offer for that breed, one for the best of each sex.

A dog has to win three of these awards under three different judges to obtain the bench title of Show Champion, but one of the awards must be gained when he/she is over 12 months old. In a slow maturing breed like the Golden Retriever it is very much the exception to win a CC under the age of two years. A full Champion title will be confirmed if a dog with

3 CCs already holds, or is subsequently awarded, his/her Show Gundog Working certificate or wins a Certificate of Merit or higher award at a Field Trial.

It takes roughly 4–6 weeks for The Kennel Club to confirm a CC and bench title and issue the appropriate certificate. A Reserve CC is also awarded under the same criteria, in case the CC winner is disqualified. The dog winning a second prize to the CC winner can be considered in the Challenge if invited to do so by the judge, provided he/she has not been beaten by any other breed class winner. The Kennel Club does not confirm a Reserve CC.

Stud Book Numbers

The term 'stud' may confuse the beginner as it does not apply solely to males but both sexes. Qualifying for a stud book number and entry into The Kennel Club Stud Book is a mark of achievement which can be gained at Championship Shows, Field and Working Trials and Obedience Championship shows. The Championship Show criteria for Golden Retrievers is currently restricted to 1st, 2nd or 3rd in the Open or Limit classes, the CC and Reserve CC winner and a Junior Warrant winner under the new rules.

Only one number is awarded to a dog meeting the criteria for the first time. The Kennel Club usually takes 4–6 weeks to confirm the number. Once a dog has won a number, his/her registered name cannot be changed and affixes cannot be added as a suffix (that is, at the end of the dog's registered name) if the dog changes ownership.

Junior Warrant

This can only be obtained by a dog aged 6–18 months of age:
- Achieving 25 points in breed classes.
- Winning three points for a Championship Show 1st prize where CCs are on offer and achieving 1 point for an Open Show 1st prize. First prizes won at limited or lower level shows are ineligible. Three dogs or must be present in each class for the point to count. One point may be claimed if this is not the case and the dog is awarded BOB.
- A minimum of 12 points must be won at Championship Shows where Challenge Certificates are on offer and a minimum of 10 at Open Shows.
- Points can only be claimed from one show per day with three clear days between qualifying shows.

Unlike CCs and Stud Book numbers, it is necessary for the owner to apply for a Junior Warrant using the appropriate Kennel Club form. The Kennel Club normally confirm a Junior Warrant and issue a Warrant Certificate within 1–4 weeks. Under the new rules, Junior Warrant winners will also be issued with a Stud Book number and can add the letters 'JW' after the dog's registered name.

The Irish Kennel Club Green Star Judging System
- written by John B Lennon and Alistair M Scott of Largymore Goldens.

As the system of judging dogs in Ireland is quite similar to our own and as there are no quarantine restrictions between Britain and Ireland, in recent years an increasing number of Golden Retriever owners are furthering their hobby by exhibiting in Ireland. Any British exhibitor may show their dog in the Republic of Ireland provided that they are registered with the Irish Kennel Club, except in the case of the British citizens of Northern Ireland who must have their dogs registered and also be Associate Members of the Irish Kennel Club before they are permitted to exhibit at any show under the jurisdiction of the IKC.

Unlike Britain, with its Challenge Certificate system, the Irish Kennel Club issues Green Star Awards. These are certificates won at Championship Shows held under the Rules and

Regulations of the Irish Kennel Club, and go towards the title of Champion. Each Green Star carries a value of points commensurate with the Green Star index prevailing on the date of the show on which certificate was given. The judges are required to certify that the dogs to which they award the Green Star and the Reserve Green Star are of sufficient merit to become Champions. Green Stars of five points or more may be considered to be the equivalent of a Challenge Certificate under The Kennel Club system.

An index figure will be allocated to each sex, also to mixed dog and bitch classes in each breed. This index figure is arrived at by dividing the total number of valid exhibits at Championship Shows by the number of shows at which Green Stars were offered during the previous year ending 30 June in that breed.

Where the total number of eligible exhibits actually shown (in the dog, bitch or mixed class, as the case may be) is equal to the index figure, then five Green Star points is awarded; for every 20% below the index figure one point is deducted and for every 20% above the index figure one point is added. All points will be rounded up or down to the nearest whole number. No Green Star awarded will have a value of less than one point or greater than 10 points and no breed will be allocated an index figure of less than five.

Before a dog can become a Champion, it must win a total of not less than 40 Green Star points, including one of the following combinations:
(a) By winning 4 x 5 points in the breed under 4 different judges, or
(b) By winning 2 x 5 points and 1 x 10 points in the breed under 3 different judges, or
(c) By winning 3 x 5 points in the breed and 1 group under 4 different judges.

Dogs disqualified for any reason whatsoever cannot be awarded Green Stars. However, the only disqualifications which can lower the value in the calculation of the index figure are that for non-registration and exhibition in the wrong breed.

Where two Green Stars are offered in any breed, the award to the Best Dog or Bitch shall entitle the winner to a Green Star, the value of which shall at least be equal to the value of the Green Star awarded to the best opposite sex. Also, a dog winning a Group or Best in Show will be entitled to a Green Star equal in value to the highest value won by any dog eligible to compete and competing in that Group or Best in Show.

The Green Star points which have contributed to the title of Champion may not be used again towards any other Champion title except that of Annual Champion and where a dog is disqualified then the Green Star may be awarded to the winner of the Reserve Green Star.

At least two Green Stars towards the title of Champion must be gained after the dog reaches the age of 12 months. A dog in a breed where the Green Star is withheld shall not be entitled to compete in the Group, the only exception being the Any Variety Not Separately Classified Best of Breeds in that Group.

A Green Star will not be offered under a judge who has previously judged that breed (and a Green Star or Green Stars were offered) within a period of 12 calendar months.

The Irish Annual Championship Titles

An Annual Championship shall be awarded in each breed to the dog or bitch which has won, in each calendar year, the greatest number of Green Star points in its breed with a minimum of 30, to be won under not less than three different judges. Each dog or bitch winning an Annual Championship shall be entitled to be described as '**** (year date) Annual Champion' in brackets after its name. In the case of a tie for Annual Championship, each exhibit shall be designated '**** (year date) Annual Champions'. An exhibit which has won such Annual Championship, as aforesaid, in 2 consecutive years shall be awarded a Full Championship.

CHAPTER NINE

Working Goldens

Introduction

Each element of working involves specialist training and, in order to handle a dog, you need to learn what is required and be taught how to train your dog. The first dog anyone trains usually is the 'guinea pig' on which the process will be learnt and only limited success may be achieved competitively. Greater success is usually obtained with subsequent dogs, provided it is appreciated that no two dogs are alike; each will have individual training needs.

I have heard of some owners paying vast sums of money for their dogs to be trained, for example to pick up at shoots. At the end of the course, the trainer demonstrates what the dog is capable of and returns him to the owner. Within 2–3 weeks the dog is no better for the task than before. The money would have been more wisely invested if the owner had been trained instead!

Many Goldens with the correct upbringing, encouragement and training are capable of some degree of work, but much will depend on the individual and his breeding. If you decide you may or definitely want to work your dog, then consider acquiring one from working lines, or lines that have achieved success in the field of work you wish to pursue. You must appreciate that this is no guarantee of the dog's abilities and you may find he is very active and does not settle so easily into the family way of life. If he is to live as a pet and also work, then it may be prudent to find a Golden from a blend of lines.

To undertake any form of specialised training you need to understand the breed in depth as well as the dog as an individual. This is particularly important if you have owned other breeds previously. In the main, Golden Retrievers are sensitive and need firm but gentle handling. Training requires much patience, understanding, dedication, enthusiasm and application. To achieve success normally involves even more time. If you wish to compete in more than one form of work, or work and show, you may have to choose which discipline will take priority.

Time and dedication are important, as training needs to be continued between training classes. There is nothing worse than those owners who attend for the social occasion or will not practise between classes, no matter how much their instructors impress upon them the importance of doing so. Conversely, care should be taken not to be over-enthusiastic and train too rigorously. Training sessions should be short and sweet to maintain the dog's interest and enthusiasm. Whatever your choice, basic obedience control is essential.

If you are uncertain which discipline to choose, spectate at some of the various events as well as read specialist articles, books, and familiarise yourself with the rules and requirements. The same applies to training. Before you enroll at any club, attend one or two training sessions without your dog to see if you feel happy about the methods used by the trainers, their attitude and the club atmosphere.

Ron Hare at the Southern GRS Scurry Test, 1994. The lengths owners go to in order to have fun!

Wherever possible, I recommend that you find out if the trainers have owned or understand Goldens. The last thing you need with a sensitive, but disobedient, Golden is for him to be harshly handled by the trainer. This has been known to happen, and may finish a Golden's career before it even starts and leave a novice handler angry and bewildered.

The cost of participating in most disciplines is reasonable. If you choose to compete around the country, then obviously the costs of travel and accommodation will give rise to a higher outlay.

As with anything, there will be peaks and troughs, but it should be remembered that, if the dog has sufficient intelligence to learn to work, many of the problems will be due to the handler not being able to instruct clearly what he/she requires the dog to do, or be the result of a lack of training, rather than be the dog's fault. Kennel Club Working Test Regulations state *'No person shall carry out punitive correction of a dog whilst within the boundaries of the test'*. Anyone who does so, for any reason, will be reported to The Kennel Club and suitably disciplined which may include being banned from participating in any other Kennel Club-licensed event. This applies at all working events. At all grounds and venues, the facilities and hosts should be treated with the utmost respect.

Kennel Club Rules and Regulations

Everyone who competes, judges or stewards in any form of work should be fully conversant with the current rules and regulations for their specialist interest. These can be found in The Kennel Club Year Book (available from the Publications Department at The Kennel Club). Some of interest can be found in this chapter.

Gundog Training Classes

Most breed clubs, but not all, organise gundog training classes so you need to contact the secretary of your nearest club. The club should be able to help you to locate the most appropriate class for this, or any other, form of work. Alternatively, you can contact The Kennel Club or your breeder.

When you attend classes or tests, always take a bowl of water, towels for the dog in case he has to enter water, and a first aid kit for emergencies. For safety reasons, collars should be removed when training and **must** be removed when competing.

Gundog Working Tests

Working tests are held by gundog societies, including breed clubs, for the purpose of assessing competitively (without game being shot) the working abilities of retrievers. They can be held at any time but in the United Kingdom are mainly held outside the shooting season. Cold game or dummies may be used for the retrieving exercises designed to simulate shooting day conditions.

Most judges mark out of 10 or 20 for each test. Judges should have experience of dog work under shooting field conditions and there must be one judge for every 20 dogs competing. In an Open test one Kennel Club Field Trial Panel judge must officiate.

Dogs must be registered with The Kennel Club and a draw determines their running order.

The organisers should ensure that the tests are designed to further good gundog work and that they do not inhibit dogs from showing natural working ability. The exercises must be designed by a person(s) with experience of dog work under shooting conditions and agreed with the judges before the start of the test. The final decision on their acceptability lies with the judge(s). This includes the dummies and cold game.

If shots are fired, the gun should not be further away than 40 yards from any retrieve and should always precede the dummy being thrown. Gunfire is optional for unseen retrieves.

Serious faults must disqualify a dog from the awards and may lead to elimination.

Judges should **always** be careful for the safety of dogs and not require them to negotiate dangerous obstacles. Those in charge of the dog should ensure it is fully under control.

At the start of a Gundog Working Test, judges should make sure that they have the correct dogs in the line, lowest number placed on the right. Wherever possible, all dogs should be tested at a drive, walking up and in water. A dog must walk steadily to heel, be steady to shot and fall and retrieve on command.

Good marking is essential with a quick pick-up and a fast return. Judges should not penalise a dog too heavily for putting down a retrieve to get a firmer grip, although this must not be confused with sloppy retrieving. Dogs showing gamefinding ability and initiative should be placed above those which have to be handled on to their retrieve. A dog should not be asked to pass too close to another retrieve in order to make a specific retrieve.

The code of conduct for participants is the same as at field trials.

Credit Points

Natural marking ability, nose, drive, style, speed in gathering retrieve, control, quiet handling, and delivery.

Summary of Faults

Refusing to retrieve, whining or barking, running in and/or chasing, out of control, failing to enter water, changing retrieve and poor heelwork.

Working Test Definitions

(Open/Novice - KC regulate. Remainder are guidelines.)

Beginners: This can vary from club to club but tends to be for handlers and dogs who have never entered a test previously and/or won any prize in any test at any level or field trial.

Puppy: A puppy is any dog or bitch which is under two years of age on the day **before** the test is held.

Novice dog/handler: Neither dog nor handler to have won any award, including a certificate of merit, at a field trial or 1st, 2nd, 3rd or Reserve in an Open or All Aged working test or 1st in **any** working test.

Novice: Any dog or bitch of any age not having won:

(a) a field trial award, including a certificate of merit, at a field trial.

(b) a 1st, 2nd, or 3rd in an Open or All Aged working test.

(c) a 1st in a Novice test or any test above Novice level.

(d) a 1st in Puppy and Novice Test at which one set of awards is given. (A 1st in Puppy Stake or a 1st in a Novice Dog/Novice Handler is discounted for this purpose.)

Puppy and novice: Where only one set of awards is given, namely Novice. For any dog or bitch not having won:

As for (a) to (c) in Novice.

(d) a 1st in a combined Puppy and Novice Test where separate awards for puppies were **not** given.

Intermediate: Any dog or bitch not having won:

(a) a 1st in any intermediate, Open or All Aged working test.

(b) a 1st, 2nd, or 3rd in any field trial, **except** for a novice dog/novice handler field trial, where first only would be excluded.

Open: Open to all dogs of a specified breed or breeds. Preference may be given to dogs which have won a Novice test or a Field trial award. Cold game tests are usually at this level.

Veteran: Open to all dogs aged eight years or over on the day before the test is run.

All Aged: An Open test which may be restricted by the regulations or agreement of the organising club.

Exercises

Exercises vary slightly from test to test, partly as a result of the terrain, the test classification and the use of double or multiple retrieves and jumps. A test usually comprises four exercises:

- A walk-up with retrieve and gunfire;
- A marked retrieve, that is, seen;
- A water retrieve, either from or over the other side, marked or blind;
- A blind retrieve, that is, unseen.

A walk-up usually includes 4–6 dogs in line off the lead together, equally spaced as in a field trial. They will be marked on the heelwork, steadiness and retrieve. The exercise is only completed once the judge instructs the handlers to replace their dogs on the lead. Beaters may also be used in cover to simulate a shoot.

The thinking behind the difficulty of the exercises varies from club to club and judge to judge. Some wish the dogs and handlers to succeed in completing the exercises in order not to discourage anyone, especially in the lower level of tests and may only include one or two of the four tests with more difficulty to find the best on the day. On the other hand, in the case of a Novice test, I have heard it said that not only do the judges wish to find the best but, as the winner will have to compete at Open level from then on, all the tests are set at Open level.

Most judges are very helpful and encouraging, and can be approached after the test to answer questions on how to overcome any difficulty you may have experienced during the day. Much can be learnt from attending working tests and watching the handlers and their handling techniques or by helping to throw dummies or steward for the judges. By helping, you can see the dogs working at closer quarters than you would as a spectator.

Working tests are a means of assessing your dog's ability, progress in training and can be used as practice to move on to other work at shoots, either competitively (at field trials) or

Judge explaining a test exercise to a competitor.

picking up. However, you may find that once a dog has moved onto retrieving warm game, his enthusiasm for working with dummies and/or cold game wanes.

Gundog Training Terminology (also see Chapter 3 for basic control commands)

The terminology is used together with whistle commands and hand signals by the handler.

'Mark': to attract dog's attention to a dummy being thrown.

'Get on', 'Get out', 'Cast out' or 'Out': given to send your dog out for a retrieve.

'Get back': to send your dog back for a retrieve if he begins to return without the dummy.

'Get over' or 'Over': given to the dog when you want to encourage him to jump an obstacle such as a fence, or go over a stream or ditch to retrieve.

'Hilost': hunting command given to the dog when you need to encourage him to search the area where the dummy or game is. It needs to be given as the dog approaches the area if he is at full speed, or where he is likely to wind the dummy if it is fairly close.

'Stop' or 'Stay': given to halt a dog if he is working in the incorrect area and has yet to be taught the equivalent whistle command or has refused to obey the whistle command.

'Hold': to encourage the dog to hold the dummy without dropping it, especially at the point of delivery. It only needs to be used if the dog has a tendency to drop the dummy.

'Dead' or 'Give': when the handler wants the dog to release the dummy or game.

Gundog Training Hand Signals (see photos overleaf)

Stay/stop: raise a flat hand, palm showing, to the dog's face (see photo 1).

Heel close: tap your thigh with your left hand (see photo 2).

Recall/present: hold arms out in front and just below shoulder height and withdraw them as dog approaches.

Get out, etc: use left hand and move it forward at the dog's eye level to encourage dog to move out in front, but only when the judge tells you to send your dog (see photo 3).

Move and search to the left: move left arm outwards until it is fully extended, several times if necessary (see photo 4).

Move and search to the right: as above but with right arm (see photo 5).

Get back: use left or right arm fully extended in front of you at a 45° angle. The choice of arm depends on whether the dummy/game is slightly on the left or right of the dog's position (see photo 6).

Hunt: flutter a hand at a low level.

Click the fingers: to return close with the retrieve or sit the dog.

The teaching of hand signals is discussed on page 161. If you cannot be seen clearly by the dog against the backdrop, holding a small white hanky will enable you to be picked out by the dog.

Whistle Commands

'Recall': two or three quick 'pips' on the whistle for the dog to come to you. Pause and repeat only if the dog is not coming back.

'Stop' or 'Stay': long blast on the whistle to make the dog stop if required. Do not overuse as this may interfere with the dog's natural speed.

1. Stay/stop.

2. Heel close.

3. Move out in front.

4. Move and search to left.

5. Move and search to right.

6. Get back.

Some owners also develop a hunt whistle signal instead of using the command 'Hilost' and for left and right directions instead of hand signals. When training, sometimes place the whistle in your mouth without blowing it. This will help to prevent your dog anticipating whistle commands as soon as he sees you place the whistle in your mouth.

Other Terminology

'Blind': a dummy that has been placed without the dog seeing it. The owner will be told where it is if he did not see it placed.

'Blind with diversion': judge informs handler that a dummy has been placed in cover or elsewhere. A marked dummy is thrown and the dog has to ignore the marked dummy and retrieve the blind. Another variation is where two marked dummies are thrown and the dog is asked to retrieve the first mark. This is known solely as a 'diversion'.

'Blinking': when a dog finds the shot game but will not pick it up and goes on hunting.

'Drive': dogs sit with the handlers and the guns whilst birds are shot around them. The dog must remain perfectly steady until given the command to retrieve one of the birds.

'Eye wipe': if a dog fails to find game and then another one picks it, this is called an eye wipe.

'Eye wipe by judge': if a dog fails to find game but it is picked up by the judge.

'Technical eye wipe': when the first dog sent for the retrieve does not get to the fall or hunt the area, but the second dog does. (An eye wipe on a runner will be marked as an excellent retrieve.)

'First dog down': (in a walked-up trial) is when a dog is sent straight away for a shot bird. If the first dog fails, the next dog is 'second dog down'. If for any reason there is a lapse of time then, although it is the first dog sent he will be deemed to be the second dog down on a runner.

'On ice': dogs designated for certain awards before the competition is over.

'Runner': wounded game where the dog has to pick the fall of the bird, follow its fall scent trail, find the bird and retrieve it to the handler.

'Running in': when a dog goes of his own accord for a retrieve, without the judge or handler asking him to be sent.

'Steadiness': dogs must remain steady while a drive or walk-up is in progress.

'Walk-up': dogs, guns, handlers and judges walking in a straight line. When the bird is shot or dummy thrown, the judge nominates which dog should be sent to retrieve it.

Gundog Training Equipment

In addition to a rope slip lead and whistle, you will also require canvas dummies. For young puppies I usually use a small, lightweight dummy to check if they will retrieve, and retrieve canvas without weight being the problem. Later on I introduce the standard dummy which should be a minimum of 458kg (1lb) in weight. You will need at least two, but a few more will be useful for steadiness and hunting exercises.

Just occasionally, dogs are required to retrieve dummies with fur or feather on them so, if you can, acquire a rabbit skin or game bird wings for your dummies. This will also help to prepare the dog for cold game test work, picking-up at shoots, the SGWC and field trialling.

Dummy launchers are also used at tests occasionally, but more as a training aid for an owner who finds it difficult to obtain the help of a dummy thrower; to improve a dog's marking ability; and to get him used to gunfire. It is not essential to have your own as some training classes use them and, by attending them, you will be able to acclimatise your dog there.

Early Training

I cover only some of the elementary gundog training in this section and would recommend you read the books written by more experienced trainers and handlers (see Bibliography). Gundog training should only be started in earnest once the basic obedience and control is established.

Retrieving

I referred to this in Chapter 3.

- Use the commands given earlier, using the dog's name first.
- Begin in a confined area, so that the dog cannot run off.
- Begin to use the recall whistle pips when the dog is coming to you, so the dog associates the noise with returning to you. Can also be used when heeling the dog from a moving off position.
- Ensure the dog returns and presents the retrieved article to you. In gundog work it is not

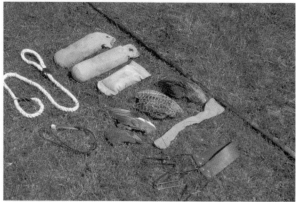

Gundog training equipment: Top right: thumb stick. Centre from top to bottom: 2lb dummy, 1lb dummy, puppy dummy, bird wing selection (pheasant, pigeon and partridge), nylon stocking, game carrier. Bottom top to bottom: rope lead, bone whistle (with pea removed).

essential that he sits first and this should not be insisted upon if the dog is likely to drop the article. It is also not necessary for the dog to 'finish', that is, sit by your left hand side after giving up the article, as in Obedience. If the dog is reluctant to come towards you, encourage him with a treat. The disadvantage of this is that the dog may spit out the article in order to gain the treat. However, the treats can be discontinued once the dog returns to you without a problem. Another method to get the dog to return the article to you is to lie down on the ground or run away from the dog. This usually gains his attention and makes him come to you, then you can gather up the article when he is close enough.

- Once the dog is reliable in a confined space, progress to an open space. I recommend that you use a field or park rather than your garden as the dog will associate the garden with being a play area.
- Retrieves should only be performed over a short distance initially.
- Increase the distance gradually, provided the success rate is good and your dog's confidence grows. One method is to drop a dummy whilst heeling a dog, ensuring he sees you do it, and then send him back. This helps with memory and scenting. Or, sit the dog, throw a dummy in front of him, turn him around with his back to the dummy, put him on a stay and leave the dog. At the distance of your choice, turn and face the dog and

command him to retrieve the dummy and/or to 'get back'. This exercise also teaches the dog what 'get back' means.

- Use straight hedges or fences to encourage the dog to retrieve in a straight line; this helps greatly with later training.
- Vary your retrieves so you practise in cover and woodland, as well as open space. Also use dry ditches and banks.
- Do not always throw the dummy yourself as the dog may expect only you to do so. If you have no one who can do this, it will help to go to gundog classes.
- Class attendance is necessary to give the dog the opportunity of training alongside other dogs. This helps with steadiness and provides the opportunity to practise on neutral and unfamiliar terrain. You will get help with any problems you may be encountering and will also gain tips on improving and also learning alternative exercises.
- When setting retrieving exercises for your dog, try to ensure he can see what you want him to by checking his line of vision from his head height, not your standing height.
- Do not forget to praise your dog when he completes an exercise correctly, both in training and at tests. Do not do so part way through a test, such as after one retrieve of a double exercise, as the judge may penalise you for touching or talking excessively. This does not prevent you encouraging the dog to enable him to complete the exercise at lower level tests.
- Introduce second/double retrieves only when single retrieving is being done successfully.

Encouraging a dog to hold the dummy. Tilt his head up, rub his chest and praise him.

Receiving a dummy.

Steadiness exercise.

Steadiness

This is very important as judges will not award any points where a dog has run in unless they have specified otherwise. It is essential if you are to teach direction and diversion work.

One of the best methods of teaching this is to put your dog in a 'down stay' and throw dummies around him, far away to begin with and, when steadiness begins to be achieved, gradually nearer and over his head, then in the sit position and then with other dogs.

'Blind' Retrieving

The great difficulty with teaching blind work is gaining the dog's confidence to retrieve something he has not seen being thrown. Initially the exercise should be very short and distance increased gradually.

One method is to throw a marked retrieve and, whilst the dog is on the return, have another placed in the same area. Alternatively, throw a marked retrieve within a short distance of a dummy that is already on the ground, send the dog for the seen dummy and he should see or scent that a second one is available to retrieve.

The difficulty of the terrain should be increased gradually as you progress to purely blind work.

When placing blind dummies, always throw the dummy as far as you can rather than walking to the place of the drop, and vary your route as dogs with good scenting ability will follow your trail. Be sure to have the dog well away from the area, so he does not see or hear the placement of a blind dummy. If possible place a blind some time before taking your dog to do the retrieve.

Hunting and Scenting

Teaching a dog to hunt and use his nose can begin in the home using toys. Initially take the dog into a room on his own and let him see you hide a toy. Command him to hunt and retrieve it to you. He will think this is great fun. Then hide the toy in the room without the dog watching, but not always in the same place, and let the dog bring it to you. I find more and more devious places to hide the toy and not always on the ground. It helps to get the dog to look off the ground, as some dummies and birds become caught up in cover. Once you know the dog understands the exercise, transfer the exercise out-of-doors and use dummies or toys to begin with. The dummies should also be the dog's own, as they will have more scent on them.

Practise retrieves into denser cover, coupled with the hunt command 'hilost'.

Once the dog understands this command and finds the dummy, you can begin to encourage him to hunt blind retrieves, increasing the distances and difficulty gradually. Some Goldens who use their noses will quarter the ground to pick up a scent, others may work towards the direction the wind is blowing from, after being cast out. When training or competing, owners can help their dogs by knowing the way their dogs work, checking where the wind scent is coming from and casting their dogs out accordingly. Always check wind direction just prior to an exercise as the direction can change quite quickly. Also check for things such as wild garlic and mint, which make it difficult for dogs to scent.

Sending dog out on a blind retrieve.

Directions and Hand Signals/Diversion work

These should only be taught once you know your dog is steady and you have his attention. There are two methods of teaching.

(a) You can use the appropriate hand signal when the dog moves to the left or right if he is watching you, so that he begins to associate the action with your signal. This method is based on established sheepdog training methods.

(b) Sit the dog in front of you on a stay, move back a few paces, face the dog. Command him to stay again. Throw a dummy either to the left or right. After a few seconds, use the appropriate arm/hand signal and command the dog to retrieve the dummy. Repeat this once or twice at follow-up training sessions and then try the opposite direction a few times.

Once the dog understands, move further away and repeat a few more times. The next stage is to throw two dummies, one to the left and one to the right of the dog. Send the dog with the appropriate signal for the first dummy, as nearly every dog will try to go for the dummy thrown last. To begin with, always throw the second dummy close enough for you to

Jump retrieve over firm fence of plank boards.

Water retrieve training in calm water with easy entry.

pick it up if the dog tries to retrieve it before the one you have commanded him to fetch. When the dog obeys your command and repeatedly retrieves the correct dummy, you will know that you have control and he is learning the command. You can then increase your distance from the dog gradually, until you are practising the exercise at the distances used in tests for both marked and blind or a mixture of both. These can vary but are anything from 25m to 135m. The angles of the thrown dummies can be reduced to increase the difficulty.

Whichever method you use, you need to be able to use the technique to send the dog from your side. For some the transition is easy. The dog is cast out in a straight line in front of you and once you stop or gain the dog's attention at roughly the appropriate place, then the hand signal is given and the dog should respond. Not all respond correctly and need further practice to build the confidence and trust between dog and owner.

Other trainers initially turn the dog's head to the left or right in the direction of the dummy to cast him out in the line of the retrieve. Eventually the cast out signal direction is sufficient for the dog to know which way he should run. Bear in mind that, at tests, judges do not usually want the handler to touch their dog in order to direct them. Some owners will stand on the other side of the dog to cast him out for a retrieve on the right.

Be careful not to chastise a dog too much if he picks up the wrong dummy and certainly not afterwards as this may encourage him to drop the dummy if he is a little submissive and discourage him from returning to you with the retrieve. It is better to find a method of making certain he picks up the correct dummy rather than scold him or you may undo a lot of training and the rapport you have built with your dog.

Jumping

I would not recommend that dogs are taught to jump until they are about 18 months old and their joints are finally set. Some will not need teaching! For those that do, begin with very firm, low obstacles or fences so the dog only needs to hop over them. If necessary, climb over them yourself and encourage the dog to follow using the command 'over'.

Introduce the retrieve after the dog begins to jump the low fence, as holding an object in his mouth may make him reluctant to jump at first. Increase the height gradually. It helps if you can build your own jump to practise with, but check it is safe and that the take off and landing areas are also safe. If the dog is jumping a good height but he is touching the top of the jump with his feet and you would prefer him to clear the obstacle, add a small strip of chicken wire across the top of the fence. Show the dog it is there and this usually makes him jump more cleanly.

Water

- **Never** push or throw your Golden into the water, as most will never go in again voluntarily.
- If you can let him swim when he is young (3–4 months), the lesson is much easier. At this age the puppy will not be fully grown and he will be out of his depth while you can walk in water to encourage him.
- Choose a warm day, preferably in the hotter months of the year, and a safe, clean, quiet stretch of water with no strong current or waves.
- It may help to take another dog that can swim but do make sure that the youngster is not put off by too much splashing about.
- Find a narrow stretch of water where the dog will be out of his depth. Take an extremely

Correct water retrieve: the dog has delivered the dummy prior to shaking.

Incorrect water retrieve: the dog has dropped the dummy to shake off excess water.

long piece of rope to clip to the dog's collar. You need a second person to hold the dog whilst you go to the other side of the water and call the dog. If he fails to cross on his own, the other person throws the rope to you and you gently pull the dog over towards you. As you are his owner, most will come and, eventually, you can dispose of the rope. I have resorted to this method with a few of my Goldens and all have swum with no problem once they had the confidence to be out of their depth. You can also throw a dummy as they are swimming towards you. This will help those who have not the confidence to enter the water and swim away from their owner.

- Once the dog can swim and he is retrieving on land, retrieves can begin from water, and then across water. Vary the training so that the dog does not anticipate the same routine.
- Water is a great temptation for most retrievers. This is where many will run in at tests, so great control needs to be exerted and they should not be allowed to go for every retrieve.
- Do not do too many water retrieves. Swimming can be tiring and, if a dog is in the water too long on a cold day, he may get 'wet tail'.
- Each year, there are a few tests based purely on water. To compete in these your dog will need to be of a fairly high standard as control and directing in water demands a great deal more training than on land, together with time and access to such facilities.

Gunfire

There are several ways of introducing your dog to gunfire. I have already referred to dummy launchers. Other methods are to use a starting pistol (a method first used in my family), to fire blank cartridges from a shotgun, to fire .22 blanks with an adapter in an old shotgun (as black powder residue is difficult to clean out from the barrels) or, my preferred method as the sound is authentic, to shoot live cartridges from a shotgun.

All methods need to be done at some distance, say 90m (100yd) or more to begin with, particularly with my preferred method. The distances are gradually reduced over a number of sessions, provided the dog shows no signs of extreme anxiety (gun shyness). Throwing a dummy after the shot will encourage the dog to associate the gunfire with retrieving. He should be allowed to retrieve the dummy. If he does, this will help to reassure him, but not every Golden will come round and some may be gun shy for life. If a Golden is upset by storms and fireworks, do not assume he will be gun shy as well without trying it out, as this does not always follow.

If you do not have a gun:

(a) Enlist the help of a friend who has a gun. In my experience, you will only need about 2–3 sessions to train dogs for the SGWC (to acclimatise dogs to gunfire if they are not affected by it).

(b) Find out where clay pigeon shoots are held in your area. Most gunsmiths know of events which also will be advertised in clay shooting magazines. Park some distance away and remain in the car with your dog for a while, to see if he reacts to the sound. If not, take him out on a lead and walk him closer to the sound of the gunfire. **Do not** get too close on the first one or two occasions, as it is likely that several guns will be fired simultaneously.

(c) Find a local gundog training class which uses an introductory method as part of its training.

Competing

Remember, it should be fun for you both, not just the dog. Do not expect instant success even if you have done exceedingly well at training classes as you undoubtedly will have more adrenaline flowing than when you train. Your dog will sense this and may exploit the situation! There may be exercises which you have not covered, and so on.

One of the best pieces of advice I was ever given was from Olive Hickmott (Stubblesdown) who told me to treat each test as a training class. I find it very difficult, especially when starting out with a new Golden, but she was so right.

Show Gundog Working Certificate (SGWC)

The SGWC is an award made to dogs that, in the opinion of an A-panel field trial judge, meet a minimum set of criteria which ascertain if they are capable of working in the field with freshly-shot game. Unlike field trials and working tests, it is not a competition where judges assess the dogs on their performance against each another.

Dogs that achieve the award together with three Challenge Certificates under three different judges are credited with a full Champion title, not just a Show Champion title. However, a Certificate of Merit or higher award at a field trial supersedes the SGWC award.

A Gundog which has won one or more CCs may be entered for a SGWC at a Field Trial Meeting for its breed provided that the Society holding the meeting is recognised for the Championships or Champion stake for its breed and that one of the Judges awarding the SGWC is on the A Panel of the Official List of Panel Judges for the breed

All dogs entered for SGWC must be tested during the morning.

Dogs that have won a Championship first prize (where CCs were on offer) are also permitted to take a SGWC at a SWGC Trial.

The introduction of the Show Champion title in 1958, when it no longer became necessary to prove a dog's working capability in order to acquire a bench title, has led to a significant decline in the number of full Champion title holders in the breed, particularly since the mid 1980s. Personally, I feel this is such a shame for a breed that was developed for work, and would like to encourage owners to have a go or ask for an experienced handler's help to take the SGWC.

The criteria

The SGWC clearly sets out what is required of a retriever. The requirements are:

1. *For a dog to be tested in line; that is, a line of guns shooting interspersed amongst other handlers, their dogs, (which may be retrieving), judges and possibly stewards.* Usually it takes the form of a driven shoot, where the guns are stationary at about 32m (35yd) apart as opposed to a walked up shoot. The dogs would also be spaced equally between the guns with the lowest numbers on the right.

2. *For a dog not to be gun shy and to be off the lead during gun fire.* That is, the dog should not make any noise, whining or barking or exhibit any behaviour or tendency to indicate it is frightened of gunfire. A dog that runs from the line whilst off the lead to retrieve shot game will not be eliminated, as it would in a field trial competition, because absolute steadiness is not essential, just reasonable control. Judges at recent SGWC trial meetings have required only a few dogs at a time to be off the lead during gunfire for a very short while. Other than that,

or when they are retrieving under the direction of the judge, they are to be on the lead the rest of the time.

3.   *For a dog to hunt, face cover and retrieve tenderly to hand.* Some dogs may be able to prove their hunting and retrieving capabilities on one retrieve depending on the situation of the game, but quite often two retrieves are required. Hunting capabilities will be assessed on the way the dog uses his nose and covers the ground or plough. Retrieving tenderly to hand means the dog needs to find and pick up freshly shot and, preferably, unhandled game without too much hesitation, and return it undamaged to their handler. Birds are shot mainly, but occasionally a rabbit or hare may need to be retrieved. The game is then handed to the judge to inspect for damage, if any, done by the dog, mainly to the ribcage. If a dog is proved to be hard-mouthed and has crushed game, he will not be awarded his SGWC. If a hard mouth is suspected, the other judges must examine the game before the dog is eliminated. The handler should also be allowed to inspect the game in the presence of the judges, but the judges' decision is final.

Retrieve on a dummy with a rabbit skin taken at one of the GRC Working Tests in 1966 at Northolt, home of Mrs Wentworth Smith (Yelme).

Handlers participating at a SGWC meeting should be aware that most of the game will be dead, but this is not always the case. The judge will despatch the game if you are unable to once it has been retrieved.

Once all the dogs have been given every opportunity to complete the criteria, the judges announce which have been successful or failed. The award is entirely at their discretion. The organising club then inform The Kennel Club of the position and SGWCs are issued by them to the successful dogs.

Eliminating faults
- Whining and barking when in line.
- Gun shyness.
- A dog that fails to hunt.
- A dog that fails to retrieve at all or tenderly to hand.
- A dog that fails to enter water if directed to do so.

Preparation
Make sure you and your dog are thoroughly prepared.
1. Attend some shoots and a SGWC trial to see what is required of the dog and handler and to find out if you can cope with seeing and handling shot game. Not everyone can. If not, see if you can find someone else to handle your dog.
2. You will require a rope slip lead, whistle, a 453g (1lb) canvas dummy and, if possible, a 1kg (2lb) dummy (see 5 below), some game birds wings and rabbit skin (see 4 below) and, finally, some cold game.
3. Much of the elementary training should have been done, including heelwork, sits, stays, recalls and simple retrieves. If you have done these only at home, I strongly advise that you attend classes to train alongside other dogs, which can be a major distraction once a dog has to work off a lead. It would also be more beneficial to be outside at gundog training classes where there are less constraints and a greater variety of tempting smells, all of which need to be overcome before considering taking the SGWC. I believe it is essential to use a whistle to recall a dog and direction training is helpful but not essential.
4. Acquire some pheasant, partridge or duck wings to attach to dummies so that you can check the dog has no objection to carrying feather. It may be necessary to gently tease the dog with a wing before attaching the latter to a dummy. Wings can usually be obtained from anyone who shoots or picks up at shoots.
5. Most dummies only weigh about 0.5kg (1lb) but pheasants and ducks can weigh anything from 1–1.5kg (2–3lb), so I advise using a heavier dummy in your training programme. This helps the dog to cope with the additional weight before introducing game.
6. The next stage is acclimatising your dog to gunfire as described under the Working Test Section.
7. It is advisable to introduce a dog to cold game, firstly because it is firmer for dogs to carry and secondly because the smell of blood will not be as potent as on warm game. Pheasants are the best bird to use. Game can normally be purchased from gamekeepers and butchers. Not every Golden will instinctively pick up game and may need to be helped or encouraged.

Some methods that can be employed are:

(a) Exciting the dog so much that he believes holding the bird is the best thing he has ever done. Once the bird is in the dog's mouth, tilt his head up so he cannot drop it. Stroke the dog under the chin and give him a lot of praise for a few seconds before accepting the bird.

(b) Place the bird in a nylon stocking and tie a knot at the end so it does not come out when thrown for a retrieve.

(c) If you have another dog that will retrieve the bird, he may be able to show the youngster what should be done or make him jealous! However, watch that the novice dog does not act submissively and drop the game for the more experienced dog.

Mr & Mrs Stevens Pearlbarn Lucky Star at Stevandorn retrieving pheasant from water.

Mr Ray Hardie's Rayleas Extra Cover seen here retrieving over a jump at the Utility Gundog Society's Kent & East Sussex branch Open Working Test in 1997.

Comments

Before training and entering a SGWC Trial, assess your dog to see whether he is ready mentally. Some mature later than others. As a guide, I would advise most owners of show dogs to wait until their Golden is at least 18 months or, preferably, 2–3 years old before attempting a SGWC. I would also recommend after the training and prior to entering a SGWC that, if possible, you attend a shoot and arrange for your dog to pick up some warm game.

At all the SGWC Trials I have attended, the judges have been very helpful and kind to their dogs and owners. They want them to pass the set criteria, not fail.

I always feel a sense of pride and joy when one of my Goldens achieves the award or someone I have helped does, whether or not they go on to take their bench title.

Picking up

I believe that those that pick up should have proven their ability to work at gundog working tests. The guns' dogs usually deal with the simple work in the open, whereas the picking-up dogs usually deal with the more difficult task of finding the wounded game that has flown further and the runners that have just been pricked. The object is to retrieve the game tenderly to hand as quickly as possible.

The dog should have also been introduced to gunfire and cold and warm game and be totally controllable before you accept an invitation or an opportunity to pick up. Most people pick up with their dogs for the pleasure it gives them both. Anyone wishing to pick up with their dog must appreciate that they will be required from time to time to kill wounded game. Picking up means hard work and a long and exhausting day, depending on the terrain to be covered. Some people are paid a token fee for picking up and/or are given a brace of birds. You normally have to provide your own lunch.

Introducing your dog to picking up in his first shooting season should be done carefully so he does not become 'too hot' and therefore the number of retrieves should be restricted. The dog must never chase live, unshot game.

Equipment

Apart from the equipment already mentioned, there are three other items that I find essential. They are either a game carrier or bag, a strong stick (thumb hole stick), and a priest or other suitable hard object that can be used to dispatch a bird. The stick may be required to help you beat as well as pick up, and get you out of difficulties, for example to test the depth of a stream you have to cross.

Tips

- Find out what is required of you. Remember, the guns have normally paid a large sum to shoot and will not want their day ruined.
- Learn the shoot's terrain as soon as possible. Some cover wide areas of woodland and you may need to work an area quite separately on your own.
- Find out if the shoot is driven or walked up or both. A *driven* shoot is where the guns stand in line and beaters drive the game towards the guns from some distance. A *walked-up* shoot is where the guns and beaters walk forward in line together putting game up in front of them.
- Find out if the guns are to shoot birds only or ground game. If the latter is included, you will need to be more vigilant as Goldens could be mistaken for a fox by an over-zealous gun. Safety is paramount at most shoots but mistakes can happen. A few years ago, a friend's yellow Labrador was shot whilst out picking up for wildfowlers. She survived but her eyesight was damaged.
- For safety, always let nearby guns know where you are.
- Keep an eye on nearby guns to check on their gun and shooting safety (do they unload between drives, walk with closed barrels or swing through at low birds bringing you and your dog into range). Being a clay pigeon shooter has made me far more aware of the safety aspects.
- Check when the gamekeeper wants the game retrieved. At some shoots or drives they may want you to wait until the drive is over, as it may affect the next drive. Others may want you to retrieve the game behind the guns during the drive. Game in front of the guns is normally picked by the guns' dogs, the guns or beaters.
- Take a very small energy snack (as well as the usual drinking water) for your dog.

After the shoot, check your dog thoroughly for burrs, thorns and skin wounds, particularly feet. Clean him up and wash his paws to prevent mud drying and causing discomfort, before giving him his meal and a well-earned rest.

Field Trials

Field trials are held for the purpose of assessing competitively the working abilities of retrievers on freshly-shot game in the shooting season. Handled game cannot be used unless it is to be used for a water test. Trials are held at both driven and walked-up shoots, or a mixture of both depending upon the shoot's conditions. The ground covered varies greatly around the country and at walked-up trials there will be a lot of walking for both the dog and handler.

What is Required

Dogs should be steady whilst being shot over until commanded to quest for dead or wounded game, from land or water, and retrieve tenderly to hand. Dogs should also be able to retrieve all sorts of game from duck to hare, not just pheasants. Hare can weigh double that of a cock pheasant and are frequently shot in East Anglia.

Credit points

Natural gamefinding ability, nose, marking ability, drive, style, quickness in gathering game, control, good retrieving and delivery and quietness in handling.

Elimination and Major Faults

Dogs must be excluded from further participation in the Stake if they have committed an eliminating fault. The judges may also discard dogs for major faults.

Eliminating faults: hard mouth; whining or barking; running in and chasing; out of control; failing to enter water; changing game whilst retrieving.

Major faults: failing to find dead or wounded game; unsteadiness at heel; 'eye wipe'; disturbing ground; slack and unbusinesslike work; noisy handling; poor control.

Stakes

Open: dogs have the opportunity to gain a qualification towards the title of Field Trial Champion or towards entry in the Championships or Champion Stake for their breed and in which entry is open to all dogs of a specified breed or breeds; it may be limited to a prescribed number of runners, in which case these shall be decided by a draw conducted in accordance with Regulation J 6g so that preference is given to previous performance.

All-aged: open to all dogs of a specified breed or breeds without restriction as to their age, but which may be restricted by any other conditions determined by the Society.

Novice: confined to dogs which have not gained the following awards: First, Second, Third or Fourth in a 24 dog Open Stake; or First, Second or Third in a 12 dog Open Stake; or First in an All-aged or Novice Stake, or two Second awards in All-aged or Novice Stakes if gained prior to 1 July 1993.

Puppy: confined to dogs whelped not earlier than 1 January in the year preceding the date of the field trials. (For January Stakes, a dog which was a puppy in the previous year shall be deemed to be still a puppy.)

Non-winner: for dogs that have not won a non-winner or Novice Stake or two second prizes in a Novice, or a first, second or third in an Open Stake.

Novice dog/novice handler: this Stake is run for newcomers and is mainly confined to handlers who have not yet gained any awards. (Sometimes lower awards are permitted.)

The usual requirements for the Open Stake are:

- For a dog to have won a first in a Novice or All-aged Stake, or a second in these Stakes if gained prior to 1 July 1993, a first, second or third in a 12 dog Open Stake or a first, second, third and fourth in a 24 dog Open Stake;
- Preference may also be given in a draw to members of the society whose dogs have gained such awards. However, members' dogs that have gained other awards cannot take preference over non-members' dogs who have gained any of the awards listed above.
- Competitors entering more than one similarly qualified dog must indicate which has preference. Second and subsequent dogs must be placed in separate ballots before entries are drawn from other categories.
- Whilst all are eligible to enter the All-aged Stake, preference is normally given to those dogs who have some award in a Non-Winner or Novice Stake and particularly in an Open Stake.
- The standard of work at Novice and Non-Winner Stakes can be very high as good new youngsters are brought out but the retrieves will be less difficult and judging will not be so hard as in an Open Stake.

Awards

Judges may award a first, second, third or fourth in a Stake. They also have the discretion to award either a Diploma of Merit at a Championship or Champion Stake Meeting or a Certificate of Merit in any other Stake; or withhold an award if in their opinion the dogs do not show sufficient merit.

Handling and Competing

All competing dogs and handlers must be present when it is announced by the Chief Steward that the trial has commenced. They must also be available when required by the judges. Dogs that are not present when required will be discarded, save in exceptional circumstances.

All handlers must carry out the instructions of the judges who are empowered to turn out of the Stake any dog whose handler does not obey them or whose handler wilfully interferes with another competitor or his dog. There is an established code of conduct expected at field trials and those taking part in them shall not openly impugn the decision of the judge or judges or criticise the host, ground or guns.

Judging

- The task of the judges is to find the dog which, on the day, pleased them most by the quality of his work from the shooting point of view. They should take natural game-finding to be of the first importance. A good working knowledge of the breed(s) is also important.
- The standard of work in Stakes carrying Field Trial Championship Status should be higher than in other Stakes.
- It is the duty of the judges to give dogs every opportunity to work well by seeing that conditions are in their favour as far as possible. In all Stakes the work of the dog is much affected by the way the handler behaves. Noisy handling is a major fault. A good handler will appear to do little while maintaining at all times perfect control over his dog.
- Judges should keep their opinions strictly to themselves and act on what happened on the day or days of the trial at which they are judging, forgetting past performance.

All sorts of game, including pheasants, may be shot.

- At the end of each run, judges are advised to place each dog in a category such as A, B, or C (+ or -) according to the work done. When all dogs have been seen by more than one judge or pair of judges, the judges may confer to assess which dogs they should discard or retain. It is advisable to take short notes of each dog's work and not to trust memory.
- Judges should be careful for the safety of dogs and should not require them to negotiate dangerous obstacles, such as barbed wire fences, ice, roadways and walls with high drops.
- Judges on the 'A' panel should bear in mind that in future they may be asked for assessments of 'B' panel or unlisted judges with whom they officiate.

173

For those required to retrieve

- A dog should be steady to shot and fall of game and should retrieve on command. Handlers shall not send their dog until directed by the judge.
- All wounded game should be gathered and dispatched at the earliest opportunity. Wounded game should normally be tried before dead game. If game cannot be gathered, the judge must depute this task to the official handler and dog (picker-up) appointed for this purpose.
- If game is shot very close to a dog which would make a retrieve of no value, the retrieve may be offered to a dog under another judge. During the first round of the Stake dogs should, whenever possible, have the opportunity to pick game shot by their own guns.
- Handlers may be instructed where to try from and given reasonable directions as to where the game fell. If the dogs fail to complete the retrieve, the judges should search the area of fall and, if they find the game, the dogs should be eliminated, save in exceptional circumstances.
- Good marking is essential in a retrieving dog as he should not disturb ground unnecessarily. Judges should give full credit to a dog which goes straight to the fall and gets on with the job.
- The perfect pick-up should be quick with a fast return. The handler should not snatch or drag game from the dog's mouth. Judges should not penalise a dog too heavily for putting down game to get a firmer grip, but this must not be confused with sloppy retrieving. A

Mrs June Atkinson with Holway Quilla winning the GRC's 2 Day Open Stake in 1995 prior to her gaining her field trial title.

good game-finding dog should not rely on the handler to find the game but should be obedient and respond to his handler's signals where necessary. Dogs showing game-finding ability and initiative should be placed above those which have to be handled onto

Riversdale Chorister bred, owned and handled by Miss J Hunt, waiting to be called into line at the 1995 ECGRC's All Aged FT Stake. He was the guns' unanimous choice for the day and won a Certificate of Merit.

their game. Usually, the best dog seems to require the least handling. He appears to have an instinctive knowledge of direction and makes a difficult find look simple and easy.

- If a dog is performing indifferently on a runner, he should be called up promptly. If more dogs are tried on the runner, the work of all these dogs must be assessed in relation to the order in which they are tried. The handlers of the second and subsequent dogs down may be allowed to take their dogs towards the fall, as may the handler of the first dog if he has not had a chance to mark the game. Game picked by the second or a subsequent dog constitutes an 'eye wipe'. All eye wipes should be treated on their merits but dogs which have had their eyes wiped during the body of the Stake should be discarded. If a dog shows ability by acknowledging the fall and making a workmanlike job of the line, he should not automatically be barred from the awards by failing to produce the game, provided the game is not collected by another dog tried by the judges on the same game.

- All game should be examined for signs of 'hard mouth'. A hard-mouthed dog seldom gives visible evidence of hardness. He will simply crush in one or both sides of the ribs. Blowing up the feathers on a bird will not disclose the damage. Place the game on the palm of the hand, breast upwards, head forward and feel the ribs with the finger and thumb. They should be round and firm. If they are caved in or flat this is evidence of hard mouth. Be sure the game reaches the co-judges for examination. There should be no hesitation or sentiment with 'hard mouth' – the dog should be discarded. A certain indication of good mouth is a dog bringing in live game whose head is up and eye bright.

Competing

Dogs must walk steadily at heel and sit quietly at drives. If the game situation permits two retrieves under the first judge or pair of judges, then one retrieve in the second round is the usual procedure. The judges may then confer and discard any dog they no longer require. The dog steward should be informed of any dogs eliminated or discarded for any reason. This will allow him to have the right dogs in the line.

The dog steward should be instructed to send in the second round dogs when there is a vacancy in the line. Second round dogs should have their opportunity to be tried against the first round dogs when the situation arises.

Judges should be most careful to see that each dog gets his chance in the correct order, starting with the lowest number on the right. Should dog No 1 fail, and dog No 2 be successful, No 2 still has the first chance in the next retrieve. It is quite unfair to give a dog two first chances in succession and the other dog two second chances. If the two dogs fail on game, the judge should not call fresh dogs into the line to try for it until the other dogs already in the line have been tried. In the concluding stages of a trial, judges may use their own discretion as the situation arises.

If one part of the line is starved of game and the dogs have been down under that judge for quite some time then another judge could offer all game shot by one or both of his guns to the judge who is short of game. The handlers should be made aware of these arrangements. It is quite unfair in the body of the Stake to offer dead game to a co-judge, then to ask your own dogs to try for the runners.

Run offs may be required to determine the final placings of the top few dogs. It should be expected that judges will stretch the dogs to such a degree that they may fail and be eye wiped. An eye wipe at this stage will incur penalty but the dog may still remain in the awards.

Field Trial Champions

This is a much coveted title. All wins towards the title are confined to Open Stakes for which a Field Trial certificate will be awarded to the winner. The dogs which will be accredited with the title must either be the winner of:

- The Retriever Championship
- Two 24 dog stakes   )These wins must also be under two different A
- One 24 dog stake & one 12 dog stake   )panel judges with a minimum of 20/10 runners
- Three 12 dog stakes   )respectively and one open to all Retrievers.

Before any retriever is entitled to be described as a Field Trial Champion he must also have sat quietly at a drive and have passed a water test. The special water test must have been fulfilled at the Championship, in a Field Trial Stake before two Panel 'A' judges or at a subsequent special test before two Panel 'A' judges.

Retriever Championships

To qualify for the annual Championships a dog must have either won:

- a 2-day open stake which counts as an 'A', or
- have 3 'B's. 'B's are gained by either winning a 12 dog open stake or a 2nd in a 2-day open stake.

The winner of the previous year's Retriever Championships is also eligible to defend his title.

General

There is a lot of luck in field trialling, which begins firstly with trying to obtain a run. Most trials are over-subscribed which makes it difficult and then there is so much luck involved on the day itself. Most field trial handlers give their dogs the opportunity to pick up prior to trialling, but limit their retrieving greatly so they do not become overkeen when trialling begins. If you wish to obtain information on how to train your dog to trial, I recommend you read some of the many books by working gundog specialists.

Obedience

I have already suggested how to teach your dog basic obedience and how to locate training classes run by local dog clubs to help or improve on the basics. Some of these clubs also run more advanced classes if you wish to compete in obedience or take The Kennel Club Good Citizen Dog Scheme.

Private trainers may be located through the two specialist obedience publications, Dog Training Weekly and Obedience Info.

Retrieving a dumb-bell in obedience competition.

Dogs in a Down stay at one of the GRC's Obedience Tests in July 1995.

Competitive Obedience

Various levels of shows are permitted to run obedience classes under Kennel Club licence.

Championship Obedience Shows: open to all competitors, except where a qualification for entry has been approved by the General Committee of The Kennel Club, and at which Kennel Club Obedience Certificates are offered.

Open Obedience Shows: open to all competitors.

Limited Obedience Shows: entry is limited :

1. to members of the show society
2. to competitors resident within a specific area
3. to specific breeds
4. by numbers (such numbers to be stipulated in the schedule) or otherwise subject to the approval of the General Committee of The Kennel Club

Obedience Certificate/Champions

A Dog Obedience CC and a Bitch Obedience CC will be on offer from The Kennel Club for winners of first prizes in Championship Class 'C' Dog and Championship Class 'C' Bitch at a Championship Show, provided they do not lose more than 15 points out of 300.

To obtain the title of Obedience Champion, a dog must win three CCs under three different judges or win The Kennel Club's Obedience Championship at Crufts.

The classes on offer at the 3 main types of show may include Pre-Beginners, Beginners, Novice, Test A, Test B, Test C and Championship C. Please refer to The Kennel Club Year Book for the definitions of each class.

Obedience Test Exercises and Points
General
In all classes the dog should work in a happy and natural manner but should not impede the handler and prime consideration should be given to judging the dog and handler as a team. The dog may be encouraged and praised except where specifically stated.

In all tests the left side of a handler will be regarded as the 'working side' unless the handler suffers from a physical disability and has the judge's permission to work the dog on the right hand side. To signal the completion of each test the handler will be given the command 'test finished'.

It is permissible for handlers to practise their dogs before going into the ring provided there is no punitive correction; this is similar to an athlete warming up before an event. The dog should be led into the ring for judging with a smooth collar or slip chain, lead attached (unless otherwise directed) and should be at the handler's side.

Pre-Beginners
Heel on Lead	15pts
Heel Free	20pts
Recall	10pts
1 minute Sit Stay	10pts
2 minute Down Stay	20pts
Total	75pts

Beginners
Heel on Lead	15pts
Heel Free	20pts
Recall	10pts
Retrieve any article	25pts
1 minute Sit Stay	10pts
2 minute Down Stay	20pts
Total	100pts

Novice
Temperament Test	10pts
Heel on Lead	15pts
Heel Free	20pts
Recall	10pts
Retrieve a dumb-bell	15pts
1 minute Sit Stay	10pts
2 minute Down Stay	20pts
Total	100pts

Class A
Heel on Lead	15pts
Heel Free	25pts
A Recall	15pts
Retrieve a dumb-bell	25pts

2 minute Sit Stay	10pts
5 minute Down Stay out of sight	30pts
Scent	30pts
Total	150pts

Class B

Heel Free	40pts
Send Away	40pts
Retrieve judge's article	30pts
1 minute Stand Stay	10pts
2 minute Sit Stay out of sight	20pts
5 minute Down Stay out of sight	30pts
Scent	30pts
Total	200pts

Class C

Heel Free	60pts
Send Away	40pts
Retrieve judge's article	30pts
Distance Control	50pts
2 minute Sit Stay out of sight	20pts
10 minute Down Stay out of sight	50pts
Scent	50pts
Total	300pts

Agility

Agility has existed in the United Kingdom for roughly 20 years and is a fast growing sport, soon to be granted Championship status. Sponsored competitions have been televised and some

The weave.

of the entrants feature in the annual Crufts programme. The object is for a dog to follow a set course over various apparatus with his handler in the fastest possible time, without incurring any penalties.

Obedience training and control is essential before undertaking agility training. You will also need a fit, healthy, active, exuberant and outgoing dog in order to compete. The handler needs to be fit too!

Some clubs offer agility training mainly for fun and others are more competitively-minded. Competition is more expensive as you will need to build or purchase equipment to train between classes if you wish to be successful. Otherwise all you will need is a smooth collar with a long detachable lead. It is not safe to use rope slip leads for agility training.

Training should not begin on apparatus with Goldens until they are about 18 months old and their joints are set. Apart from the basic obedience terms, your dog will have to learn additional words such as 'tunnel', 'weave', 'left', 'go on', 'steady' and so on.

Before you consider starting in agility, I would recommend you read Ruth Hobday's book *Agility is Fun*.

Classes

Classes are usually offered for standard, midi and mini dogs. (Goldens are 'standard.')
The standard classes are:

Elementary: for owners, handlers or dogs which have not gained a third prize or above in Agility and/or a Jumping Class at a licensed Agility Test.

Starters: for owners, handlers or dogs which have not won an Agility and/or a Jumping Class at a licensed Agility Test (Elementary excepted).

The yellow areas indicate contact points which the dog must touch.

Novice: for dogs which have not won a total of two first prizes at least one of which must be gained in an Agility class at a licensed Agility Test. (Starters and Elementary excepted.)
Intermediate: Open to all except dogs eligible for Elementary and Starters Classes at a licensed Agility Test.
Seniors: Open to dogs having won at least two first prizes, one of which must be an Agility class, at a licensed Agility Test (Elementary and Starter wins excepted).
Advanced: Open to dogs having a minimum of four wins at a licensed Agility Test, two of which must be gained in Intermediate, Senior or Open Agility (not Jumping) Classes (Elementary, Starter and Novice wins excepted).
Open: Open to all.

Courses

The judge is responsible for the design of the course. The course will consist of a minimum of 10 and a maximum of 20 obstacles. No practice is allowed on the course by competitors with their dogs but competitors are permitted to walk the course without their dogs before the test(s) begins.

Obstacles

Those which meet with The Kennel Club's approval are:
Hurdles, Rising Spread Jumps (2 elements only), Brush fences, Hoops (Tyres), Tables, Pause Boxes, Long Jumps, Water Jumps, Wishing Wells or Lych Gates, Collapsible Tunnels, Pipe Tunnels, Weaving Poles (minimum of 5, maximum of 12), A Ramps, See Saws, Dog Walks (a walk plank set off the ground) and Cross overs. As the dimension regulations change frequently for these obstacles, refer to The Kennel Club for up to date details.

Marking

All course faults are marked in units of 5. Standard marking set out by The Kennel Club must be used in the standard classes defined earlier. Faults incurred for failure to negotiate obstacles will be added to the faults incurred for failure to complete a course in a set time. A single fault or part thereof will be added for each second over the set time. Actual time is recorded. Rounding up/down is not permitted. If other marking variations are used in non standard classes they must be clearly defined to all competitors prior to the competition.

Incorrect entry into the weaving poles or alights from see saws, ramps or dog walks before the specified section are regarded as refusals.

Elimination faults are: three refusals/run outs; taking the wrong course; fouling the ring and dogs out of control.

Flyball

This is another fun competition, involving a team knockout competition. It is a relatively new sport in the United Kingdom, having been invented in Canada. Most dogs can be taught to do Flyball if they are interested in catching a ball. As with any other discipline, it is important to have basic control over your dog; the top teams will have dogs racing at speeds of 30 miles per hour!

Most breeds can attempt Flyball if they are interested in catching a ball.

Each dog in a team jumps four hurdles in succession before proceeding to the end of the run to a box containing a ball. The dog has to trigger the release of the ball by jumping on a pad and retrieving the ball in its mouth, then jump back over the four hurdles to the start/finish

The smallest dog in the team is called the 'height' dog because he determines the height of the hurdles to be cleared by the team.

183

line. Only when each dog has crossed the start/finish line completely may the next dog commence its run.

The first team of dogs to cross the finish line wins the race. The best of three runs decides which team proceeds to the next heat until there is an outright winner.

Equipment

Hurdles: The height of the hurdles must be 30.9cm (12in) in all classes and for all sizes of dog. The hurdles must be white, have an inside width of 61cm (24in) with posts not more than 91.4cm (36in) high and the hurdle rail must not exceed 1.27cm (0.5in) in depth. In the interests of safety the top bar must be flexible, padded and/or spring loaded.
Box: The design drawing with dimensions for the flyball box are available from The Kennel Club. Alternatives may be used provided safety is observed. Each team must supply its own box with one to spare.
Backstop board: A backstop board must be provided. Minimum height 61cm (24in) the design must be clearly visible and positioned a minimum of 213cm (7ft) behind the boxes.
Balls: All balls used must be tennis balls, which must not be punctured. Each team must supply its own.

Judging

(a) The judge has overall responsibility for the competition and will control both the start and finish.
(b) A steward must be positioned at the end of the start/finish line.
(c) Two stewards must be appointed to ensure that the box and hurdle rules are not infringed. Re-runs must be clearly indicated.
(d) If in the opinion of the judge a box malfunctions during a race, the race must be stopped, a spare box must be substituted and the race re-run. If the spare box also breaks down the team forfeits the race.
(e) A dog must attempt to clear every hurdle. However, if a hurdle is knocked down, the dog must not be penalised, provided he clears the hurdle as if it were standing.
(f) A dog must re-run at the end of the line if: an early start is indicated; he does not attempt every jump; he does not trigger the box; he does not return with the ball; his handler's feet cross the start line during his run (with the exception of resetting a jump or retrieving a lost ball); in the judge's opinion he started his run before the preceding dog had reached the start/finish line; the box loader is faulted for assisting the dog.
(g) If a dog or any team member obstructs the opposing team during a race, the offending team will forfeit the race. A dog chasing a loose ball is not necessarily causing an obstruction.

Competing

Each dog jumps the four hurdles in succession, triggers the box and returns over the hurdles with the ball in his mouth. Only when each dog has crossed the start/finish line with any part of his body may the next dog commence his run.

Box loaders may only give verbal encouragement to the dogs and, except when loading, must stand at the rear of the box in an upright position with their hands behind their backs. A runner or handler may reset the hurdle but must not interfere with or guide the dog in any way.

Working Trials

Working trials were recognised as beginning in the United Kingdom in 1927. Entries of up to 200 may be expected at a Championship Trial which may be held over a week or more.

Some of the tests incorporate a mixture of elements from other fields of work and, whilst some Goldens compete, it is a wonder that more do not. (As in Obedience, the most popular breeds are the Border Collie/collie type and German Shepherd Dog.) The requirements are: agility, biddability, good scenting, intelligence and soundness.

The stakes are graduated according to ability. They are Companion Dog (CD) Stake, Utility Dog (UD) Stake, Working Dog (WD) Stake, Tracking Dog (TD) Stake, Patrol Dog (PD) Stake. Goldies are only eligible to compete from 18 months old and do not usually compete in PD Stakes due to their friendly nature. Basic exercise details are given below.

Schedule of Exercises and Points

Companion Dog Stakes

	Max. Marks	Group Total	Minimum Group Qualifying Mark
Group I Control			
1 Heel on leash	5		
2 Heel free	10		
3 Recall to handler	5		
4 Sending the dog away	10	30	21
Group II Stays			
5 Sit (2 minutes)	10		
6 Down (10 minutes)	10	20	14
Group III Agility			
7 Clear jump	5		
8 Long jump	5		
9 Scale (3) Stay (2) Recall (5)	10	20	14
Group IV Retrieving and Nosework			
10 Retrieve a dumb-bell	10		
11 Elementary search	20	30	21
Totals	100	100	70

Utility Dog Stakes

	Max. Marks	Group Total	Minimum Group Qualifying Mark
Group I Control			
1 Heel free	5		
2 Sending the dog away	10		
3 Retrieve a dumb-bell	5		

	Max. Marks	Group Total	Minimum Group Qualifying Mark
4 Down (10 minutes)	10		
5 Steadiness to gunshot	5	35	25
Group II Agility			
6 Clear jump	5		
7 Long jump	5		
8 Scale (3) Stay (2) Recall (5)	10	20	14
Group III Nosework			
9 Search	35		
10 Track (90)			
11 Articles 10+10 (20)	110	145	102
Totals	200	200	141

Working Dog Stakes

	Max. Marks	Group Total	Minimum Group Qualifying Mark
Group I Control			
1 Heel free	5		
2 Sending the dog away	10		
3 Retrieve a dumb-bell	5		
4 Down (10 Minutes)	10		
5 Steadiness to gunshot	5	35	25
Group II Agility			
6 Clear jump	5		
7 Long jump	5		
8 Scale (3) Stay (2) Recall (5)	10	20	14
Group III Nosework			
9 Search	35		
10 Track (90)			
Articles (10+10 =20)	110	145	102
Totals	200	200	141

Tracking Dog Stake

	Max. Marks	Group Total	Minimum Group Qualifying Mark
Group I Control			
1 Heel free	5		
2 Sending away and directional control	10		
3 Speak on command	5		
4 Down (10 minutes)	10		
5 Steadiness to gunshot	5	35	25

	Max. Marks	Group Total	Minimum Group Qualifying Mark
Group II Agility			
6 Clear jump	5		
7 Long jump	5		
8 Scale (3) Stay (2) Recall (5)	10	20	14
Group III Nosework			
9 Search	35		
10 Track 100 articles			
(10+10+10=30)	130	165	116
Totals	220	220	155

Patrol Dog Stake

	Max. Marks	Group Total	Minimum Group Qualifying Mark
Group I Control			
1 Heel free	5		
2 Sending away and directional control	10		
3 Speak on command	5		
4 Down (10 minutes)	10		
5 Steadiness to gunshot	5	35	25
Group II Agility			
6 Clear jump	5		
7 Long jump	5		
8 Scale (3) Stay (2) Recall (5)	10	20	14
Group III Nosework			
9 Search	35		
10 Track (60) articles (10+10=20)	80	115	80
Group IV Patrol			
11 Quartering the ground	45		
12 Test of Courage	20		
13 Search and escort	25		
14a Recall from criminal	30		
14b Pursuit and detention of criminal	30	150	105
Totals	320	320	224

The eligibility for Open Working Trials is:

Companion Dog (CD) Stake: for dogs which have not qualified CDex or UDex or won three or more first prizes in Open CD or any prize in UD Stakes, WD Stakes, PD or TD Stakes at Open or Championship Working Trials.

Utility Dog (UD) Stake: for dogs which have not been awarded a Certificate of Merit in UD, WD, PD, or TD Stakes.

Working Dog (WD) Stake: for dogs which have been awarded a Certificate of Merit UD Stakes, but not in WD, PD, or TD Stakes.

Tracking Dog (TD) Stake: for dogs which have been awarded a Certificate of Merit WD Stakes, but not more than one Certificate of Merit in TD Stakes.

Patrol Dog (PD) Stake: for dogs which have qualified WD Excellent at a Championship Trial but excluding dogs that have qualified PD Excellent at a Championship Trial.

The eligibility for Championship Working Trials is:

Companion Dog (CD) Stake: for dogs which have not won three or more first prizes in CD Stakes, and not more than one prize in UD Stake, or any prize in any other Stake at Championship Working Trials.

Utility Dog (UD) Stake: for dogs which have won a Certificate of Merit in an Open UD Stake. A dog is not eligible for entry in this Stake if he has qualified WDex or has been entered in the WD Stake at the same trial.

Working Dog (WD) Stake: for dogs which have qualified UDex and have won a Certificate of Merit in Open WD Stakes. A dog is not eligible for entry in this stake if he has qualified TD or PD Excellent or been entered in the TD or PD Stake at the same trial.

Tracking Dog (TD) Stake: for dogs which have been awarded two Certificates of Merit in Open TD Stakes and have qualified WDex at two Championship Trials.

Patrol Dog (PD) Stake: For dogs which have been awarded two Certificates of Merit in Open PD Stakes and have qualified WDex at two Championship Trials.

Working Trial Certificates

A Kennel Club Working Trial Certificate will be awarded to any dog winning a TD or PD Stake at a Championship Working Trial provided that he has obtained 70% or more marks as indicated in the Schedule of Points and has also been awarded the qualification 'excellent' by obtaining at least 80% of the possible total marks for the stake.

Certificates will be awarded by the judge or judges at a Championship Working Trial PD, TD, WD, UD and CD Stake to dogs that have obtained 70% or more marks in each group of exercises in the Stake entered, provided that the dog has complied with any additional requirements for that Stake. The added qualification 'excellent' shall be awarded should the dog also obtain 80% or more marks for the total for the Stake.

Two wins in a TD or PD Championship provided the necessary marks are achieved will gain the title of Working Trials Champion. To date no Golden has ever achieved this.

Certificates of Merit are awarded at Open Working Trials to dogs gaining an 'excellent' qualification.

Dogs eligible for entry in the Working Trial Championships are:

TD Championship: a dog must have been placed 1st in Championship TD Stake with the qualification 'excellent' in the Stake during the period week no. 35 to week no. 34 the following year.

PD Championship: a dog must have been placed 1st in Championship PD Stake with the qualification 'excellent' in the Stake during the period week no. 35 to week no. 34 the following year.

The winners of the previous year's Championship Stakes qualify automatically.

CHAPTER TEN

Stewarding and Judging

Stewarding

Stewards and helpers are required at all competitive events to undertake various tasks, some more demanding than others. Most, if not all, volunteer their time and help without any financial recompense and, if it were not for these people, the events which many in dogdom enjoy would be unable to take place or run smoothly.

Although some clubs organise teach-ins on various matters, most of what is required is learnt through participation in events and observation of others. Many volunteers are those who have gained from their hobby, either through success or by showing they understand what is required by other means, and wish to put something back into the sport. Many others wish to learn as much as they can by stewarding, which can assist them in training and handling to achieve greater success with their own dogs, and help them when they go on to judge, if they so desire.

If you want to steward but are uncertain whether you have sufficient experience, most societies would probably allow you to be a trainee steward and place you with an experienced steward who can teach you what is required.

In this chapter I will consider, for the most part, the role of stewards and judges at Breed shows. As always, The Kennel Club Year Book is the definitive guide for all activities that are run under its jurisdiction and should be referred to for details of the current rules and regulations. Details of amendments to these, new rules, and so on are also published in the Kennel Gazette. (The Kennel Club Year Book and the Kennel Gazette are available from the Publications Department, The Kennel Club, 1-5 Clarges Street, Piccadilly London W1Y 8AB.)

From 1st July 2001, new judges at Championship shows where CCs are on offer must first have stewarded for 3 years and at a minimum of 12 shows.

Stewarding at Dog Shows
Things to remember before you go to the show
- Directions and start time.
- Pens and pencils.
- Clipboard (optional).
- Clear polythene bag to cover clipboard, in case of wet weather.
- Wet weather clothes.
- Schedule.

Things to check before you start
- Meet your judge.
- Ask the judge if you should check the ring.

- Make sure the ring is rubbish-free, safely roped and has a table and chair.
- Ask the judge where the new and old dogs are to stand; where they are to be seen; where the line up is to be; and in what order, if any, he or she wishes the dogs to be in, particularly the old dogs.
- Get the box of awards and prizes for the ring.

Things you will find in the ring box
- For the judge: judge's rosette, judge's book, dog press envelopes (pre-paid postage) for their write up, and a catalogue.
- For you: steward's badge, steward's sheet, catalogue.
- Ring numbers (if not on the benches). Sort them into class order if this has not been done already.
- Prize cards, rosettes, cup slips – check they are all there.

Ensure exhibitors are aware that judging is to commence and have the correct number clearly displayed. Make sure that no unauthorised person or dog enters the ring, then advise the judge that all those present are in the ring.

Things to check once the first class is in the ring
- How many places do you have cards for?
- What awards do you have for the challenge?
- What dogs are in subsequent classes?
- Write the absentees in the judge's book and on the steward's sheet.
- Inform exhibitors when the last dog is being seen.
- Be ready with cards and rosettes once the judge has made his/her placings, but do not give anything out until the judge has written the numbers down in the judge's book.
- Call out the numbers in your loudest voice, remembering to face the audience as you do so. Write down the numbers as you go.
- Get the next class in while the judge writes up the critique. Stand the new dogs by themselves and the old dogs in whatever order requested by the judge. When the next class is being judged, sort out your paperwork.
- Check that you and the judge wrote down the same numbers.
- Clearly mark awards on award board (if one is provided) and the secretary's slip (ditto).
- Fill in the judge's book results slips. Some judges prefer to do this themselves.
- Ensure the judge has signed the slips (at some shows it is necessary to take the award slips to the award board if it is not by the ring).
- Fill in both your and judge's catalogues with results and absentees.
- Put any information on your result chart to help you identify unbeaten winning dogs, placed dogs coming through from earlier classes, and placed dogs which have met indirectly.

The Kennel Club's Regulations state that:
- Stewards are not authorised to allow any exhibit into the ring unless it is entered in the class as recorded in the judge's book and/or catalogue or unless a notice of transfer authority is provided by the Show Secretary/Manager.
- Stewards are not authorised to transfer dogs from classes or allow unentered exhibits into

classes without the necessary authority from the Show Secretary/Manager.
* Stewards are not authorised to instruct exhibitors concerning a dog's eligibility to compete in a class and should never prevent a dog which is entered in the class or has the necessary authority to be exhibited from competing even if it is considered that the dog is ineligible.
* Stewards must be aware of the order in which breeds are to be judged in the ring, ensure that exhibits are not attracted from outside the ring, and report any persons doing this to the judge.

The Challenge

Ask the judge if he/she would like all unbeaten dogs in the ring, where and in what order. Make sure you know exactly who you expect in the ring; if an unexpected dog appears, double check everything before you ask for it to be removed.

Be ready to call in any seconds (only beaten by the winning dog, or dogs beaten only by the other sex), for a Best Opposite Sex challenge or as required by the judge.

Remember to write all the challenge results on the show secretary's slips. The slips may have to be taken to the secretary during judging rather than waiting until the breed is completed as catalogues have to be marked up for The Kennel Club. Ensure the judge completes and signs the CC, RCC, BOB and BOS cards, where these are on offer, after the decision has been declared.

Golden rules to remember
* The judge is in charge of, and responsible for, everything that happens in the ring. You are only there to assist.
* You must not take it upon yourself to make any decisions; always refer to the judge, show manager or chief steward.
* Do your best to make sure everyone has an enjoyable day, and don't panic!

Judging

Please refer to my general comments on stewarding which are relevant to anyone who wishes to judge in any capacity; particularly the points on familiarising yourself with the appropriate Kennel Club Regulations, Societies' event rules and gaining stewarding experience.

Usually judges are selected from persons who are competent and who may have achieved good results, thus demonstrating their knowledge of the breed, training and handling skills and what is required. It is not usually a matter, or should not be, of self invitation!

From 1st July 2001 it will be mandatory for new CC show judges to have undergone seminar training on relevant KC show regulations, ring procedure, practical aspects of judging, anatomy, conformation, movement and breed points. This, together with a formal assessment of their first appointment, are two recent KC innovations.

In certain working elements (Obedience, Working Trials and Field Trials), it is actually laid down by The Kennel Club what the requirements are in The Kennel Club Year Book.

Judge's Invitations

Kennel Club Regulations state specifically that for most shows and working events, invitations should be in writing. Societies should ensure written acceptances are received and, once received, should supply a written confirmation of the appointment. This will then be deemed to be a 'contract'.

Before accepting any invitation, ensure you meet any criteria laid down and that you agree in writing any financial expenses for which you want recompense. It saves any misunderstanding or embarrassment at the end of the day.

Judging at Shows

The Kennel Club can supply on request a copy of their 'Guide for Judges' which should be read in conjunction with the Show Regulations published in their Year Book. One example from the Guide for those who do not know is that 'Judges must not smoke at any time in the judging ring'.

What To Do
Before the show
- Decide whether to charge expenses and/or travelling and confirm this to the society.
- Check schedule; society's rules and prizes (number of places, trophies, and so on); time of judging and venue.
- Know steward's duties (now a KC requirement for first time CC judges).
- Take pen and note pad, schedule, waterproofs, change of shoes.
- Decide on your priorities according to the Breed Standard, such as whether you consider good shoulder construction to be more important than a high tail carriage, and so on.
- **Know and understand the Breed Standard.**

At the show
- Go to the cloakroom and make yourself comfortable.
- Report to Secretary, collect judging particulars, rosette, judge's book, *Dog World* and *Our Dog* envelopes (some may be in the steward's ring box).
- Check which dogs you have to write about. (Usually 1sts at Open and 1st and 2nd at Championship Shows and Breed Club Open Shows. Crufts also includes 3rds.)
- Check judge's book on numbers and second entries.
- Check ring and decide how you want the dogs stood, run and placed, and inform your steward. If judging outside, remember to have the sun behind you for yours and the dog's sakes. On completion of judging, the dogs to be given awards should be placed in the centre of the ring in descending order from left to right, but take note of where exhibitors are seated. Move the table if it helps.

Judging
- Decide on method of examining the dogs, and be consistent throughout the day.
- Allow more time for puppies (about two minutes), for adults 60–90 seconds per dog. Take 10 minutes approximately for choosing and write-ups per class at Championship Shows and five minutes for Open Shows. These speeds may seem fast to judges of numerically smaller breeds but are required for the large entries in Goldens.
- Do not talk to exhibitors and only when necessary to the steward, especially if you are a husband/wife or partnership team.
- Ensure exhibitors have ample space to set up dogs (steward's job).

- Try to select five dogs, if possible, or fill the places required. If you need to shortlist, do not choose six if there are only five places, try to select a minimum of seven.
- Be clear to exhibitors if you are placing or selecting only (touch dogs, do not point as this can lead to misunderstandings) and then check they are positioned correctly, so that you are not relying solely on the steward.
- Try not to change places if you have placed already and not indicated you are not placing.
- Try to be decisive. You may not be happy with exact results after the show, but that's natural, given time restrictions and often close decisions. A confident, decisive judge looks efficient.
- Try not to be intimidated by big name breeders/handlers – judge the dogs.
- If a dog has a good or a bad point and you wish to remember it without making it obvious, make a mental note of an article of clothing being worn by the exhibitor.
- Note numbers of winners in the judging book. Any changes must be initialled by the judge with a time and date.
- Prepare your write-up notes (I also take a photo to help me).
- Repeat winners in judge's book for secretary and award board slips or check your steward has done this for you and then sign them. Do not pre-sign. Check that the absentees are marked on the slips for the first class they are absent from. The Kennel Club requires this information and so will you when you are under consideration to award CCs.
- Carry on until all classes are completed.

Awards at Open shows – Dogs that can be considered:
BOB: 1st prize winners only.
RBOB: 1st prize winners and second to BOB.
BOS: 1st to 4th places only can be called, if beaten by opposite sex.
B Puppy: 1st prize winners in puppy classes but check for other puppies in higher classes that have only been beaten by dogs older than 12 months.

Awards at Championship shows – Dogs that can be considered:
CC: 1st prize winners only.
RCC: 1st prize winners and 2nd to CC if unbeaten in other breed classes.
BOB: Dog and Bitch CC winners.
BOS: Goes to whichever CC winner does not take BOB.
BP: As for Open shows.
RBIS: (Breed Clubs only) the RCC winner to the BOB can challenge the BOS winner.

Hand out top prizes in order, for example, CC before RCC (signed) at Championship Shows and BOB before BP at any show. Between classes, check your placings to see if any previously-seen dogs have not come in for their class (especially unbeaten 1st prize winners) as they will not be eligible to challenge for BOB at Open shows or a CC at Championship shows.

After the show
Return to secretary, claim expenses if any were agreed, collect your marked-up catalogue from the steward or secretary. **Say your 'thank yous'.**

Prepare your critique, which should preferably be typed. Try not to be over-critical. Bring out good points. Your report must be sent to *Dog World* and *Our Dogs* within 4 weeks/1 month respectively.

The Breed Standard for the United Kingdom

General appearance: Symmetrical, balanced, active, powerful, level mover, sound with kindly expression.

Characteristics: Biddable, intelligent and possessing natural working ability.

Temperament: Kindly, friendly and confident.

Head and skull: Balanced and well-chiselled, skull broad without coarseness; well set on neck, muzzle powerful, wide and deep. Length of foreface approximately equals length from well-defined stop to occiput. Nose preferably black.

Eyes: Dark brown, set well apart, dark rims.

Ears: Moderate size, set on approximate level with eyes.

Mouth: Jaws strong, with a perfect, regular and complete scissor bite, i.e. upper teeth closely overlapping lower teeth and set square to the jaws.

Neck: Good length, clean and muscular.

Forequarters: Forelegs straight with good bone, shoulders well laid back, long in blade with upper arm of equal length placing legs well under body. Elbows close fitting.

Body: Balanced, short coupled, deep through heart. Ribs deep, well sprung. Level topline.

Hindquarters: Loin and legs strong and muscular, good second thighs, well bent stifles. Hocks well let down, straight when viewed from rear, neither turning in nor out. Cowhocks highly undesirable.

Feet: Round and cat-like.

Tail: Set on and carried level with back, reaching to hocks, without curl at tip.

Gait/movement: Powerful with good drive. Straight and true in front and rear. Stride long and free with no sign of hackney action in front.

Coat: Flat or wavy with good feathering, dense water-resisting undercoat.

Colour: Any shade of gold or cream, neither red nor mahogany. A few white hairs on chest only are permissible.

Size: Height at withers: dogs 56–61cm (22–24in), bitches 51–56cm (20–22in).

Faults: Any departure from the foregoing points should be considered a fault and the seriousness with which the fault should be regarded should be in exact proportion to its degree.

Note: Male animals should have two apparently normal testicles fully descended into the scrotum.

Interpretation

I hear many exhibitors and judges say, 'It is a matter of the judge's opinion and interpretation'. As a judge myself, I believe this to be true. If judging dogs was a science with exactly the same results over and over again, most dogs would be discarded and showing would not be the fun that it is (most of the time). The interpretation leading to different results (in the 'judge's opinion') can occur due to:

- The judge giving priority to one part of the dog's construction compared to another part.

My priorities are based on the fact that Goldens were bred to work and need to be well constructed for this purpose. For instance, I would give far greater priority to good shoulder construction than a low tail set;
- The coat, handling, presentation and showmanship on the day.

Faults

I have given below my interpretation of the 'departures' from the Breed Standard.

Faults in General appearance
Symmetrical/balanced
Disproportionate properties are seen either when the dog stands or moves, such as head size to overall body size, neck length to body length or forehand angulation to hind angulation.

Active/powerful
The dog is lacking in both. It is sometimes difficult to determine 'active' given the restraints of a show ring. Power can normally be seen both standing and/or on the move.

Level mover
This can only be seen in profile, not when coming and going. If level is taken to mean with a good head and neck carriage, that is, held above the back line, with the back level from the withers to the tail set and the tail set and carried level with the back, then unlevel would be any departure from this outline.

Soundness
Interpretations of soundness can vary, but the term generally covers the dog's overall make-up, standing and moving. The unsound dog may be lame or favouring a limb.

Kindly expression
Hard/coarse expression.

Faults in Character:
Biddable/intelligent and possessing natural working ability
It is very difficult to assess these in the show ring. Biddability may be seen from behaviour and the rapport the dog has with his owner, but in many cases its lack may be due to the owner's training, not the dog.

Any prior knowledge you may have of a dog's working ability should be ignored, as it is unlikely that you will have the same information about every dog in the class. This will not be a problem if the class is specifically for dogs that have achieved an award in the field.

Faults in Temperament:
Kindly, friendly and confident
Usually, this can be assessed only by how the dog reacts to the judge's approach, examination and with other exhibitors and dogs for the duration of the class.

Head and skull faults

See definition given in the Standard. Faults are: foreface too long or short compared to skull length when viewed in profile, domed skull, coarse skull, too large or too small, level foreface (lacking chiselling), dish face, no stop, snipey muzzle, too wide in the cheek, pronounced occiput in adult, too much flews.

Pigment faults

The Standard only states 'preferably black'. I would not over-penalise a dog lacking in pigment if it had other very good properties, unless it became a deciding factor between two dogs of otherwise equal merit. It is purely for appearance and makes no difference to a dog's working ability.

Eye faults

Light eyes, and eyes set too close. Nothing is stated about the size or shape, although judges have been known to penalise eyes set on the slant, too small an eye, round or almond shape.

Ear faults

Too large, too small, set too low, set too high. If the ear set and size are correct and the eye set is correct the ear tip should just cover the eye to the far corner (tear duct area).

Mouth faults

Undershot (top set behind lower set), overshot (top set well in front of lower set), even (top set level with lower set), incomplete denture, teeth out of line and partly out of line, including dropped teeth. The latter usually applies to the two middle front teeth on lower jaw. Veterans may be expected to have some wear and tear on their denture but the dog's age should not affect his 'bite'.

Neck faults

Too long (sometimes referred to as a 'swan' neck), too short, excessive loose skin from back of jaw bones to beginning of neck which is called unclean or throatiness, not muscular or too muscular, curved or arching, and incorrect set. The neck needs to be assessed carefully as many dogs have a good neck, but can tuck it back into their shoulders. The appearance of a short neck can be made worse if there is insufficient shoulder layback.

Forequarter faults

These can only be assessed when the dog has been set up correctly with his legs centrally in line under the shoulder blade (scapula). The correct front width is about that of a cupped hand between the front legs.

Faults from front view are:

- Wide front and out at elbow.
- Narrow front and too tightly fitting elbows.
- Bowed front.
- Pastern weakness causing feet to turn outwards (may only affect one foot).
- Knuckling over (wrist joint set over feet when viewed in profile).
- Poor bone.

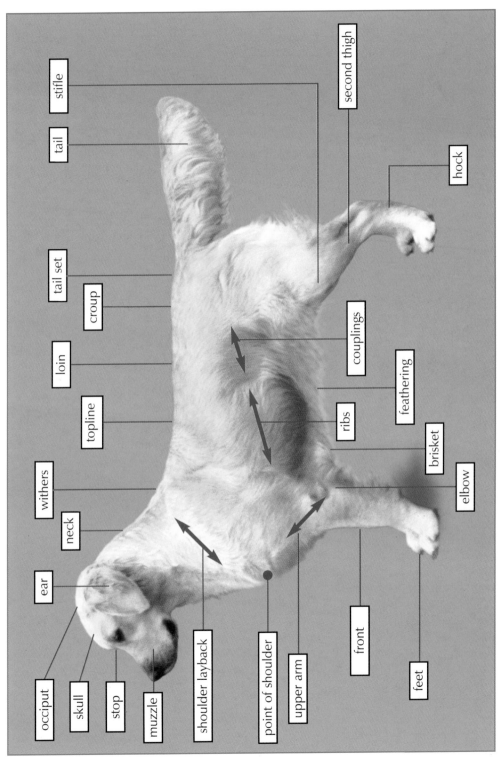

ANATOMICAL POINTS OF THE BREED STANDARD

Faults from profile view are:

- Shoulder lay set too far forward when an imaginary line is drawn from the top of the shoulder blades down the leg and is well in front of the elbow.
- The width between the blades can also be too narrow or too wide (the measurement between should be about the width of two fingers for a man and 2–3 fingers for a lady).
- The shoulder blade and the upper arm are not of equal length and are placed too far forward.

Few of our breed have too much blade and upper arm lengths but may have too much upper arm compared to blade length or vice versa.

Body faults
- Unbalanced, that is, ribs to loin and depth to length.
- Long coupled. 3–5 fingers' length is about right between end of ribs and the rump.
- Too short-coupled.
- Too deep in brisket (ie below elbow level).
- Lacking depth in brisket – opposite to above.
- Barrel ribbed, that is, too much rib spring.
- Flat ribbed – sometimes termed 'slabsided' but meaning insufficient spring of rib.
- Too short in rib – will usually mean a longer loin.
- Too long in rib – will make the dog look long in the back, especially if long in the couplings as well.
- Unlevel topline – can be due to conformation (such as length of ribs to loin being incorrect causing a weakness), a dog being overweight or if the fore or hindquarters are set at different heights or are of disproportionate lengths.
- Sloping croup, where the dog's hindquarters drop off excessively from loin to tail set (not to be confused with a low tail set).
- Roach back, that is, upward arch like a Bedlington Terrier but not so pronounced.

Hindquarter faults
Soft condition, that is, not muscular. You can check firmness of muscles on back of thigh or second thigh to determine this.

Faults in profile view
Narrow thighs, wide thighs, too short/long in second thigh, straight stifle, over-angulated stifles (which may cause crouching and hocks to be set behind the upper part of the leg), too long/short in hock or sickle hocks.

Faults in rear view
Cow hocks (hocks turning inwards at the top and feet turning outwards), hocks not straight under the dog when viewed from the rear. Sickle hocks, narrow rear, spread hocks (wider at the top with feet turning slightly inwards).

Foot faults
Open, splayed, down on pasterns or too long in the pastern, harefoot (where the foot is elongated like a hare's with no rise in the toe level).

Tail faults

High set, low set, too long/short (tip should reach the top of the hocks, if length is correct compared to rest of the dog's appearance), no curl at tip as stated in Standard, too high a carriage when standing/ moving, too low a carriage when moving.

Coat faults

Poor feathering, curly, no undercoat, lacking coat.

Colour faults

Red, mahogany or white blazes anywhere, other than a few hairs on the chest as stated in the Standard.

Size faults

Any male or female which does not conform to the heights given when assessed from the withers.

If you want to check a dog's height, previously calculate where the heights are on your own leg to make a rough comparison when close to the dog. Work it out wearing the shoes you will judge in.

Male faults
- Monorchids (only one testicle has descended into the scrotum).
- Cryptorchids (neither testicle has descended into the scrotum).
- Castrated males can be shown with Kennel Club permission, but the Standard still requires a dog to have two testicles descended into the scrotum.

Gait/movement faults

Profile view

Short strides (front and or rear), lacking drive and power, unlevel, pacing. Has a very awkward/ wobbly gait.

Profile or viewed from front

Hackney action - the wrists are raised with a short pace instead of a good length of stride and reach of stride. Pounding - the front stride is shorter than the rear stride, making the forefeet strike the ground heavily. Padding - the front feet are raised higher than necessary to avoid heavy contact with the ground (cause: strong rear action and upright shoulder construction).

Profile or viewed from front or rear

Crabbing, where a dog has unbalanced angulation either at the front and rear causing either to move on a different track to the other so the feet do not hit one another or are trying to catch up. Mostly seen in Goldens with good rear and poor front angulation.

Front and/or rear view

Close movement, wide movement. Feet or front turning inwards or outwards. Plaiting/knitting/weaving when moving. Unwillingness on dog's part to move.

Weight faults

Guides are no longer given in the Breed Standard for this, but severely overweight dogs will be very noticeable when they stand. Do check with your fingers, as a dog with a good coat with undercoat, particularly on correctly short-coupled Goldens, can give the outward appearance of being overweight when it is not.

Judging Abroad

Mrs Brenda Lowe (Davern) judging in Sweden, 1978.

You should only accept a judging invitation in a country whose Kennel Club has a reciprocal arrangement with our own Club and for a society that is officially recognised by its own country's Kennel Club. Accepting other invitations may, if it comes to light, jeopardise your own judging career in the United Kingdom. The normal reciprocal arrangement between the Kennel Clubs is that judges only accept invitations to judge abroad for breeds in which they are approved to award CCs in the United Kingdom.

Make certain all the paperwork relating to the invitation is received in good time, with details of travel arrangements, accommodation, expenses confirmed and so on. Some societies will make travel bookings for you and pay up front and others will expect you to make your own and claim expenses after you have judged. At International Shows, societies are required also to pay a fee by the FCI. Always take out travel insurance for every appointment If you are going into a country in the European Community, also take your Form E1.11.

Find out the method of judging used. Many countries use an entirely different system of classification and procedure than in this country. Normally societies will supply this in advance or immediately upon arrival.

Most European countries use a similar method of grading the dogs with an Excellent/Very Good/Good and Fairly Good, with the best being placed 1st to 4th. Judges usually provide a dictated critique immediately after examining each dog, before grading, which is handed to the exhibitor. The Certificates CACs or CACIBs are then decided from the top classes mainly (some are exempt), but can challenge for BOB later. Good stewards are usually provided to guide you on procedure.

Exhibitors will wish to hear the good and bad criticism. I usually start with some good points then the bad points, followed by one or two more good points at the end, before grading. It may help to decide how to grade the dogs by seeing the whole class together at the outset, to determine quickly what the standard of entries is.

Most countries provide fantastic hospitality to judges from abroad, so remember that you are an ambassador for this country and do not abuse their hospitality.

Joan Gill (Westley/Standerwick) dictating her critique on a dog at the 1993 Luxembourg Retriever Club Show to the late Pat Busch (of Mill Lane).

In Conclusion

Before you embark on any show judging career, I would certainly recommend that you:

- Go to breed seminars on judging (now a KC requirement for judges wishing to award CCs for the first time).
- Read up on interpretations of the breed standard, such as *Golden Retriever* by Lyn Anderson and *The Golden Retriever* by Wendy Andrews.
- Do further reading on dog construction, movement and gait including *The New Dogsteps* by Rachel Page Elliott and *The Dog in Action* by McDowell Lyons.
- Obtain a copy of the video *Dogsteps* by Rachel Page Elliott, distributed by Ringpress Books. They have also issued a video on the American Breed Standard and on conformation and movement. The Kennel Club have also issued their own video on conformation and movement.

Breeding Goldens

Introduction

When carried out properly, breeding is very time-consuming and is a responsible undertaking for the owners of both the brood bitch and stud dog, especially as society has become more litigious. If you follow the procedures described here in the interests of the breed, the individual dog and prospective purchasers, you will realise that the idea that breeding is profit making could not be further from the truth, especially as the owner's time and the maintenance of the dogs involved are never costed. The paramount aim should be to breed strong, healthy puppies conforming to breed type and temperament as set out in the Breed Standard and to find caring, responsible purchasers who will remain their custodians for life.

Both breeders and purchasers of Goldens, as with all breeds of dog, should realise that it is impossible to breed a perfect specimen and to know exactly how each specimen will turn out, because rearing and environment can also affect the dog after he is sold.

Screening programmes for hereditary diseases, depending on their genetic nature, can help breeders to reduce the incidence or eradicate the diseases. In Goldens, the breeders voluntarily submit their stock for screening, and have to pay an appropriate fee set by the British Veterinary Association (BVA). Difficulties arise where conditions have a late clinical onset, such as after the dogs are bred from, or those that do not show themselves clinically for several generations due to their recessive genetic nature. DNA testing for various conditions affecting dogs is gradually being introduced. These will help future breeders to identify carriers, and decisions will have to be made whether to exclude them from breeding stock. However, as further conditions are identified that affect the breed, compromises may have to be made in breeding plans. This may result in problems for breeders selling puppies under current legislation and, perhaps, insuring them.

At present, at least 300 conditions affect dogs and, alarmingly, on average one further condition is being identified nearly every month.

In the United Kingdom, the Golden Retriever is screened for Hereditary Cataract, Multifocal Retinal Dysplasia, Progressive Retinal Atrophy (General and Central) and Elbow and Hip Dysplasia but, in the case of eyes alone, is also under investigation for four other conditions. This leaves breeders with many difficult decisions about other conditions which are not screened but may have been identified as being hereditary. Progress can be made only with breeders and vets co-operating, and by funding being made available for the research required for each condition.

This information may be very depressing to the breeder but, to quote a practising vet speaking at a symposium on hereditary diseases in dogs in 1997, "It is surprising how many normal dogs I still see at my surgery."

Stud Dog

As the owner of the stud dog, your responsibilities are greater prior to the mating of a bitch.

1.   Decide if your male has enough good breed attributes to pass on to another generation, such as type, temperament, working abilities and appearance? If you are not sure, contact the breeder or ask your nearest breed club secretary to put you in touch with some experienced, reputable breeders.

2.   Have your dog screened for all the hereditary conditions under official schemes available for the breed, and determine if the results are acceptable. I always recommend that eyes are done before elbows and hips, as fees are far cheaper for eye checks and, if your dog has the misfortune to fail at an early age, you will not have the further expense of elbow and hip X-rays. In the United Kingdom, elbow and hip X-rays cannot be done until a dog is at least 12 months and in America, the dog has to be 24 months old. (See also point 4 under Brood Bitch.) Eyes have to be done annually or at least prior to a mating, and only a pass is acceptable. For hips the decision is based on the dog's score in relation to the breed average, currently 19.8 in the Golden Retriever. A dog used regularly has more influence on the breed than a brood bitch because of the number of puppies he can sire, so the consensus is that stud dogs should have scores lower than the breed average. This does not mean that males with higher scores should not be used if they have many other breed attributes, but hip results from their offspring may determine if they continue to be used. As results for individual stud dog's progeny are available, owners of brood bitches can take this into consideration without difficulty. It is difficult to advise on elbows as so few have been screened in the United Kingdom to date, so it is not known how badly the breed is affected clinically and radiographically. Until this information is collected it will not be possible to find out whether the breed average is 0, 1, 2 or 3. Dogs certified with a 0 score are the best option.

3.   Be honest with yourself in the interest of the breed and do not use a dog that passes all the screening programmes but is suffering from another condition which is believed to be hereditary.

4.   Consider whether the dog will have the opportunity to be used regularly. A one-off request to service a bitch or only a few opportunities in a lifetime will arouse his sexual awareness. This is not only unfair to the dog, but may result in him being more difficult to control if kept with bitches that still come into season, or other males whether or not they are used at stud. The same may apply if neighbours have un-neutered bitches. Some owners of pet males believe all dogs should be used and have been known to offer their dog's services, not appreciating that it is the usual procedure for a brood bitch's owner to approach the owner of a male.

5.   Can you cope with the inconvenience of when a bitch may need to call on the stud dog and are you prepared and have the time to help and advise the inexperienced breeder after his bitch has been mated?

6.   Is your skin thick enough to cope with the criticism that always seems to fly in the direction of the stud dog or his owner? The greater the success of the stud or his progeny, the more likely that flack will fly! Also, if his progeny have any screening failures or problems, usually the stud dog is blamed rather than the brood bitch, although it has taken both to produce stock.

7. No matter who owns the brood bitch, decide if you are happy with her temperament, pedigree, screening results and so on.
8. Determine whether your stud dog's lines and attributes are suitable to the bitch's requirements. Certain lines do not always come together well. It is only possible to find this out from experienced breeders or through your own experiences of your line's breeding.

Details of stud work can be found at the end of this chapter.

Brood Bitch

As owner of the brood bitch, you have more responsibilities following the mating of the bitch. Consider the following points.

1. Have you the space to whelp a bitch, and a suitable location in the premises where she can remain reasonably undisturbed by family life and callers?
2. Have you the time to carry out 4 months work, 2 months of which are labour-intensive?
3. Have you the right temperament to cope? Much patience is needed despite fatigue and there may be distress if puppies are born dead or die later.
4. Can you finance the proceedings? There is quite a lot of outlay prior to selling the pups.

Owners will also have to consider points 1, 2 and 3 under 'Stud Dog'. If the bitch passes her first eye examination, I have the elbows and hips X-rayed by my vet and sent away for scoring. If your vet has little experience in X-raying hips/elbows, you can use another vet with a radiographic qualification. In the UK this is done under anaesthetic or heavy sedation but not all countries use this system. Some countries use a grading scheme.

The bitch has to be at least 12 months before scores can be given to hip or elbow X-ray plates. My bitches are done between 12–18 months of age. I avoid their season by at least 2 months either side, but preferably for 4 clear months if possible, just in case the season has any effect on the result. There are various views on this but, without veterinary evidence, it is easier to give it the benefit of the doubt and just be aware that higher scores may result if the X-ray is done too close to a season. Vets do not recommend that it is done whilst a bitch is in season.

Once the scores are known (usually after 2–6 weeks), I decide if they are low enough for the bitch to be bred from. On the continent, this decision is not always left entirely to the bitch's owner, as some countries have breeding control committees.

The results of the eye test for both the sire and dam are printed on The Kennel Club Registration Certificate for each puppy, so I ensure that the bitch is tested again at least 12 months before the puppies will be registered, not 12 months before mating, for my own peace of mind. This means the dam cannot have an eye failure prior to the registration of her offspring. It is not practical to request this of stud dog owners as they would be perpetually bringing the annual eye test screening forward and a dog used regularly would be tested all the time.

If the bitch meets all these criteria and is in good health, the breeder will probably decide to breed from her. Timing can be critical as the market can be very slow prior to school holidays, especially during the summer. Some breeders do not mate bitches if the pups will be ready to go at Christmas, or hold on to them for an additional 1–2 weeks.

Your responsibilities for the brood bitch following the mating are to:
- Care for her during gestation;
- Prepare for and carry out the whelping;
- Look after the dam post-whelping and rear the puppies;
- Vet and advise prospective puppy purchasers;
- Maintain contact with puppy owners to monitor the dogs' progress throughout their lives;
- Help and advise the owner if required on any issue or problem;
- Assist the owner in rehoming his dog if the need arises.

Breeding Definitions

Inbreeding

This is an intensive form of line breeding using the same gene pool. I would classify matings in this category as, for example, father to daughter, mother to son and brother to sister.

Line Breeding

A more moderate form of inbreeding with some outcrossing depending on the closeness of the pairing. Examples on a decreasing scale of line breeding are: half brother to half sister; grandfather to grand-daughter (this appears to have greater success than grandson to grandmother); uncle to niece; nephew to aunt; several common ancestors in the 4th generation; several common ancestors in the 5th generation.

The fewer the common denominators in both the sire and the dam's pedigree, the less the degree of line breeding that takes place.

An alternative line breeding option is to pair two closely line-bred dogs of unrelated lines.

Outcrossing

Where there are no common dogs in a four or five generation pedigree or only a few in the fifth generation.

Advantages and Disadvantages

There are advantages and disadvantages with any of the three options.

Inbreeding can stamp in or even intensify the good traits of a line, but it will not produce any characteristic which did not exist already in the common dogs in the pedigree. Equally, faults will not occur unless they were carried by the original stock. This would be disastrous if temperament was a failing. To have any degree of insight into this, a breeder would have had to have been in the breed for many years and known the specific dogs intimately. It follows that, unless the breeder owned all the dogs in question, it is probably impossible for everything to be known. Also, original stock will not necessarily have been screened for the increasing list of conditions affecting the breed.

In future, DNA testing may assist with a particular condition, such as cataract, but I am not certain it could be used for something such as temperament. I feel very strongly that inbreeding as I have defined it should *not* be used in our breed.

Line breeding is really a combination of inbreeding and outcrossing. There is less chance of faults appearing, but the risk is not totally eliminated. Breeders still need to know the merits and faults of the dog they are planning to double up on if this method is to provide success. To improve a particular component in their stock, particularly if it is line bred, a breeder needs to ensure that the line to which they are out-crossing has the required factor but does not add any undesirable factors.

Outcrossing can be useful to eliminate undesirable factors as it can be used to dilute lines but, again, it helps to know the dogs in the first two or three generations to prevent the risk of introducing an undesirable factor that may be common to several unrelated dogs. Puppies from this method usually show much more variation in type than from the other methods.

One has to also bear in mind two other facts when breeding:

- A rare genetic mutation can occur with any method at any time, introducing an unexpected factor, be it faults or virtue, and;
- Certain lines and individual dogs appear to have more dominance when they are bred from. On-the-ground and photo research can help the inexperienced breeder to identify these dogs.

My policy where possible has been to line breed on a third generation and outcross alternately. When I outcross, I try to use dogs of a similar appearance to reduce the type variation in a litter.

Preparing for a Litter

If you decide to breed from your bitch, you may like to consider the procedure I follow.

I decide at what age and which season to mate the bitch. I normally like her to have her first litter between the age of two and three years, but this is subject to how regularly she comes into season. I do not like to mate much before the age of two, as Goldens may be physically mature but are seldom mentally mature. If you mate before the age of three and the bitch misses on the first attempt, another attempt can be made before she reaches four years. First litters after the age of four are possible but there may be more risk for the bitch and her pups.

To select a stud dog I draw up a shortlist for each bitch and make my final selection based on:

- Type, kennel type, temperament, character, intelligence, construction, movement, working ability, coat, elbow and hip scores and eye passes;
- Hip and eye progeny data of stud dog and bitch if she has produced offspring – elbows will be included when available;
- Progeny attributes and failings of sire and dam;
- Pedigree (whether to outcross, line breed or outcross to a line bred dog);
- If I want to keep a dog or bitch whether the lines produce mainly good dogs, bitches or both.

I would expect to have different priorities for each bitch.

I also try to conduct my enquiries discreetly as, having been a stud dog owner, I know that raised hopes are so often dashed. However, eventually I may need to go direct to the stud dog owner to find out some information. Do not rely on rumour or hearsay.

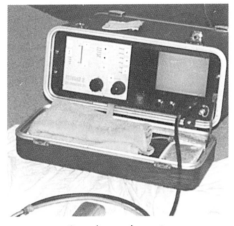

Scanning equipment.

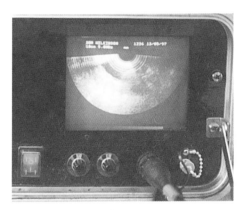

Scanning screen.

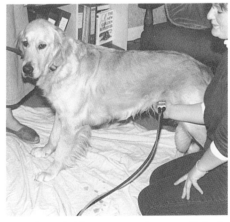

Scanning a Golden at 4-5 weeks to see if she is in whelp.

When you have made your final choice of a stud dog, contact the owner in good time with all the bitch's details to check that the bitch will be accepted and that the dog will be available when she is due to come into season. It is wise to have a second choice should the first stud be unavailable or not wish to mate the bitch when the time arrives.

If the bitch's booster inoculation is due during the period from her season to rearing the puppies, either bring the date forward and ensure that it is done before she comes into season or wait until the litter is reared. Worm the bitch before she comes into season.

If you believe you may breed more than one litter and want the progeny to have a common identity you will also need to apply to The Kennel Club for an affix. The process can take a number of months, so send off for an application form at least 6 months in advance.

When She Comes into Season

Check you know the first day of the bitch's season and, if you have not wormed her recently, do so immediately. Make provisional arrangements with the stud dog owner. Have the bitch swabbed by a vet as soon as possible to check she has no infection. Some stud dog owners request this to reduce failures and to prevent their dog catching or passing an infection to subsequent bitches. Antibiotics can be given before she is mated to clear the infection and reduce the risk of her missing. You may also consider asking the stud dog owner to have the dog swabbed as it is likely he will be mating other bitches in his lifespan, not just yours.

Most bitches are mated around the 13th day but I know some that have been mated as early as their 8th and as late as their 20th day. To reduce the risk of arriving too early or too late, particularly if the stud dog is some distance from home, I sometimes have a pre-mate test done by my vet, to check the correct day. I have found that quite often I have had to add 36 hours to the vet's advice on when to take the bitch to be mated to get a good mating and puppies. If she has ovulated it is advisable to have the bitch mated immediately. Do not forget to keep the stud dog owner informed of the position if you have the test done. Check which test your vet uses as several are available.

I keep an eye on the bitch to see how she reacts to being touched on her rear. If she begins to turn her tail she may be ready for mating. I also own dogs, so sometimes check their reaction to the bitch, but you must be careful that you are fully in control of the situation, otherwise you may find out how efficient a stud your own dog is! The vulva will also soften when the bitch becomes ready for mating. You may find it difficult to mate your own dog and bitch together, as some bitches do not like being mated by dogs they live with.

Take your bitch to the stud dog on the pre-arranged day, time and place.

Show the stud dog owner all the bitch's official documents (eye, elbow and hip certificates) and ask to see the dog's current certificates before proceeding further.

Find out what routine the stud dog owner likes to follow so that everyone is prepared.

Make the bitch comfortable by allowing her to relieve herself before she is introduced to the stud dog. Most stud dog owners allow the bitch to get used to the room or area where the mating will take place before introducing the stud dog.

Most stud dog owners will check the bitch internally to make sure she has no strictures that may prevent the dog from penetrating and tying. If all is well, the dog and bitch can be introduced. You could, of course, get your vet to check this when the bitch is swabbed.

Reactions of bitches vary and sometimes will be very much out of character. In most cases, the stud dog owner will be able to advise to ensure a mating takes place either on this occasion or at another time if the bitch is not quite ready. Most stud dog owners will want the bitch to be held whilst she is mated (see Stud Work).

If one successful mating occurs you must decide whether you would like a second mating and check with the stud dog owner if he is prepared to allow this and when it will be convenient. Sperm can last for 2–3 days, so it is likely to cover the bitch even if she is mated a little early. For this reason, if a second mating is required then it would be advisable two days later but only if the bitch is still of interest to the dog. The gestation period is 9 weeks (63 days). A chart showing mating and likely subsequent whelping dates can be found at the end of this chapter (p.232-233).

After the mating(s), complete any necessary paperwork, pay the stud fee, obtain a receipt and establish whether a further service will be honoured should the bitch miss.

Ensure the bitch is kept away from other males until her season is finished, normally at 21 days. If she is mated by another dog, the vet can inject her but there may be some risk to the bitch. It will also be necessary to have every puppy born from such an incident DNA-tested to prove the parentage if any are registered for Kennel Club events.

Do not allow the bitch to swim while in season, before she whelps and while she is still feeding her puppies as her vulva will be open after mating and infections may occur. She can be exercised as normal to begin with but, as she increases in size, she will take more care of herself and is unlikely to want so much in the last 2 weeks.

I keep the bitch on her normal quantities of food until the sixth week of pregnancy, but gradually change over to a food with a higher protein content. Many well-known brands have an identified diet for bitches in whelp. Also see Vitamin C, Chapter 7.

Bitch 6 weeks in whelp with seven puppies.

Same bitch, 7 weeks in whelp.

In the past, I have given a calcium/phosphate supplement (obtained from the vet to make sure it is of the correct balance) from the day of mating. Some vets are now of the opinion that this may prevent the bitch from triggering her own calcium production during the final days of pregnancy, possibly causing eclampsia, and that it should only be given a week before whelping. This you must decide for yourself after consulting your own vet. I used to give just a small amount for the first 5 weeks, increasing it gradually up to the ninth week.

At 3–4 weeks, signs that the bitch may be in whelp are if she goes off her food for about two days, her nipples enlarge and her coat flicks on her flanks, just below her loin, outwards and towards her front. These are only possible indications, not definite signs, and may also be associated with false pregnancies.

From 21 days a bitch can be ultra-scanned by a vet or another specialist (see previous photographs), to confirm if she is in whelp. For the best results it should be carried out between 4–5 weeks. This can be carried out at your home, but then the fee will usually be higher. Some vets shave some hair off the bitch but I think it is unnecessary. I do not see that it is absolutely necessary to scan unless the bitch's health is in question or you are concerned there may be something wrong with the pups, such as if there is no feeling of movement in the last 2 weeks of pregnancy. However, it can be helpful to know, from the scan, how many puppies to expect and whether the litter is likely to arrive early.

At 28 days, the vet can palpate the bitch to see if she is in whelp. I do not have this done as I try to avoid visiting the vet as much as possible to prevent the risk of the bitch becoming infected. In any case, the outcome will not be altered.

At 42 days/6 weeks, worm the bitch if you have not already done so. Worming products are available from your vet which can be used at any time during the 9 weeks, provided the dosage is accurately measured to the bitch's weight.

At 6 weeks I increase the bitch's food by about 50g (2oz) if she is on meat and mixer. If you are giving a high protein, all-in-one product, follow the manufacturer's instructions. It is better to increase the protein, not the carbohydrates, so the goodness is absorbed by your bitch and the pups do not become too large for the whelping. Very large puppies of over 0.5kg (1lb) in weight may give a bitch added difficulty and discomfort in trying to produce them, especially on her first whelping. If the bitch is on a meat and mixer diet, I continue to increase the protein by 50g (2oz) each week.

As I give all my dogs two meals a day, I add the extra food to the bitch's breakfast when she normally only has a cereal meal. This helps to sustain her and the pups throughout the day and particularly later in the pregnancy, when she may be unable to eat the increased volume of food. In fact I find it easier to divide her food into three meals during the last 10 days when I also increase the carbohydrates by about 50–100g (2–4oz). I also give cooked eggs with glucose during this period as part of the protein (often as the lunch meal). The glucose is to sustain the bitch's energy levels as she may not wish to eat much (if anything) during the last 2–3 days if she is carrying a large litter. The bitch going off her food is usually another sign that whelping is imminent.

At 7–8 weeks, you can usually begin to feel the pups move. If not, I suggest you consult your vet who will check the bitch and listen for heartbeats to reassure you all is well. I have also found that from this time onwards, bitches may have urinating accidents in the home if left for any length of time or in the night. This is due to the pressure on their bladders from the weight of the pups, so do not be cross with your bitch if it happens.

The extra pressures in the bitch's body in the latter stages may also cause her eyes to bulge. Probably she will also begin to dig, usually somewhere secretive if possible. It is her way of preparing a place to have her brood, even if it is not where you want her to have them!

The Countdown

Ten days prior to the expected day of whelping I begin to record her temperature. If possible, I recommend doing this three times a day, but at least twice daily. If there is any doubt about her being in whelp, because she may have a small litter and has not been scanned or checked by a vet, still carry out the procedure. By doing this, you will establish the normal temperature of your bitch and should be able to establish the temperature drop that will occur about 12–36 hours prior to the onset of labour. Normal temperature is 38.6°C (101.5°F) but most of my in-whelp bitches are slightly lower than this, about 37.8–38.3°C (100–101°F). The drop should be to 36.7–37.2°C (98–99°F).

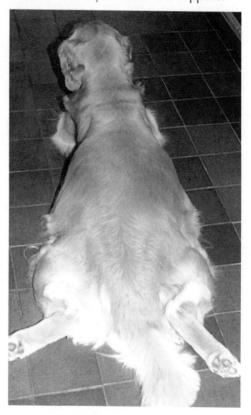

Same bitch, 7-8 weeks in whelp.

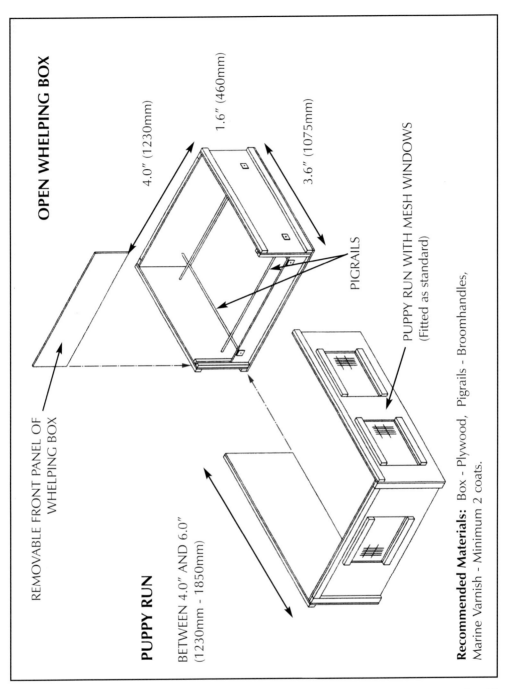

OPEN WHELPING BOX

4.0" (1230mm)

1.6" (460mm)

3.6" (1075mm)

PIGRAILS

PUPPY RUN WITH MESH WINDOWS
(Fitted as standard)

REMOVABLE FRONT PANEL OF
WHELPING BOX

PUPPY RUN

BETWEEN 4.0" AND 6.0"
(1230mm - 1850mm)

Recommended Materials: Box - Plywood, Pigrails - Broomhandles,
Marine Varnish - Minimum 2 coats.

At this same stage you are likely to know whether your bitch is in whelp, so you should check the following points:
- Have you all the things necessary to whelp and look after the bitch and her puppies for the first few weeks (see Whelping List)? Bitches can whelp anything up to seven

days early or two to three days late, but most will whelp 63 days following their first or second matings. If the bitch goes over 66 days and there is no sign of labour starting, the vet should examine her.

- Is your whelping box ready? I have mine in place a week before the due date in case a bitch whelps early but also so she can get used to it. I always wipe it thoroughly with a disinfectant immediately before its use. (See diagram on previous page for dimensions.)

Whelping List

- Whelping box in place layered with newspapers just prior to the commencement of whelping. I do not put the rails in place until after the bitch has finished whelping.
- Veterinary surgery's telephone number (for help and emergencies). I also find out which vet is on duty when the bitch is due to whelp and tell the practice when she is due.
- Newspaper – a lot – to be used for bedding in the box throughout the duration and under bedding.
- Towels for dog and human use.
- Bowl of water with a little antiseptic added (Savlon) to wash your hands as required.
- Black refuse sack.
- Baby talcum powder to help dry the bitch's feathers once cleaned.
- Hot water bottle to keep the puppies warm if they have to be removed from the dam.
- Medium-size cardboard box to place puppies in, if required, whilst changing the bedding.
- Thermometer.
- Milton Sterilising Fluid.
- Sterilised scissors in a basin of sterilised fluid.
- Surgical gloves if you require them.
- KY Jelly or Vaseline for your fingers if you need to do any internal work to assist the bitch have a puppy or to check if there is a puppy in her passage.
- Gripe water.
- Liquid paraffin.
- Milk of Magnesia.
- Brandy/water mix at 50/50 for the bitch.
- Cold or hot ready-made meal for you should it prove difficult to leave the bitch.
- Scales to weigh a puppy. You may need to line it with kitchen roll paper to prevent the puppy slipping.
- Note pad and pen to record pups' birth weights.
- Puppy colostrum feeding pack for emergency hand rearing.
- Baby feeder and teats.
- Enough vet beds to use alternately. I use the first only when the whelping has concluded.
- Pig lamp/bulbs (at least one spare) and grill for safety to be placed about 1m (3ft) above the whelping box, but so it can be lowered if necessary. The bulb should be a dull emitter 150/250 watt or 450 watt. How much this is used depends on whether you have a summer or winter litter. For my last summer litter I only used it for the first few hours whilst the puppies dried out. For winter litters, greater usage may be

Whelping box and lamp in place.

required, but it will depend on the room temperature if the pups are indoors. A constant 22°C (72°F) with ordinary heating should be ample without using a pig lamp. It will be essential for litters born or kept outside, and then used almost continually, particularly at night.

- A run to fix to the whelping box and another if the weather permits the pups to go outside. Wood shavings or some alternative for the indoor run.
- Disinfectant.
- Lectade sachets for emergency rehydration of puppies.
- Also make certain you have plenty of petrol in the car in case of an emergency journey to the vet in the middle of the night when a petrol/gas station may be shut.

Feeding the Dam

For the first day or so only light meals will be required: gruel containing oats, glucose, Complan, eggs, milk, water and honey; fish; rabbit; chicken; egg custard ingredients; milk pudding ingredients. To drink: water, goat's milk, Lactol or some other powdered milk.

Later on, give her whatever brand of food she normally eats, but the variety recommended for a dam that has whelped. You will need to give greater quantities if she has three or more puppies, according to the number in the litter. You may need to give a calcium (balanced) supplement, especially if eclampsia has occurred.

Other Items

- Kennel Club Form to register the puppies (plus export pedigree) if required. The stud dog owner has to complete a section of the registration form and most have copies they can give you either on completion of the mating or on whelping once you have notified them.
- Insurance forms.
- Pedigree forms.
- Toys/bones/empty toilet rolls make wonderful short-term toys. I save plenty and change them when they become soiled or flat.
- Worming liquid paste or pills (only use brands available from the vet). The puppies will need to be wormed at least three times before they leave you. The first time will be prior to weaning, so a liquid or paste administered directly onto the mouth is best and easiest and ensures every puppy is done. Pills can be crushed into the puppies' food for the second and third times. However, you must ensure each puppy eats his own food, so that they are all done and receive the right dosage. A rota system is useful to prevent the same puppy being done twice.
- Copies of sales documents for information and, later on, owner's/breeder's signatures.
- Sale receipts.
- General information on puppy care. Some of the leading pet food manufacturers provide free puppy packs if you are registered with them.
- Diet sheets.
- Any other hand out-literature.
- Puppy food and spare puppy food for new owners – enough for about a week.
- Photos of sire and dam for new owners.

Whelping

(For convenience, puppies are referred to as 'he' in the following text.)
I do not leave my bitches unattended after their temperature drops, which often means sleeping with her wherever she will be whelped. As I whelp my bitches indoors, this presents me with much more comfort.

There are two stages of labour. When things begin, do not panic – easier said than done sometimes – but your bitch will need you to be as relaxed and calm as possible. If you are prepared there is nothing more you can do than observe the bitch and wait for nature to take its course. Most Goldens whelp easily and make good mums.

Stage 1

The first stage is where the birth passage has to soften and dilate to enable the puppies to be born and may last from 2–24 hours. The bitch will be restless, pant heavily with brief pauses, have glazed eyes and a disorientated look. Do not deny her access to the outside as she may wish to continue digging the holes that she probably started a few weeks previously, to prepare herself. In the wild they would whelp in a hole in the ground in a secluded place.

If this stage lasts longer than 24 hours, I would speak to a vet or take the bitch to the surgery to check that all is well. You may need to be insistent with some vets. Some inexperienced breeders have lost litters because they have not been insistent enough about their concerns or worries about whelping. There is also the risk, of course, that if something is seriously wrong you could also lose the bitch.

The bitch's water will also break towards the end of stage 1. This may occur when she urinates. It should be understood that she will have no control over where it will occur. She may be a bit concerned before it happens, and try to urinate without anything happening or keep flashing round to her behind to investigate.

She may also lose her appetite, vomit or have a clear white mucous discharge from her vagina.

Stage 2

This is when the first puppy enters the pelvis. The bitch will begin to have contractions, straining downwards and maybe grunting. This is the commencement of labour.

In my experience the first contraction can occur from 30 minutes to 2 hours after the waters break. I would be concerned if nothing had happened within 2–3 hours at the most. If the bitch goes outside at all during this stage, day or night, accompany her with a towel just in case she drops a puppy accidentally on the ground. It has been known to happen.

Make a note of the time of the first contraction. If the first puppy has not appeared within 1–2 hours, consult your vet for further advice. Some bitches may have only a few contractions and others more. The contractions normally become more regular and stronger just prior to the birth of a puppy.

A very large first puppy can be a problem for a maiden bitch, as she will have not passed anything of this size through her channel before. A maiden bitch may be distressed by what is happening to her. Reassure her, but check that everything is all right. Most of my bitches want to whelp on the comfort of the settee! I find it helps to allow this for the first puppy, but then insist the whelping box is used. If you allow this you will need to cover your settee with something waterproof plus washable sheets or blankets to prevent it being soiled.

The textbook birth is a puppy born in a fluid-filled membrane bag with his (or her) own afterbirth (placenta) attached to him by an umbilical cord. He should appear head first with everything intact. The bitch should break the bag with her front teeth and clean the puppy. She will sever the cord and may eat the afterbirth. (There is nothing abnormal about this; it is full of nutrition and will help keep the dam's energy levels up.) She will then clean the pup by licking and he may find his way to her teats to feed.

Some bitches need to have a little help with their first born as they may not know what to do or be in a little shock. The membrane should be broken near the puppy's mouth to enable him to breathe. The cord should then be cut with the sterilised scissors (not too sharp) 5cm (2in) from the body to prevent it rupturing. A check should be made when the bitch does it herself. Many can be over-zealous and break the cord too close to the puppy. I intervene to prevent this. Within 1–3 days the remaining cord dries up, shrivels and eventually drops off.

If the bitch does not want to eat the afterbirth, wrap it up in newspaper and dispose of it later. You many need to rub the puppy with a towel, to partly dry him, keep him warm and stimulate his breathing before offering him to mum and encouraging her to take an interest or placing him on a teat for his first feed. You may need to prise open the puppy's mouth gently with a finger to place him on a teat. Once on, normally all will be well and very quickly the pups will learn to feed and obtain the colostrum they require in the first day or so from their mother.

Newborn puppy still in his bag with afterbirth.

Some puppies may come without a bag or afterbirth. If you can see a pup with no bag in the birth passage, he will probably be born within a few more contractions. Do not allow him to be there too long if you can assist your bitch, otherwise he may have breathing difficulties and die.

To help with a difficult birth, place some KY Jelly on one or two of your fingers. Place one or both in the bitch's passage and gently ease them around the puppy's body in a downward

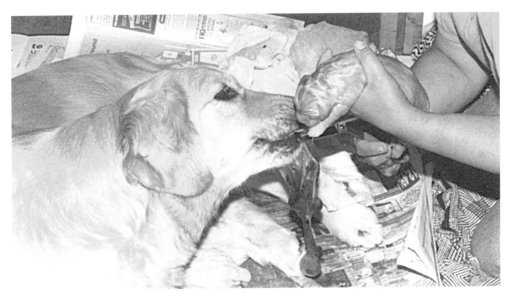

I am assisting the cutting of the cord whilst mum attends to her pup.

movement. Never pull on any part of the puppy. Repeat if necessary, with the bitch's contractions. If the puppy is lying awkwardly or across the passage, veterinary help will probably be needed. This can occur at any time through the whelping, not just with the first born. Some puppies may come the wrong way round with their tail and hind feet first. Do not be alarmed; most will be perfectly all right.

If a puppy has had a difficult birth and looks a little limp, remove the membrane, cut the cord, place him in a towel, wipe his head and nose to remove excess liquid/mucous and, keeping him in the towel, shake him head-downwards to remove any excess liquid from the lungs. He may begin to snuffle or cry so wipe his head and nose again, and place on a teat as soon as possible.

Puppies are quite robust once born, and can be worked on quite vigorously to get life back into them even though they may appear totally lifeless. If this occurs, the breathing will need to be stimulated by rubbing the puppy's full body length vigorously both ways with a towel. It may take anything from a few minutes to about quarter of an hour. If weakness is still apparent, administer one to two drops of the brandy mix to assist his revival and keep him warm and separate for a while to monitor him. If after 15 minutes a puppy is still lifeless, although it is distressing I normally cease my efforts, as the longer it takes the more risk of brain damage, and further efforts are likely to be in vain.

These are the rules I follow for every puppy born:

- Weigh and record his weight to check whether he is gaining or losing over the next few days. Many puppies lose a little weight from birth to day 1, but they should gain from then on. If they continue to lose weight, you should be concerned and have the puppy checked by a vet. When the puppies are over a week old, I only weigh them about twice a week, unless any give me concern.
- Record whether an afterbirth has arrived, or if any have been retained. They sometimes follow on or perhaps several appear after all the puppies have been born.

- Check the mouth for a cleft palate. This can be done by gently placing a finger in the mouth to check there is a roof. If you find a cleft palate, it would be kinder to have the puppy put to sleep. Palates can be perforated, which may cause a little difficulty with feeding but, as the puppy grows, the holes may seal and the dog will live a normal life. This will not be possible with a cleft palate.
- Record the sex.
- Ensure he is warm enough.

Once the whelping is over, arrange for the vet to visit the dam and her puppies to check them all over. I never take the bitch to the vet unless there is an emergency. I inform the vet of any retained afterbirths. Some will give the bitch an injection to clear out the uterus and, if they are worried about an infection, place her on a short course of antibiotics, which will not affect the puppies.

There is no set pattern to a bitch giving birth. Some can produce eight puppies in 2–3 hours, others may take much longer with one puppy appearing every hour. Some bitches may produce about half their brood and then take a 1–2 hour break before having further contractions. If a bitch strains for 2 hours or there are no further labour signs and you know more puppies are to be born, consult your vet for immediate assistance. The bitch will probably be given a pitruitin injection to encourage her chemistry to produce further puppies more speedily. In most cases it works, but not necessarily for the whole of the rest of the litter and the vet may need to be recalled. If you suspect major problems or no births occur after a couple of injections, a Caesarean section may be required. The bitch and her other puppies will then need to be transported to the vet's surgery. The vet will probably require your assistance once the initial cut is made, so be prepared. Puppies are produced much faster than normal, and many hands will be required to dry the puppies and make sure they are breathing and kept warm.

Dam cleaning a puppy whilst the rest of her litter sleep or suckle.

Most vets give an anaesthetic so the bitch may be disorientated when she comes round. If she required a Caesarean before any pups were born, and this is her first litter, she may take a while to come to terms with a litter of puppies appearing from nowhere wishing to feed from a sore, cut stomach!

During the whelping, offer the mother a whelping drink of milk, water and glucose but no food. This should sustain her. If she is disinterested in the milk, try just water and glucose or add a teaspoonful of brandy.

Most Goldens prefer their owners to be present during the whelping but not the whole family, and certainly not unfamiliar people. I would recommend a maximum of two people at a home whelping.

Leave the puppies with the dam during most of the whelping otherwise she becomes disturbed by their absence, however brief. The only exception is if you need to change the bedding paper.

If the bitch totally rejects a puppy that seems normal but has accepted the rest of her litter, from my experience I would recommend you do not try to rear this puppy separately. Without doubt, there will be something wrong with him, which may not show up for several days or weeks. It is much easier to make such a difficult decision earlier than later.

Caring for the Dam and her Puppies
General
I clean the box with disinfectant daily and change the paper and vet bed daily. The rails are to prevent the bitch from lying on and suffocating a puppy.

Check the milk is flowing from the bitch's teats and all the puppies are feeding well. Her rear end may appear weaker after whelping and rearing a litter but she should regain her condition later on. She will probably have a vaginal discharge lasting from several days up to 2 weeks, but it should become less obvious during that period. If it does not, or is particularly odorous after the first few days, consult a vet. Trembling may be due to shock or eclampsia.

Check her teats daily to make certain there is no hardness.

You will probably have to take her on a lead to get her outside to urinate and defecate as she will not wish to leave her litter. This tie is very strong in the first week but gradually lessens as time passes. She should not be taken out for a walk off your property until the puppies have left for their new homes.

I stay and sleep with the bitch for about 8–14 days to ensure she is coping and does not accidentally lie on any of the puppies. If she is not coping I stay with her longer, until I think she can. Some breeders sleep with their bitch for 4 weeks but I find I'm usually exhausted by this time. For the early weeks try not to disturb her unnecessarily. I do not allow any visitors for the first 3 weeks and only a few until the pups are 4 weeks or more.

I take the bitch's temperature twice a day after whelping for about 10 days. The temperature is likely to be higher than normal for several days but, if it exceeds 103°F or drops very low very quickly, I would consult the vet immediately. There maybe an internal complication, a problem with her milk flow or a lack of calcium (see also Eclampsia, p.230).

Each time the bitch leaves and returns to the box, make certain she lays on the opposite side to before. This should help prevent her getting mastitis in any of the teats as the pups will use all the teats that have milk. A bitch usually has 10 teats but may have less. There may not always be milk in all of them. She will soon get used to the routine of alternating, and may do it naturally from the outset.

Puppies will be more active from 3 weeks and toileting more of their own accord. The indoor run should be erected; I use a plastic sheet at the base, heavily laden with newspaper and then woodshavings. I find it keeps the pups very clean and it is easy to clean up their stools. How often it needs changing will depend on the litter size but it will be weekly for the first 2 weeks and then at about 2–3 day intervals from 5 weeks until the puppies go to their new homes.

Day 1

Once the whelping has finished, offer the bitch a nourishing whelp drink. Let her sleep for several hours before you attempt to change the bedding, clean her rear end and add the box rails. After a few hours she will also welcome a small, light meal. I usually give her a whelping meal such as Gyrima Gruel (courtesy of the late Mrs Timson).

Recipe

Place 1 cup of oats, 1 tablespoon of Complan and glucose, 2 cups of cold water in a saucepan and cook as you would porridge until thick. Add one egg (only one per day) to the mixture and cook. Once cooked, add one tablespoon of honey and stir until dissolved (if added prior to cooking this often burns). Finally, add 1 cup of cold milk to cool the mixture.

Once the gruel is cool enough, give it to the bitch. All my bitches have loved it and it has helped to restore their energy and strength quickly. I make a fresh batch for each meal and give it three times during the first day at about 7-hourly intervals. Fresh water should also be available for the bitch but not left unattended in the box.

If a bitch has had a Caesarean with anaesthetic, it is best to keep the puppies warm and separate, and let her sleep it off in comfort, then offer her a whelp meal before introducing her to her brood. When you introduce the puppies, stay with her for reassurance and to make certain she is coping with them. Keep an eye on the stitched area to make sure it does not become sore. If it looks sore, bathe with Savlon dilution and add Savlon cream. If the skin is perspiring and causing soreness, add a little baby talcum powder to dry the moisture.

You will also need to ensure that the bitch is cleaning the puppies and stimulating them to urinate and defecate (most dams are fanatical about this!). If not, you may need to give assistance. To stimulate the puppies you will need to mimic the dam's tongue action. Dip a piece of cotton wool in warm water, wipe over the puppies' genital areas and this should help them to go.

Day 2

Offer the bitch a white fish/meat meal. Meal 2 is gruel, meal 3 another white fish/meat meal with a mixer.

Day 3 onwards

Introduce the bitch back to her normal foods or the food she was on prior to whelping (if it was also intended for nursing bitches), at the quantities recommended. If her stools are firm all should be well; if not, you may need to reintroduce foods more gradually as though you

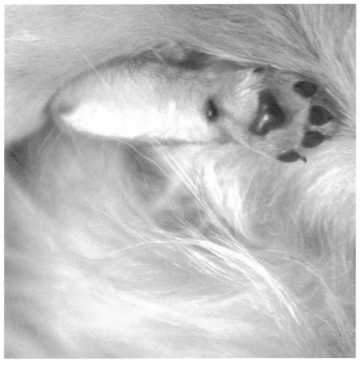

Pigment on a pup's pads after only a few days.

were dealing with diarrhoea. If loose stools persist, consult a vet. The stools are likely to be darker for a day or so, especially if she consumed any afterbirths. She should now be on two protein meals, one in the morning and one late evening, with two gruel meals between.

The quantity of food given to the dam will need to be increased as the puppies get older, depending upon the number in the litter, until weaning begins. Then it will need to be reduced gradually to normal levels once the bitch has finished feeding the puppies. In the case of complete foods, follow the manufacturer's guidelines. If a bitch has only two puppies to feed, her normal intake should be adequate.

When born, the puppies cannot see or hear but will grow well and most will double their birth weight in the first week. If not already black, the pigment on the nose, eye rims and paws should eventually go black. Some pups are born with black pigment.

If you need to identify puppies that are not already clearly distinguishable by sex, colour and pigment on their feet, you will need to use some colour system. Some people use a small dab of different nail varnishes because felt tip pen marks rub off easily.

If puppies are hungry or cold they will cry and screw themselves up, but contented pups will lie with mum or in clusters. They will spread out if they are too hot. If you have no way of reducing the temperature, spray a little water into the air with a fine water spray bottle. Gripe water is good to help wind or tummy ache. A little liquid paraffin administered through a syringe can be used if they become constipated. If the dam's milk is too rich, give her about 5ml Milk of Magnesia a few times to see if it helps. Continue if necessary.

Each puppy will need to have his nails trimmed after the first week – 18 in all including dew claws. This prevents them clawing their mum when feeding, and making her teats sore. It also helps to maintain the shape of the puppies' feet. From the first cut the task needs doing every 4–5 days until the puppies leave for their new homes. I use my dog nail clippers. Ordinary scissors will do the task initially but, as the nails become harder and thicker, you will need proper clippers.

I do not find it necessary to have dew claws removed from Goldens but, if you wish to have them removed, you will need to arrange it sooner rather than later with your vet.

If all the puppies are well during the first week, notify any breed clubs of which you are a member and organisations that can help you sell your puppies, rather than advertise in the local press. Also contact any people who have pre-booked a puppy to let them know about the litter and to check they still want one.

Week 2 onwards

If you are feeding her on meat and biscuit and not the complete foods, you will need to increase the bitch's meal intake by 170g (6oz) meat for every puppy she is feeding, but keep the mixer/carbohydrates at about normal levels. She will be on four meals still:

Breakfast: one-third of total daily meat/carbohydrate.
Lunch: gruel.
Tea: as for breakfast.
Supper: as for breakfast.

Some bitches may go off the gruel in the second week. If so, replace it with a light meal such as egg custard, scrambled egg or fish. During this week, the puppies' eyes will begin to open and see. Do not let them be in bright conditions for about a week. They will also begin to hear soon.

Register the puppies with The Kennel Club. You will have to use ordinary names if you do not have a kennel affix. There will not be time to apply for an affix at this stage as the process can take several months. If you can, borrow an affix book so that you do not use registered affixes as names as these will be rejected. Now is the time to begin preparing all the paperwork – pedigrees, diet sheet, notes and so on, so that it is not left till until later on when the puppies are more time-consuming.

Outdoor run for puppies aged over 4 weeks.

The first two weeks of a puppy's life are spent sleeping and feeding.

Sexing: Dog pup on the left, bitch pup on the right.

Week 3

(If required), book the tattooist to come for when the puppies are 6 weeks. Identification by microchipping or tattooing is not compulsory in the United Kingdom but is recommended. Arrange a date to have the litter screened for MRD at 4–6 weeks. The dam's food intake as for Week 2 should be adequate.

I usually begin to wean puppies when they are 3 weeks old, whether the litter is large or small, or earlier if there is a problem with one puppy or the dam. The worming needs to be done about 3 days before weaning so that it has had time to take effect and the goodness of the food is not wasted. Worms can be responsible for many problems including loose stools, so they need to be dealt with early on and throughout the pup's rearing. To administer most worming products you need to weigh the puppies to find out the correct dosages.

Weaning

At 3 weeks I start puppies on about (25g) 1oz of fatty mince rolled into a ball which they can eat off a clean piece of newspaper – they usually learn fast. I find it is much easier than teaching them to lap. I use mince initially no matter what my long-term feeding plan is. I use it for about four days with a multi-supplement then, if stools are firm, change over to my preferred choice of food(s). Every breeder has their own ideas and preferences. (See Chapter 3 on feeding.) I would not choose any product with too high a protein content for Goldens although, at the puppy stage, it needs to be higher than that for a normal adult. Complete foods are certainly easier to manage and they require no supplementation. Whatever your choice, make certain it is something that can be purchased easily by the new owners for their pets so a change of diet is not required later.

I weigh, measure and feed all meals separately for each puppy, to make certain all have the correct quantity. It is much harder and more time-consuming, but communal feeding may result in the stronger puppies eating more and becoming even stronger and vice versa.

At 3.5 weeks I introduce a second meal, so one is given first thing in the morning and the other in the evening, and ensure fresh drinking water is available in a safe vessel the puppies cannot lay their heads in.

At 4.5 weeks I introduce a third meal, and a fourth at 5.5 weeks.

As the pups are weaned, so the bitch's food intake needs to be reduced. When the pups are on one meal a day, reduce her overall quantity by one-third; when they are on two meals a day, reduce her overall quantity to about one-half of the amount she was eating when she was feeding her entire brood. When the pups are fully weaned at 5–5.5 weeks, cut her intake back to normal. She will probably dislike you for it, but it is necessary. During the weaning period, the puppies will continue to demand milk from mum. As part of the routine, I try to feed the puppies and then allow mum to go in to them. This way the pups should have full tummies before they have a drink off mum and will not hurt her so much.

From 4 weeks on and as the puppies get their teeth, the dam may be less inclined to feed the pups so regularly and attend to them. This is not always the case and some may regurgitate food to help wean their young. When they are in the run, the pups gradually learn the geography, and soil their bedding less and the wood shavings more. Give them some toys to play, carry and crawl over. Introduce the puppies to being combed to help them get used to being handled later.

By 5 weeks I allow the bitch to feed the pups only twice per day, in the early morning and late afternoon so that they drain her. The bitch should go back on her normal diet. With less food intake she will eventually dry up. The puppies will need to be wormed again.

By 6 weeks the dam should not be feeding them at all so they have at least one week before going to their new homes without relying on their mother. It helps their transition greatly and prevents the insecurity and trauma that occurs if this has not happened.

Some breeders think that if the mother is still producing milk they can leave her with the pups as long as possible as the easy way out, but this is unfair to both the dam and puppies. I find it helpful to give a pet cal tablet for a few extra weeks after the bitch has finished lactation to assist with the restoration of bone in her limbs. Calcium is drawn from the long bones for her puppies, and is particularly noticeable on the front legs

Other Activities

Have the litter screened for MRD by 6 weeks and the puppies tattooed at 6 weeks. Tattooing usually takes less than an hour to do an average size litter, together with the paperwork. Each puppy will need the inside of one ear shaved prior to having a number tattooed there. It is advisable to have someone with experience to hold the puppies still during the procedure. They do cry for half a minute or so – the males are usually worse than the bitches – but a quick cuddle and a biscuit to eat usually makes them forget. I have the small calipers and black dye as I find it far clearer once the hair returns. Care should be taken for up to 14 days not to let the ear get wet and remove the dye.

At 7 weeks the puppies will need to be wormed again. Make certain it is at least 3 days before they go to their new homes so any upset stomachs can be sorted out. If necessary bring it forward. I also ensure a puppy is fed a couple of hours prior to collection so that he has the chance to be clean before the journey. Continue to comb, trim nails and handle the puppies from 4 weeks to departure and, if necessary, to trim the hair around the feet.

Selling the Puppies

Finding suitable owners for Goldens can sometimes be easy and at other times a nightmare. Whilst the main aim is to find an owner who will love and care for their puppy as you would, the other is to find someone whom you believe will remain the dog's owner for a lifetime. Vetting prospective owners and their circumstances can be difficult, but you owe it to the puppies to try to get it right from the outset. Breeders learn how to do this mainly from experience, but a few questions should enable you to decide if you want to meet prospective owners. The initial enquiry is usually over the telephone and you can ascertain the following.

- Do they want a dog or a bitch?
- Do they work and, if so, what hours? A young pup really can't be left longer than 4–5 hours in the daytime due to his feeding routine, training and socialisation.
- Do they have children, how many and how old? You will probably need to meet them to decide if they are well behaved, responsive to parents, are not frightened of dogs and so on.
- How much garden space is available and is it completely secured with fencing and gates? How high are the fences? If you can visit or find someone you know to have a quick look it will help but this is not always practical and you may have to accept their word.

- Are there places nearby where they can exercise the dog as he is growing?
- Where do they intend to let the puppy sleep (indoors or outdoors)? For me, the latter would be out of the question.
- Do they have any other dogs or pets and what are their ages.

If you are happy with the answers provided, take their name, address and telephone number and agree a date when they can visit, when the pups are about 4 weeks. I insist on meeting the whole family. I prefer as few visitors as possible up to 4 weeks to lessen the risk of infection and keep disturbances to the dam to a minimum.

The owners are likely to have questions for you, probably including the price. You must decide before taking enquiries what you are going to charge and what that will include; for example, KC registration, insurance, pedigree, photos of the sire and dam, diet sheet, general information, a week's food supply, tattooing, bones and toys. Also have to hand details of the parents' hip scores and other screening checks they have had, should you be asked.

You may be asked if there is a choice and when they can choose. You must decide if that is what you want. I do not permit this until after I have selected and only then if I'm not trying to match the right puppy and owners together.

First visit

I try to time this when the pups are active, not asleep, but not so that they will get overtired. I double check most of the information given on the telephone and see if anything else comes to light and that I am happy with the enquirers. The puppies are not so active or interesting at this age, so I discuss many things the owners will need to know in the first few weeks, such as feeding, worming, bedding, inoculations, teething, training (including the retrieving instinct), toys, grooming, moulting, upset stomachs (why and what to do), exercising, leads, collars, the law, trimming and the paperwork.

If at the end of the first visit I am still happy with the enquirers I will make an appointment for a second visit so that they can see the pups aged 6–7 weeks and perhaps make their choice. I will also inform them about my sales document and its contents. I stress that if anyone has any questions to contact me in the meantime, rather than wait until the next visit.

I do not take deposits any more. If someone wants to pull out of a deal, I'd rather he did so than provide an unhappy life for a dog he felt obliged to have because he had paid a deposit. Equally it gives the breeder the opportunity to decline selling a puppy, if at any further stage he is unhappy about the prospective purchasers.

Second visit

This takes place when the puppies are 6–7 weeks. This visit will be mainly so that prospective puppy owners can see the puppies which will be much larger, more active and interesting.

At this stage, you can go over anything the owners are not sure of. If I am still happy with them, I let them have a copy of the diet sheet so they can buy in advance what they will need for the puppy, the sales document which they can take away to check the contents and confirm that they will be happy to sign it, and the general notes to read in advance.

I also inform them again what the puppy leaves with and how I will require payment. Finally I arrange a time for them to collect their puppy and choose their new pet, if they have not already done so. I also inform them what they are likely to need for the journey.

Third visit

This is mainly to sort out the administration and take the puppy home. You will give the owner:

- KC Registration forms – sign and explain about transfer of ownership.
- Insurance – sign, explain cover and provide. Do not forget to return cover notes (if used) to the company as proof.
- Pedigree – explain, sign and provide.
- Tattoo registration – explain registration and transfer of ownership.
- Sales document – check they are happy to sign. Have two copies for both parties to sign and date with each keeping a copy.
- Receipt – once you have been paid.
- The parents' elbow and hip score and eye test date information if for any reason this is not on the registration certificate.

My puppy pack will include enough food for the puppy for a week, other pet food manufacturer's puppy literature, photos of the dam and sire and a calcium or bacon bone.

Ask the new owners to let you know whether their puppy has travelled and settled well, and to keep in touch with the pup's progress. Whatever happens, good or bad, the breeder should be informed as he may be able to offer help and it may influence what he does in his future breeding programme.

If you are in any doubt about any enquirer, do not let him have a puppy. You are not obliged to, and it is much easier to say no at the outset than to spend sleepless nights worrying and trying to get a puppy back.

When done properly, breeding is hard work, but can be enjoyable. I have yet to have a complete textbook litter without one emergency (minor or major) but I suppose such cases do exist.

Aftercare

All reputable breeders should provide after-sales care for the Goldens they sell as puppies or adults. Aftercare is being able to help and advise on issues that occur at any time of a Golden's life. It may entail visits and, if all else fails, either finding another suitable home or having the dog back to assess and rehome him. You may wish to include details of this in your information pack and/or sales document.

Stud Work

I have already dealt with the responsibilities of the stud dog owner. This section discusses the actual process.

Most breeders like to introduce a dog to stud work when he is about one year old if the opportunity arises, as the older he is, the more difficult it can become. As some hereditary checks cannot be done until a dog is 12 months, it may mean waiting a further 1–2 months for the results. After the dog is used for the first time, his use should be restricted to only a few times during the rest of that year. To be an effective stud, he will need to be kept in good physical condition and fed well. Vitamin E (wheatgerm) can be given as a supplement for a few days before a dog is booked.

A stud fee charge is not usually made for a proving litter, or is minimal. The first mating should be with a proven bitch, one that is easy to mate and who does not snap at the male or twist round. This can be off-putting for young and inexperienced dogs.

When starting a dog off, decide where you plan matings to take place (some dogs will be happy anywhere, others may prefer more privacy) and decide on the procedure. To gain the dog's confidence and co-operation you will need to develop a routine. Below is the procedure I follow once I have agreed to accept a bitch to my dog. Some breeders request that bitches are swabbed at the outset of their season to check for infection and are tested by vets to check which day they ought to be mated on.

- Make certain the bitch has relieved herself before the mating.
- Take the bitch and owner to the secure place where the mating will take place. Let the bitch off lead to acclimatise to the surroundings. Play with her if she is tense. I use an indoor lounge.
- Check that all the bitch's paperwork is in order.
- Show the dog's paperwork to the bitch owner.
- Explain your mating routine.
- Have seats or tables available if required.
- Have the stud dog available close by but not in the room.
- When the bitch looks relaxed, ask the owner to hold her whilst you check her internally, and then bring in the male on a lead to see her reaction. If there is none, I put the dog out of the room and prepare the bitch if I think she is ready for mating.
- The owner should hold the bitch's head with his hands through a collar. His palms should be in contact with the bitch's shoulders which gives him a lot of control over her should she attempt to move and struggle. If there is any indication that she will bite the dog or owner accidentally, a crepe bandage can be tied around the muzzle (see Emergency Muzzle, Chapter 4).
- I stand the bitch four square and kneel beside her so my left side is in contact with her left side. I then place her vulva between two of the fingers of my left hand in readiness for the dog. If I have a third person to help, they would let the dog into the room off the lead. The dog usually wants to investigate and lick the bitch's rear end initially, and may mount her several times before there is sufficient impetus for him to consider penetrating.
- You will know if a dog is off-target as you will sense with your fingers if he is anywhere near the bitch's vulva or penetrating. Your fingers can guide him in if necessary. You can normally tell if the dog is going to penetrate and tie with a bitch as he moves higher and is on tip toe at the rear. Sometimes you may need to use a little KY Jelly or Vaseline around the bitch's vulva, but it is not always required.
- If the bitch is too small or too tall for the dog, raise her rear end or the dog's standing area to compensate with additional non-slip materials such as extra carpet. If the dog is perched almost on top of the bitch's back and stops moving it is likely he has penetrated sufficiently to tie and is ejaculating sperm. This all occurs in the first few minutes.
- The bitch supposedly determines the length of a tie. It can be a few minutes to 45 minutes or more! During this time, the dog washes the sperm into the bitch with further liquid. This is why slip matings (no tie) can still produce puppies.

- I usually check the dog is tied with my fingers. If you cannot feel his penis it has probably happened. Care needs to be taken for the first few minutes. I hold the dog as close to the bitch as possible by coupling my arms around their quarters with a knee under the bitch's stomach to prevent her collapsing under the dog's weight, so that a tie and not a slip mating takes place. After a few minutes, with the help of a third person, the dog's front feet should be eased onto the floor on the opposite side to you.
- Some dogs may wish to turn back to back with the bitch. It may be unwise to let an inexperienced dog do this as he may try to do it too quickly and the tie can be broken. Some stud dog owners never permit their dogs to do this.
- Both dogs will need to be held for the duration. A male can become fidgety, so make a fuss of him.
- When the tie has finished, the bitch releases the dog. Whilst inside her, he will have swollen up immensely. If the tie has gone the full duration, most of the swelling will have subsided and the penis will retract. Be sure that the dog does not retract any of his hair, as this will be uncomfortable. The penis will just need easing out carefully. The dog is likely to lick his genitals a great deal after a mating. I place the dog in a separate room so that he can recover and ensure he has access to water.
- I tip the bitch's rear end up to prevent any liquid coming out and, with the help of the owner, carry her out to the car. She should not be permitted to urinate for at least one hour.
- Issue a receipt for the stud-handling fee to the bitch's owner and agree terms in writing should another service need to be provided if the bitch misses (this is normal practice).
- Also give the owner a copy of the dog's pedigree and a signed KC Application for Litter Registration Form. Some stud dog owners prefer to give this out when the bitch's owner confirms that the litter has arrived.
- You may need to supply a copy of the hip score sheet if the test was done some years ago, as I believe The Kennel Club have data only from about the early 1990s.
- Ask if the owner wants a second mating. To be of any benefit, it is usually done two days later as the first mating should cover the bitch for at least 48 hours. It is not essential if a good mating has taken place.
- If a slip mating occurred but the dog was not fully extended, it is possible to try again later that day. It is preferable to try a day later, particularly if the dog was fully extended. It is possible for a dog to come out fully if he is not directed into the bitch's vulva. This results in great disappointment for all concerned and causes great discomfort for the dog in standing or laying until his penis has retracted. Bathe the penis with cold water and lubricate it with Vaseline or KY Jelly and ease the sheath gently back over the penis as it reduces in size.
- If the bitch is not ready, try again 1–2 days later. Occasionally, a bitch may have gone over the best time (usually 12–13 days) in which case the owner will have to wait until her next season to mate her.
- Stud fees can vary according to the attributes of the dog, and his success as a stud dog and his progeny. Some stud dog owners will not charge a stud fee for a slip mating unless puppies are produced.

- Young dogs can be encouraged to mate a bitch by allowing more play, if the bitch permits, and holding her rear end briefly off the ground. This usually encourages the dog to get on her back, mount and perform.

Breeding-Related Ailments and Conditions

Abortion: Can occur due to infection. Miscarriages may lead to puppies' death and re-absorption, possibly without any trace. You may only know for certain that this has occurred if the bitch has been scanned previously.

Agalactia: This is where a bitch fails to produce milk immediately once she has had puppies. Causes vary from illness, hormone imbalance, stress and mastitis. The bitch can come into milk a few weeks later. If this occurs you will have to hand rear the litter – a formidable task even if the litter is small, as regular feeds will be required day and night.

Balanitis: Inflammation of the sheath that covers the penis. Seek veterinary attention.

Balanopostitis: As above but including the penis. Seek veterinary attention.

Cryptorchidism: This is where an adult male has retained his testicles in the abdominal cavity due to an abnormality. Veterinary advice should be sought. Most vets prefer to remove the testicles under anaesthetic to prevent problems such as testicular cancer later in life.

Dystocia: Term given to 'difficult births', such as an oversize puppy.

Eclampsia: Occurs in lactating bitches, mostly during the first 3 weeks, due to an imbalance of calcium or, occasionally, glucose in the bloodstream. Some vets believe the imbalance may be due to supplementing a bitch's diet throughout the pregnancy instead of just three days prior to whelping, causing her own system to fail. It can occur in bitches prior to whelping but this is far rarer than post-whelping cases. It is very serious, if untreated the bitch may die. The bitch may show signs of becoming anxious, unsettled, trembling, generally abnormal or she may collapse. **Seek veterinary attention immediately - this is an emergency.** Usually she responds to a calcium injection almost instantly but may need more later or supplementation through lactation. If it occurs, never leave the bitch unattended for long during the first 3 weeks in case she has a relapse and slips into a coma. I have experienced two cases in the few litters our kennel has had.

Ectopic ureter (wet puppies): This is the malposition of the ureter from the kidney to the bladder which can affect either or both sides of the tube. It results in involuntary incontinence most of the time and can occur in puppies in the nest. If found in one so young, the kindest thing would be to have him put to sleep rather than to try to persevere with a problem that will become greater as the puppy grows.

Fading puppy syndrome: Can affect apparently healthy puppies in the first week which begin to die in the second week. Many facts may be involved, such as hypothermia, infections, mismanagement by the owner, congenital defects, and so on. Should you incur losses, seek veterinary advice and ask for post-mortems.

False (phantom) pregnancy: A term given either to an unmated bitch who shows signs of having been mated or pregnancy, or a bitch who has been mated who shows signs of having conceived when she has not.

Mammary tumours: See Chapter 6, Growths. They are growths on the mammary glands. They can be prevented by having a bitch spayed after her first season. This is 95% effective, the percentage reducing the longer she is left unspayed.

Mastitis (milk fever): Inflammation of the mammary glands occurring in lactating bitches which can be very painful. If it is not very bad, try using a hot towel to soften it and place a puppy on the specific teat to take off the milk. If unsuccessful, or a very large area is affected, seek veterinary advice. Usually antibiotics are prescribed which will disperse it within a few days. It can happen at any stage of lactation. I have found it often occurs when you are trying to dry the bitch up at the end.

Monorchidism: A dog with only one testicle in the scrotum. See Cryptorchidism.

Neutering: The removal of a dog's testicles or a bitch's uterus and ovaries under anaesthetic to prevent them from reproducing, for health or other reasons.

Puppy head gland disease: Inflammation of the skin and head glands. Mainly it affects puppies aged under 4 months, and often while they are in the nest, but can occur up to 12 months. Swellings usually begin around the lips or just under the chin but within a short period involves the whole head. There is also a discharge. The sooner it is dealt with by a vet the better, otherwise it may scar the dog for life.

Pyometra: Caused by accumulation of pus in the uterus. Occurs from about 4–8 weeks after a bitch has finished a season, whether or not she has been bred from, although it occurs more in bitches that have not been bred from. This is one reason why vets recommend spaying. In 'open' cases, a vaginal discharge will be apparent, from cream to dark brown in colour. 'Closed' cases involve no discharge, making it harder to detect.

Other symptoms include excessive thirst, loss of appetite, increased urination (may be confused with cystitis), vomiting and abdomen distension. **Seek veterinary attention immediately** as this can be a real emergency - the bitch may die if left too long.

If you are an inexperienced breeder and do not have access to some of the available breeding data often contained in breed club or Kennel Club literature, then approach an experienced breeder for help. He or she will be able to identify features that need to be improved in your bitch and suggest some possible stud dogs from their knowledge and experience. It must be remembered that nearly all breeding is experimental and no guarantees can be given that every one of the resulting offspring will be without any problems but this assistance should help to reduce the risks.

I would be a little cautious approaching a breeder who has his own stud dogs, and particularly those who only recommend the use of their own dogs or progeny bred by them. If they suggest alternatives as well as their own, I would not be so concerned.

Whelping chart

Serve Jan:	1	2	3	4	5	6	7	8	9	10	11	12	13	14
Whelp Mar/Apr:	5	6	7	8	9	10	11	12	13	14	15	16	17	18

Serve Feb:	1	2	3	4	5	6	7	8	9	10	11	12	13	14
Whelp Apr/May:	5	6	7	8	9	10	11	12	13	14	15	16	17	18

Serve Mar:	1	2	3	4	5	6	7	8	9	10	11	12	13	14
Whelp May/Jun:	3*	4	5	6	7	8	9	10	11	12	13	14	15	16

Serve Apr:	1	2	3	4	5	6	7	8	9	10	11	12	13	14
Whelp Jun/Jul:	3	4	5	6	7	8	9	10	11	12	13	14	15	16

Serve May:	1	2	3	4	5	6	7	8	9	10	11	12	13	14
Whelp Jul/Aug:	3	4	5	6	7	8	9	10	11	12	13	14	15	16

Served Jun:	1	2	3	4	5	6	7	8	9	10	11	12	13	14
Whelp Aug/Sep:	3	4	5	6	7	8	9	10	11	12	13	14	15	16

Served Jul:	1	2	3	4	5	6	7	8	9	10	11	12	13	14
Whelp Sep/Oct:	2	3	4	5	6	7	8	9	10	11	12	13	14	15

Served Aug:	1	2	3	4	5	6	7	8	9	10	11	12	13	14
Whelp Oct/Nov:	3	4	5	6	7	8	9	10	11	12	13	14	15	16

Served Sep:	1	2	3	4	5	6	7	8	9	10	11	12	13	14
Whelp Nov/Dec:	3	4	5	6	7	8	9	10	11	12	13	14	15	16

Served Oct:	1	2	3	4	5	6	7	8	9	10	11	12	13	14
Whelp Dec/Jan:	3	4	5	6	7	8	9	10	11	12	13	14	15	16

Served Nov:	1	2	3	4	5	6	7	8	9	10	11	12	13	14
Whelp Jan/Feb:	3	4	5	6	7	8	9	10	11	12	13	14	15	16

Served Dec:	1	2	3	4	5	6	7	8	9	10	11	12	13	14
Whelp Feb/Mar:	2	3	4	5	6	7	8	9	10	11	12	13	14	15

* Adjust for leap year.

15	16	17	18	19	20	21	22	23	24	25	26	27	28	29	30	31
19	20	21	22	23	24	25	26	27	28	29	30	31	1	2	3	4

15	16	17	18	19	20	21	22	23	24	25	26	27	28	(29)
19	20	21	22	23	24	25	26	27	28	29	30	1	2	(3)

15	16	17	18	19	20	21	22	23	24	25	26	27	28	29	30	31
17	18	19	20	21	22	23	24	25	26	27	28	29	30	31	1	2

15	16	17	18	19	20	21	22	23	24	25	26	27	28	29	30
17	18	19	20	21	22	23	24	25	26	27	28	29	30	1	2

15	16	17	18	19	20	21	22	23	24	25	26	27	28	29	30	31
17	18	19	20	21	22	23	24	25	26	27	28	29	30	31	1	2

15	16	17	18	19	20	21	22	23	24	25	26	27	28	29	30
17	18	19	20	21	22	23	24	25	26	27	28	29	30	31	1

15	16	17	18	19	20	21	22	23	24	25	26	27	28	29	30	31
16	17	18	19	20	21	22	23	24	25	26	27	28	29	30	1	2

15	16	17	18	19	20	21	22	23	24	25	26	27	28	29	30	31
17	18	19	20	21	22	23	24	25	26	27	28	29	30	31	1	2

15	16	17	18	19	20	21	22	23	24	25	26	27	28	29	30
17	18	19	20	21	22	23	24	25	26	27	28	29	30	1	2

15	16	17	18	19	20	21	22	23	24	25	26	27	28	29	30	31
17	18	19	20	21	22	23	24	25	26	27	28	29	30	31	1	2

15	16	17	18	19	20	21	22	23	24	25	26	27	28	29	30
17	18	19	20	21	22	23	24	25	26	27	28	29	30	31	1

15	16	17	18	19	20	21	22	23	24	25	26	27	28	29	30	31
16	17	18	19	20	21	22	23	24	25	26	27	28	1*	2	3	4

Photographing your Goldens

Puppy pose.

The more versatile your camera and the more accessories it has, the greater the opportunity you will have of achieving better shots and special effects. It is possible to achieve good shots even with less sophisticated cameras, provided that you appreciate at the outset that they have their limitations. For instance, most have fixed speed, so your best shots will be when the dog is stationary. They may also have a fixed focal length, so close-up and distant photography will not provide satisfactory results. The camera's manual should indicate the optimum distance to stand from your photo composition and explain its other limitations.

General Tips

You should always:

- Ensure you have filled the frame within the view finder markings and check that you have not cut off anything you want in the photo such as tail, feet, ears, head.
- Check you have focused your composition.
- Check you do not have any distractions in the frame such as anything bright, reflective or cream and white. Goldens photograph best against a contrast of medium to dark colours, but not shades of red which tends to overpower the subject. They will be lost against a pale background and it may cause over-exposed results.
- For home portraits turn the camera on its side. Home portraits are best taken with a 70–120mm lens, if you have one, as it helps to balance the size of anything in the foreground of the composition.
- Ask someone to help to attract the dog when you are ready to take the photograph. Most dogs look more interested and attractive with their ears forward. A toy, squeaky toy, treat, duck caller or thrown object can help to attract the dog.
- Remember, dogs get bored easily and it may be very difficult to reason with them, no matter how well trained they are, so keep photo sessions as brief as possible. If you want a set pose, arrange everything else first and add the dog at the last moment.
- For candid shots, keep your camera at hand, already set and focused as much as possible so all you have to do is turn it on. This is always worth doing if you have a puppy, which can be so comical in the early weeks. Cameras with autofocus are obviously an advantage.

- Print film has the advantage over slide film if you want to trim off any distractions around the edges of the main subject or have a part toned down to be less distracting. With care, slides can be marginally trimmed or masked with tin foil if you remount them. It is also possible, with a little skill, to remove distractions on gloss prints with water colour paints. Do not try this on a matt finish print.
- If you want to use special effects, slide film would be best.
- If you have a digital camera, you will be able to remove any unwanted background distractions with digital imaging. Computers can also be used for the same purpose with ordinary prints and slides, but the process can be lengthy and expensive.
- Keep both eyes open when looking through the view finder and taking the picture.
- Keep as still as possible when taking the shot. Placing one foot in front of another and slightly apart achieves better balance, and take the shot after breathing out, not when holding your breath.

Mr Peter Moxon, Field Trialler and author, taking photographs in 1968.

Tips for Indoor Photography

- Use a high speed daylight film rated ISO 400/270° or more. This is especially useful in low light situations exposed in natural light, sunlight or under electronic flash. Its use may prevent the need to use a flash light.
- If you have to use a fixed flash unit, or it is an integral part of the camera that will go off automatically, never take a photo of a dog directly into its eyes. This produces the 'red eye' effect where the flash of light reflects off the retina at the back of the dog's eye. Try to compose your shot with the dog's head in profile or angled to the camera. Alternatively, place a white hanky over the flash to prevent 'red eye' but you may need to be closer to the dog to achieve sufficient light penetration.
- If your flash unit is not fixed, then experiment by pointing it to the ceiling or to the camera's side to prevent 'red eye'.
- Check you have set the camera correctly for use of a flash unit and your distances from the composition are correct for the aperture settings, not too close or too far away.
- If you do not have the specialist equipment required for studio type indoor portrait work, try a professional photographer. Most take super shots, provided you do not want a show dog pose. For these, find someone who specialises in photos for the breed or dog papers.

Outdoor Photography

Indoor male portrait with studio lighting.

- In the autumn, winter and spring in the northern hemisphere you may need to use a film rated ISO 100/21° or higher due to lower light levels.
- In the summer a film rated ISO 100/21° or less should be more than adequate for lighting conditions in the United Kingdom, Europe and other parts of the northern hemisphere.
- In the autumn, winter and spring sunlight, you will probably achieve greater colour saturation on a Golden's coat due to lower light levels. I prefer to take most of my photographs in these seasons, but not always in direct sunlight.
- In summer, care must be taken with Goldens' coats. A photo taken in direct sunlight is likely to create highlights on the coat and burn out the texture detail. Cameras can only average light readings from the light and darker parts of a composition, they cannot compensate for these areas. Better results can often be achieved from shaded areas, provided excessive amounts of light are not penetrating through the foliage as this will cause a mottled effect. Alternatively take photographs very early or late in the day, before the daylight becomes too strong or the sun is directly overhead the subject.
- If you are taking photos of dogs in water, do not forget that light reflecting off the water will tell your camera the subject is better lit than it really is, so you will need to stop down the aperture by 0.5 to 1 stop.
- Do not forget to keep your camera protected when the dog comes out of the water as he will undoubtedly shake as much excess water off his coat as possible.
- For action shots use a high speed film for better results, ISO 400/27° or higher, and slow speeds 1/60 of a second or less.
- If you want to freeze an action shot take it at 1/500 of a second or more, if lighting conditions permit.
- Video cameras really provide your best action shots and are often used by keen exhibitors to check they are showing and moving their dogs to best advantage.

Show Pose Tips

Many of the points already referred to are very relevant to this specialist field of photography whether photographs are taken indoors or outdoors, with or without studio lighting and photographic umbrellas.

- Select the place where the dog will stand and your viewpoint.

- You really need two people to assist you whilst you take the photographs. One person is needed to set the dog up in the correct stance and the other to attract his attention. I take most of my photos at the angles shown in the diagram below.

X   =   dog
            Y   =   assistant attracting dog
Z   =   photographer

- The second assistant stands either in front of the dog for a natural stance pose (but out of the frame of the photo once the dog is set up), *or* behind the dog once he has been set up, holding his tail out level with his topline. Some tension will be required to keep the tail straight.

- The tail should be held by the hair on the side away from the photographer so the hand is not visible. Sometimes the assistant wears a sock on the arm holding the tail to match the background. For instance, a dark green would be suitable for a colour photograph on grass against shrubs. However, for a black and white photo, a black sock is normally worn for dark backgrounds.

Outdoor show pose taken as demonstrated in diagram above.

- Try to take the photo at the same height as the dog. You should not be standing up fully, as this will affect the dog's appearance and make him look short-legged.
- If possible remove the dog's collar and lead, as this will affect his lines.
- Do not attempt to take photos in wet or windy weather, as both will affect the coat and overall appearance.
- Whenever using a photo for an advertisement, remember the dog should be the main feature and make certain you are entirely happy with it, whoever has taken the picture. Professional photographers can remove distractions from photographs they have taken, albeit at extra expense.
- If you are not certain whether a photo is good enough, or which is best from a selection, ask friends for their opinion.

Remember, a good photo can do no harm to a dog's reputation, but a bad one can. It would be better to use either a head study, group of dogs or even no photograph at all rather than the wrong show pose.

CHAPTER THIRTEEN

History of the Golden Retriever

Origin of the Golden Retriever

Golden Retrievers were not officially recognised as a breed by The Kennel Club until 1913, but their origins can be traced back to 1864.

For many years, and even to the present day, the true origin of the breed has caused differences of opinion amongst many notable authorities.

One of the earliest theories was that Goldens developed from a yellow 'sport' born of black wavy-coated parents from a Newfoundland/Irish Setter cross. The build, profuse coat and water work of the early Goldens does suggest some possible link to Newfoundlands. However, there is the question of where the paler-coloured Goldens originated and how they bred true if their ancestors were mainly black. Could the answers lie in the many exceptions to the rule in the field of genetics?

In the early 20th century, the original theory supported by Mrs W M Charlesworth, one of the main breed enthusiasts and a founder of the Golden Retriever Club and others, was that the breed descended from a troupe of eight Russian dogs performing in a Brighton circus. The troupe was supposedly purchased by Lord Tweedmouth (then Sir Dudley Marjoriebanks), who had seen them on a visit to Brighton and took them to his Scottish estate at Guisachan in Invernesshire for tracking deer. (Guisachan is Gaelic for 'Place of the Firs'.) The keepers at the estate were subsequently reputed to have confirmed this theory.

The late Mrs Elma Stonex.

The Earl of Ilchester's Melbury strain was founded on Ada, a bitch acquired from Lord Tweedmouth. Colonel Le Poer Trench (St Huberts), who also supported the Russian dog theory, obtained 'Sandy', a pure-bred offspring from one of the original dogs, from the Earl of Ilchester in 1883 and kept his strain pure. By 1913 the Colonel had his dogs registered separately as Retrievers (Russian Yellow) by The Kennel Club and one of his St Huberts dogs is listed in The Kennel Club Stud Book. The last entry for his kennel was in 1917 and on his death all his dogs were put to sleep at his behest.

After considerably more research into the breed's origin in the 1950s, mainly by Mrs Elma Stonex (Dorcas) and others such as James Palmer-Douglas, the Russian theory was dismissed. Lord Tweedmouth then became acknowledged as having founded the breed from his mating of Nous to Belle in 1868.

Nous had been the only yellow puppy in a litter of black Wavy-Coated Retrievers bred by Lord Chichester in 1864 and was given by the keeper at Stanmer, Obed Miles, to a Brighton cobbler in payment of debt. Later that year on a visit to Brighton, Lord Tweedmouth met Nous whilst out walking and, taken by his looks, purchased him.

Belle, recorded in Lord Tweedmouth's stud book as a Tweed Water Spaniel, was born a year earlier, in 1863. Belle was, however, half Tweed Water Spaniel and half yellow Wavy-Coated Retriever of unknown pedigree. Belle came from Lord Tweedmouth's cousin, Mr D Robertson, MP for Ladykirk on the Tweed.

The 1868 litter produced at least three golden puppies, maybe four. The male, Crocus, was given to the second Lord Tweedmouth, then The Hon Edward Marjoriebanks, and two females, Cowslip and Primrose, were retained by Lord Tweedmouth. A third bitch, named Ada, thought to have been from the original litter, was given to the fifth Earl of Ilchester, but details on her gravestone have raised questions as to whether she was the product of a repeat mating in 1872 instead.

Lord Tweedmouth never showed or trialled his Goldens, but socialised with many who did. He continued to line breed and outcross to produce yellow puppies until 1889 when Prim and Rose were born; the last two he recorded in his stud book until his death in 1894. From then until 1905 when Guisachan was sold, the second Lord Tweedmouth did not keep any records of the dogs he bred at the estate but a few Guisachan names at the turn of the 19th century were traceable through parents of stock registered later.

The oldest traceable pedigrees start in 1901, so there was a gap of almost a decade in tracing the links to the Goldens of the 20th century to those of Lord Tweedmouth. However, information contained in a letter written by John MacLennon, a Guisachan keeper, to Lady Pentland in 1946 confirmed that Viscount Harcourt, pioneer Golden breeder of the Culham kennel, acquired the foundation stock of his kennel from two puppies purchased from him at Kerrow House. Kerrow House was a neighbouring estate to Guisachan.

Culham stock is known to be behind at least 90% of all Golden pedigrees today, some of which go back to Lady who herself was proved to go back to either Prim or Rose.

Conon and Rock, also bred at Guisachan, are known to be behind several other original Golden kennels.

Mrs Stonex and the sixth Lord Ilchester, Lord Tweedmouth's nephew, presented the findings as the true origins of the breed to The Kennel Club and they were officially recognised in 1960.

'At Home and at Rest'.

'Example better than precept'.

Further research in the 1990s by Valerie Foss and Ann and Frank Weeks led to the discovery that Lady could be traced back to Rose.

One can appreciate why the Russian theory was believed for some years, until evidence to the contrary was established, particularly as Golden Retrievers bore some resemblance to such breeds as the Hungarian Kuvasz and others in Eastern Europe and Russia. It is possible even today when studying lesser-known European breeds to find some with such great similarities that it is difficult to differentiate between them.

Breed Development

Retrieving dogs were developed as a result of several historical issues.

First, came game introduced to Great Britain in addition to the indigenous varieties. For instance, pheasants were brought into England by the Romans during their 400-year occupation, but it was not until the 11th century that this fare appeared on menus and the 12th century when it became common. It is believed that birds at that time were tame and fattened in cages. The pheasant was established in the wild by the 16th century and occupied all of Britain by the end of the 18th century.

Second, came man's desire not only to eat game but to use it for sport.

Third, with the improvements in guns from cumbersome muzzle loaders to shotguns, shooting game became a fashionable pastime for the rich during the 19th century.

Game birds were originally netted and then shot on the ground but, once the gun improvements were made, birds were shot in flight. This resulted in birds being lost, and it became apparent that the hunter needed a good retrieving dog for use on both land and in water.

At the outset of the 19th century, pointers and setters were trained to retrieve. However, this affected their pointing work so there was a need for a breed to be developed solely for retrieving. Lord Tweedmouth was one such pioneer to develop such a breed, now known as the Golden Retriever.

The working requirements were: biddability, intelligence, stamina, speed, power, good scenting, a soft mouth to retrieve dead and wounded game without damage to hand and the ability to retrieve well from water.

By the outset of the 20th century, the Golden Retriever breed was known to be exceptionally good in water, had a soft mouth, showed intelligence and tirelessness but was slower than other working retriever breeds. This was due to his size, long back, heaviness and profuse coat. With these points in mind, the early breeders set about producing a more balanced, kindly, well boned, active, powerful, shorter-coupled dog with a dense, water-resisting but manageable coat.

Is this an early Golden? This appeared as a frontispiece in a book published in 1876.

Up to 1913, Goldens were registered by The Kennel Club as Flat Coated Retrievers, and only defined by colour. In 1913, the Standard of Points (original breed standard) was drawn up by Mrs Charlesworth and some other early pioneer breeders and adopted when the breed was separately registered by The Kennel Club under Retriever (Golden Yellow) in 1913.

With the continuation of pure breeding, by the 1930s there was more evenness of type, less colour abnormalities such as white feet, and the looks of the breed had improved. Goldens were achieving awards at Field Trials in greater numbers as their popularity increased, but it was an uphill struggle against other retrievers because they had different working techniques, such as scenting with a higher head carriage.

In 1936, the United Kingdom Breed Standard was amended to include ideal heights and weights and the colour cream to which reference is made later. The breed was first recognised in Canada in 1927 and by the American Kennel Club in 1932.

The outbreak of the Second World War had a detrimental effect on the breed for almost a decade as most kennels gave up breeding by 1940 due to difficulties in feeding and selling puppies. The lack of available puppies increased the sale prices and some people seized the opportunity to breed Goldens purely for financial gain with little or no concern for the dog and his working ability. Even after the end of the war, it took several years for Golden breeders with a genuine interest to re-establish themselves and produce quality specimens for working, showing and breeding.

From the 1950s to the current day, the increasing demand for the family pet and show dog and the Golden's lovely, companionable disposition, adaptability, looks and working ability led to a great surge in his popularity around the world, and exports increased. Also, the number of United Kingdom breed clubs increased from three to thirteen. However, as during the war, demand for the breed outstripped the supply available from specialist breeders and, sadly, over the last 20 to 30 years the breed has been commercially produced.

Undoubtedly this has had a detrimental effect on the temperament, health, type and quality of breed specimens and the breed's reputation, particularly in dogs being supplied to the pet market. Those who show and work their dogs are more aware of the commercially-produced Goldens. Attempts in the past to control the commercial breeders with legislation by breed enthusiasts, breed clubs, The Kennel Club, dog organisations and local authorities have had limited effect but it is hoped to have more success with the new Breeding and Sale of Dogs (Welfare) Act which came into force in 2000.

Some breeders have had colour preferences, from cream to a rich gold, even from the breed's early development. Although cream-coloured Goldens existed, the breeders at the beginning of the 20th century preferred the dark gold and the colour cream was omitted from the Standard of Points in 1913. The term 'yellow' was dropped in 1920 and the present designation of Retrievers (Golden) was adopted. It was recognised by breeders that the omission of the colour cream from the original Breed Standard was a mistake and it was included in 1936 when other amendments were made.

Breeders and the public have all had their colour preferences. In the 1970s, cream became very fashionable but, during the 1980s, the pendulum began to swing back to gold. Today, I would say the demand and preferences for cream and gold-coloured Goldens are about equal.

The start of the 1995 Eastern Counties All Aged (walked up) Field Trial Stake.

In 1952 The Kennel Club officially recognised the Golden as a British breed. In 1958 the Golden Retriever Club of America abandoned the British standard in favour of its own formulation.

Another major innovation was the introduction of the Show Champion title which has had an effect on the breed. Breeders who had worked and shown Goldens were concerned that this would create a split, with greater emphasis being put on showing rather than both. This feeling was influenced by the growing popularity and increased number of shows. With a number of breed and working clubs offering training facilities, it was hoped that the dual-purpose Golden would not decline and that owners of dogs winning their bench title would still put their dogs through a Qualifier, now known as the Show Gundog Working Certificate, to obtain their full Champion title. This was to enable Goldens to prove themselves capable of hunting and retrieving shot game tenderly to hand.

Goldens are still worked at Field Trials and Working Tests and the number of Field Trial Champions made up annually has remained almost unchanged over the years at an average of one to two a year. Initially, the number of show champions did not outnumber the Champions but the statistics for the period 1985–1999 clearly indicate that the number of Goldens with the full champion title is declining rapidly. The reduction may be due to a number of reasons. Sometimes owners do not wish to pursue the title for personal reasons but may have dogs capable if they were trained and given the opportunity. What concerns me more is the Goldens, even with training, that are no longer capable of retrieving game, particularly as the pioneer and early specialist breeders strove so hard to produce a retriever for working that was good enough to be shown, rather than the other way round. Golden owners cannot argue that opportunities to take the Show Gundog Working Certificate do not exist, as there have been a number of vacancies in recent years at the Show Gundog Qualifying Trials held for Goldens around the country. The heart of the owner, as well as the dog, needs to be willing!

A number of breeders have tried to maintain the dual role purpose of Goldens to the current day but the divide between the highest achievers at Championship shows and Field Trials has become greater in the last half of the 20th century and working Goldens tend to have a lighter frame. Although a few owners have almost reached a Dual Champion status with their dogs, the general feeling is that it is highly unlikely that it will ever be gained again. The last Golden in Britain to achieve this was Dual Ch and Irish Dual Champion David of Westley in the 1950s (see also p.249-50).

Breeders today also have more to consider in their breeding plans than in past years when type, temperament and working ability were their main concerns. With the advent of more veterinary support, conditions affecting the breed such as hereditary cataract, PRA, MRD and elbow and hip dysplasia mean that many difficult decisions and compromises have to be part of breeding plans. With the increase in litigation over puppy sales, the responsibilities for today's breeders are enormous.

The 21st century will undoubtedly bring further concerns for breeders if DNA testing is introduced to detect carriers of conditions affecting Goldens. However, on the positive side, in doing so, it may be possible to eradicate some hereditary conditions. Breeders and owners will have more opportunities, both in the UK and Europe, for breeding and competing with the greater movement of dogs permitted by the Pet Passport Scheme.

UK Breed Clubs

Introduction

The Golden Retriever Club was the only club that existed for the breed prior to the Second World War. Two other clubs began in 1946: the Northern Golden Retriever Association and the Golden Retriever Club of Scotland.

The United Retriever Club was also founded in 1946 by Mrs Lindy White (later Anderson) of the Lindys affix, for anyone interested in training retrievers. Within a year it had run its first Working Test. Shows followed 10 years later but it was not until 1963 that the Club held its first Championship show. The club was also responsible for approaching The Kennel Club for recognition of Gundog Working Tests as opposed to the Obedience Tests already in force.

With the rise in popularity of Goldens in the late 1960s and early 1970s, the demand for knowledge and help on the breed and competitive events increased greatly and existing clubs found it difficult to make provision for the boom and host activities throughout the country. This resulted in the formation of eight additional clubs by 1980 and a further two to date, making a grand total of 13.

NGRA celebrating their 50th Anniversary. Mrs Una Spratt (Secretary in 1996) made a presentation to two founder members, Ray Burnett and Marian Dawson.

UK Breed Clubs' History

Name of Club	Kennel Club Registration Year	1st Champ Show Year	1st Field Trial Year
Golden Retriever Club	1913	1946	1921
Golden Retriever Club of Scotland	1946	1946	1948
Northern Golden Retriever Association	1946	1952	1947
Golden Retriever Club of Wales	1968	1971	-
Ulster Golden Retriever Club	1969	1977	1971
South Western Golden Retriever Club	1973	1978	1989
Midland Golden Retriever Club	1976	1978	-
Berkshire Downs & Chilterns GRC	1978	1981	-
Eastern Counties GRC	1978	1980	1981
Golden Retriever Club of Northumbria	1978	1980	1985
Southern Golden Retriever Society	1978	1980	1999
North Western Golden Retriever Club	1982	1986	-
Yorkshire Golden Retriever Club	1987	1992	-

The Golden Retriever Club

Whilst researching the club's history I was immediately presented with a discrepancy as to the year it was founded. In some of the early breed books (including Mrs Charlesworth's) and club year books up to 1958 (published in 1959), the club was claimed to have been established in 1911. Other sources stated it was 1913, as did club year books after 1958. Kennel Club records confirm that official recognition was sought in 1913. One can only assume that the idea was conceived in about 1911 but did not come to fruition until 1913.

It is believed that there were four club founders but it is not clear who they were apart from Mrs Charlesworth. Two may have been Lord Harcourt (Culham) and Captain Hardy (Aucheneycheyne), who were very active with their Goldens at the time.

Mrs Charlesworth became the Secretary from the club's inception until 1921 and took over again in the late 1930s to 1946. She had considerable influence on both the breed and the club during the early years. Many other notable breeders have held office or served on the Executive Committee over the years but there are too many to list and pay tribute to.

The club held its first Field Trial Stake in 1921 and annually thereafter except during the Second World War and in the early 1990s, due to exceptional circumstances which will be explained later.

The number of stakes gradually grew and, by 1963, three were held annually with the winner of the two-day open stake qualifying two dogs for the Retriever Championship. In the 1996/7 season four Field Trials were held including a two-day open stake.

In 1936, 1937 and 1938 the club held 12 class members shows at members' homes. A retrieving and gun test and a jumping test were also held in conjunction with the shows.

After the Second World War, The Kennel Club confirmed Championship show status to breed clubs only until 1947, when the general Championship shows were permitted to hold them again. In 1946 the club therefore applied for Championship show status and held its first Championship show at Slough. The judge was Lorna, Countess Howe, who drew an entry of 444 from 150 dogs. A second was held at Workington in the same year. Championship shows became an annual event and, from 1967, two judges were appointed due to the increasing number of entries. I believe this was also the first year that Dr Keith Barnett offered his services to the breed at the show to inspect members' dogs' eyes for cataract and PRA to determine the breed incidence prior to any KC/BVA schemes being introduced.

In 1983 the club's Championship show drew a record entry of 980 (excluding 'not for competition') and the highest class entry of 77 in Maiden Bitch. A further club record occurred in 1990 with the highest number of dogs entered being 711 (excluding NFC).

Membership also has grown over the years. Initially there were only a few members but, by 1922 there were 48, with 218 by 1938. Although the membership fell during 1947 to 158, it increased again steadily afterwards. In 1963, the club's Golden jubilee year, there were 329 members. Over the next 30-year period the membership grew enormously and peaked at 2,935 in 1991. This figure also included 655 overseas members from 25 different countries. Despite the club's de-registration by The Kennel Club between 1992 to 1994 as a result of accounting irregularities, the club's membership remained well over 2,000.

Club de-registration resulted in licences being lost for all trials and shows but the club continued to produce a year book, newsletters and organise European trips, working tests, symposiums and so on. Application for re-registration was made in 1993 and The Kennel Club re-registered the club on 1 January 1995. Licences were subsequently granted by The Kennel Club for the club to hold Field Trials and Open shows in 1995 but not Championship shows. Championship status was granted again by The Kennel Club for the year 2000 after a nine year interlude.

The Golden Retriever Club of Scotland

The club was founded in 1946. Dr McKerrow was its first Chairman and Dr Acton, one of nine founder members, its Secretary.

Within 5 months of formation, the club held its first Championship show with an entry of 250. It was the first Championship show to be held in Scotland following the outbreak of the Second World War. A second Championship show and the first Field Trial was held a year later.

In 1948 the club published its first newsletter, organised a two-day Field Trial and an Open show instead of a Championship show. At some stage between 1948 and the 1950s, the club ceased holding shows of any kind. It was not until 1962 that it held its next Open show and in 1967 its next Championship show. Championship and Open shows have continued to be held each year since.

When the club was formed, its first object was 'to encourage the breeding and type of the Golden Retriever most suitable for work'. This commitment has continued through the club's history with a full programme of Field Trials and Working Tests being provided annually.

In 1996, the club celebrated its 50th anniversary.

The Northern Golden Retriever Association

This was another club founded immediately after the Second World War in 1946. Some of its early officers held office for many years. Its first Secretary, Mr W D Barwise (Beauchasse), held office for 18 years and Mrs Marion Dawson (Aurea) became its Treasurer for 12 years. She also took on the additional duties of Secretary and Field Trial clerical worker for many years. Mr Graham Holmes (Wraes) became their second Chairman and held office for 39 years (1950–1989). Altogether this provided much stability, something quite rare in dog clubs.

Their first Open show took place at Newcastle-upon-Tyne in 1947. Championship show status was granted in 1952 and, for over 30 years, Obedience classes have also been scheduled at the October Championship show. Eighty dogs were at the first Championship show and 446 at the 45th show in 1996. At the 1968 Championship show Dr Keith Barnett examined 157 dogs for eye defects; he found 18% had cataract and 2% with other defects.

The aim and object of the Association has always been 'to encourage the breeding of Golden Retrievers of a dual purpose type, ie, suitable for work and of a type conforming as nearly as possible to the Standard laid down'. Whilst therefore realising the importance of shows, equal attention has been given to the working side. Two Field Trials were run in their first year and subsequently four stakes, two confined to Goldens and two for Any Variety Retriever. Within a few years their All-Aged Stake carried qualification for the Retriever Championships. In 1995 six trials were held.

Mr Holmes provided gundog training opportunities on his ground in the early years but, in 1960, a group of people who had been training their dogs informally were given recognition by the Association at their request and became known as the Pennine Training Area. Their training is for all gundog breeds, not purely Golden Retrievers, and classes and tests are held regularly every year. Two other training groups, the Wye Valley and Burns and Becks Gundogs, were also part of the Association following their formation in the late 1960s, but subsequently went their own way.

The Association produces a year book. In 1996, it celebrated its 50th anniversary and at the Championship show made presentations to Mrs Dawson and Mr Raymond Burnett (Rossbourne), two of their founder committee members (see page 244).

Other Clubs

The history of the other 10 clubs is still in the making, with only the Ulster, South Western, and Welsh Golden Retriever Clubs so far having celebrated their silver jubilees. All run numerous events each year of an educational and social nature, shows and working activities, but not all run trials. It has also been necessary for all clubs to become involved with and run rescue and rehoming schemes for Golden Retrievers since their rise in popularity in the 1970s – an issue affecting dogdom in general.

The most significant factor affecting clubs' history in the 1990s was The Kennel Club's decision to reduce the CC allocation to a maximum of 40 sets per breed. Prior to this, all 13 breed clubs had been granted Championship status. In 1996 and 1997 three breed clubs were not granted Championship status: the GRC of Northumbria, the Yorkshire GRC and the GRC, the last due to its de-registration as Championship status cannot be applied for less than 2 years in advance.

In 1998 the three clubs affected by The Kennel Club's decision were the Berkshire Downs and Chilterns GRC, the North West GRC, and the GRC. In 1999 only two clubs were affected by The Kennel Club's decision, namely Eastern Counties GRC and the GRC, as The Kennel Club increased the maximum sets of CCs to 41 for our breed. For the year 2000 The Kennel Club increased the sets of CCs to 43 for our breed, so all breed clubs were to have one set each again but due to difficulties within the NWGRC their CC status was withdrawn.

Golden Retriever Breed Clubs' Conference

By 1980, 11 breed clubs were in existence throughout the United Kingdom. To effect some system of organisation with regard to the appointment of judges, event dates and other important matters affecting the breed, the Golden Retriever Club invited the other 10 clubs to a meeting in September. Most clubs sent representatives and it was agreed to hold further meetings. Meetings between all the existing breed clubs who wished to send representatives continued until 1991. In 1992 The Kennel Club informed the participating clubs that

(i)   the holding of a Clubs' Conference was in contravention of their rules;
(ii) that this would have to be disbanded; and
(iii) if clubs wished to continue meeting as a group they would have to form a breed council.

Golden Retriever Breed Council

Following The Kennel Club's directive referred to above, Mr Keith Young (Pyngold) set about consulting all registered breed clubs in 1992 about the formation of a Breed Council, and an inaugural meeting was held in November 1992 to discuss rules and working practices. The Kennel Club gave approval for the Golden Retriever Breed Council to be added to their register in 1993. Meetings of all clubs wishing to participate are held twice yearly. Currently all 13 breed clubs are represented on the breed council.

Mr Jim Cranston, who trained and handled Dual Ch David of Westley, is seen here taking 2nd place in the mixed Veteran Class at the AIGRC 1969 Championship Show with his wife's 10-year-old Castelnau Grandioso.

Golden Retrievers in Ireland

Golden Retrievers were introduced from England primarily for gundog work in the 1920s and the first Irish Kennel Club registrations for the breed were recorded in 1925. It was not until after the Second World War that Goldens began to be shown more, but this was confined to Northern Ireland. Little interest was shown in the breed in the South.

Achievements and breeding have been intertwined with Great Britain as a result of the free movement of Goldens across the Irish Sea, but it was not until the mid 1970s that Goldens became more popular both as pets and as show dogs. This trend has resulted in the breed developing into two types and the decline of the Field Trial dog, despite some kennels trying to maintain the dual-purpose balance. (This situation is the same in many countries today.)

Miss Lucy Ross (Buidhe), who lives in Northern Ireland, was the first notable breeder to acquire a Golden in 1932 which was one of the earliest to be bred in Ireland. Tragically, this Golden was stolen and a subsequent import from the Rossbourne Kennel died from poisoning. In 1949, Miss Ross imported another Golden from the Rossbourne Kennel but, having an increasing interest in field trialling, she decided to purchase a Golden with working potential. Her quest led her to buy David of Westley from Miss Joan Gill in 1951. He was sired by Ch Dorcas Glorious of Slat out of Ch Susan of Westley.

Jim Cranston trained and handled David, who became the breed's first and only Dual Champion in Ireland and the United Kingdom. David won 24 Field Trial awards, including a First at the first-ever Field Trial held by the All-Ireland Golden Retriever Club and a diploma in the Kennel Club Field Trial Championships. In the show ring he accumulated eight Green Stars

Mrs Twist showing Bryanstown Gale Warning at the AIGRC Championship Show in 1969, where he won the Green Star. He went on to gain his Irish and UK bench titles.

and four Challenge Certificates. He was also the sire of a Canadian and a Danish Dual Champion.

Miss Ross has also owned and bred at least three other Goldens who have gained their UK bench titles and some who have gained their Irish titles, including a Field Trial champion and Ch/Irish Ch Mandingo Buidhe Column (Alresford Nice Fella ex Buidhe Dearg), the first Irish-bred dog to win a Best of Breed at Crufts (1969). After acquiring his title he was campaigned in Great Britain by Mrs Lucille Sawtell (Yeo) and won nine Challenge Certificates.

Mrs Cynthia Twist, who lived in the South, acquired her first Golden in 1946 but it was not until her marriage to Michael in 1951 that the Bryanstown kennel was formed.

Mr Everett Massey seen here at the AIGRC 1969 Championship Show with Seamourne Honey, winner of the Reserve Green Star. She later went on to gain her Irish Champion title.

The first two Irish Champions were made up in 1953. They were Mrs Twist's dog import Pennard Golden David and Mrs O Metcalf's bitch Tullynore Linda. Mr and Mrs Twist went on to breed and/or own seven Irish Champions, one of which successfully gained his UK title following their move to England in 1970. In the 1980s they made up a further title holder in the United Kingdom.

In 1953 Mr and Mrs Twist were responsible for forming the All Ireland Golden Retriever Club, and in 1954 the club held its first Field Trial. In 1957 the club was wound up because a replacement Secretary could not be found, but it was re-established by 1962 and has continued to date. The first Championship show was held in conjunction with the Athy All Breed Championship Show.

The significant number of Goldens trialled in the 1950s and 1960s was due largely to encouragement from Mr Twist but, unfortunately, there was a rapid decline in the number of Golden owners taking part in trialling after he and his wife moved to England.

In total there have only been six Irish Field Trial Champions, including David of Westley. Although two Goldens were made up under Kennel Club rules in the 1970s, it is over 30 years since a Golden has been made up under Irish Kennel Club Rules.

It is hoped that the recent successes in the Irish Retriever Championships by Brendon

Mrs Eva Harkness, Mr Everett Massey and Miss Lucy Ross, founder members of the Ulster GRC, celebrating its 25th Anniversary in 1993 at their Championship show.

Mack with Bednall Kizzie, who was the first Golden to win an award for 20 years, and with Highseas Rocco of Glenconway who, in 1996, achieved sufficient points to become an Irish Field Trial Champion subject to qualifying in the show ring, will assist the re-establishment of the Golden on the gundog working side in Ireland.

One other kennel in the south that has spanned five decades is Mrs Joyce King's Leygore kennel. She purchased her first bitch in 1948 when living in England, but moved to County Cork in 1952. Her kennel lines encompassed both the show and working lines. Although she did not campaign her stock very often, it is behind some other notable Irish kennels that have had great success since the 1960s and 1970s such as Everett Massey's Seamourne kennel in Northern Ireland, which has had numerous Irish title holders and one UK/Irish title holder in 1994, and Michael and Mary Gaffney's Tyrol kennel in the South.

Mrs Eva Harkness began her Mandingo kennel in the 1950s. Her breeding has achieved numerous Irish titles and three dogs in her ownership have also gained their UK titles. Mandingo Marigold also started off Mrs Heather Avis' Glenavis kennel in the mid 1960s. Marigold not only won her Irish title but produced three overseas title holders in one litter when mated to Ch Camrose Cabus Christopher. Mrs Avis subsequently made up one further Champion and Irish Champion title holder and a Show Champion in 1998 who subsequently took their Irish Show title in 2000. Currently she resides in Scotland.

In 1969 the Ulster Golden Retriever Club was founded by many of the breeders based in Northern Ireland who have already been mentioned. They held their first Field Trial in 1971 and their first Championship show in 1977. The club and its events have gone from strength to strength over the 30 years. In 1998 their Championship show drew a record entry of 263 when Eva Harkness, a founder member, judged.

Mrs Kate Crosbie's (formerly Black) Lislone kennel began in the 1970s. Her first notable kennel achievement was to win Ireland's first Kennel Club Junior Warrant with an Irish-owned dog Garbank Special Edition of Lislone (Ch Camrose Fabius Tarquin ex Sh Ch Garbank Cindy). Later he went on to win both his Champion and Irish Champion titles. I also had the pleasure of awarding him a CC when he was 11 years old at the Ulster Golden Retriever Club's 25th Anniversary Championship Show in 1993 and saw him win another aged 12 years. In 1996 Kate married Jim Crosbie of Garbank kennel fame and then moved to Scotland in 1999.

One final kennel achievement of note in the 1990s is that of Mr and Mrs Gaffney's Tyrol kennel, winning Best of Breed at Crufts in two successive years. In 1994 it was the turn of Ch/Irish Ch Papeta Philosopher (Ch Sansue Golden Ruler ex Sh Ch Westley Sophia of Papeta), and in 1995 Ch/Irish Ch Galalith Crown Prince of Tyrol (Ch Sansue Golden Ruler ex Ir Ch Linchael Ecstacy at Lawpark).

With the increased popularity of the breed throughout Ireland since the 1970s, many other kennels are coming to the fore not only in the show ring and gundog work, but also in obedience and agility.

Chronological History of the Golden Retriever (plus a few other interesting landmarks)

1784:   Shooting licences introduced.
1820:   Sir Dudley Coutts Marjoriebanks was born (later 1st Lord Tweedmouth).
1835:   Sir Dudley Coutts Marjoriebanks, aged 15, began to keep a Stud Book.

1842:   First mention of a retriever in Lord Tweedmouth's stud records (now held at The Kennel Club), thought to be black.

1852:   Second mention of a retriever in Lord Tweedmouth's stud book. Only had a maximum of four retrievers in his kennels until 1866.

1854:   Sir Dudley Coutts Marjoriebanks bought the Guisachan Estate in Scotland.

1859:   First dog show held at the Corn Exchange, Newcastle-upon-Tyne.

1863:   Belle (half Tweed Water Spaniel), foundation dam of the breed, was born.

1864:   Nous (yellow Wavy-Coated Retriever), foundation sire of the breed, was born, acquired by Sir Dudley Coutts Marjoriebanks and taken to his Guisachan estate. The retriever was first shown at Birmingham.

1867:   The first retriever trials were hosted at Stafford. Belle, aged 2–3, was given to Lord Tweedmouth as a replacement for Tweed (Tweed Water Spaniel) by David Robertson MP, as Tweed had died aged about five years. (David Robertson was a relative who had changed his name from Marjoriebanks in the 1830s.)

1868:   Original mating of Nous and Belle produced three, perhaps four, puppies.

1871:   Sultan (liver coloured retriever dog) won his KC Stud Book entry by winning second in a class for retrievers other than black at Crystal Palace show in June. Born in 1867, he was by Moscow, a liver coloured dog, out of a Tweedside Spaniel. Nous died.

1873:   The Kennel Club was founded and Stud Books were compiled annually. Ada was painted by G Goddard. Originally Ada was thought to come from the 1868 Nous to Belle litter, but she may have been born in their second litter in 1872.

1875:   The Honourable H Graves painted Ada with Henry Edward, 5th Earl of Ilchester.

1880:   The KC introduced a registration system. Robin, a second generation of Lord Ilchester's kennel, was included in a picture by Van der Weyde about 1880.

1881:   Sir Dudley Coutts Marjoriebanks was granted the peerage Baron Tweedmouth and became the first Lord Tweedmouth. Honourable Archie Marjoriebanks took the first Golden Retriever to the American Continent.

1883:   Colonel Le Poer Trench had his first yellow retriever Sandy, bred by the 5th Earl of Ilchester, on whom he founded his St Huberts strain.

1890:   Lord Tweedmouth's stud book entry records end.

1891:   First Crufts held.

1894:   Lord Tweedmouth died. The Guisachan estate passed to his son Edward.

1904:   Earliest traceable entry in The Kennel Club's Stud Book of a dog with possible Golden ancestry to win at a trial, Don of Gerwyn, born in 1899. He was owned by a Mr A T Williams. He won the International Gundog League Open Retriever Stake. His sire was Lord Tweedmouth's 'Golden Flatcoat', Lucifer.

1905:   The Guisachan estate, the Scottish seat of Lord Tweedmouth, was sold to the Earl of Portsmouth. The gundogs on the estate were sold with the house. Lord Harcourt (Culham) was believed to have started his kennel with stock from the Earl of Portsmouth.

1906:   Maud Earl painted an Ilchester retriever and an early Russian retriever. Mrs Charlesworth's first Golden Retriever, Normanby Beauty of unknown pedigree, was born in April.

1908:   The first Golden Retrievers were exhibited by Lord Harcourt (Culham). Records show that they were listed as Flat Coated Retrievers and defined by colour as it was prior to the breed's Kennel Club recognition. This was the first year classes were scheduled at Crufts under the Flat Coat Retriever breed (as above). Mrs Charlesworth's kennel was founded. Her affix was originally Normanby and later became Noranby following the disqualification of her dog CC winner at Crufts in 1914 due to an incorrect spelling on her entry. In some of her advertisements, Noraby was also used!

1909:   Mrs Charlesworth acquired Normanby Beauty and began to show her Golden Retrievers with the help of Parson Upcher from Norfolk. Retrievers and some other gundogs born after 1 June could only gain their Champion title by winning three CCs under three different judges but also a prize or Certificate of Merit at a Kennel Club-recognised Field Trial. Dogs with two or more CCs were also allowed to run at such trials 'not for competition' with the sole purpose of obtaining a certificate (no entry fee was required if dogs were entered NFC). One class for Golden Retrievers was scheduled at Crufts. It was Open Dog or Bitch and listed under Any Varieties. The second Lord Tweedmouth died.

1910:   The first separate class for the breed was first scheduled at Crufts – Open Dog or Bitch. Culham Copper, born 1908 (Culham Brass ex Culham Rossa), bred and owned by Viscount Harcourt, was the first of the breed to win a Best of Breed at Crufts.

1911:   Culham Copper won a First at Crufts which entitled him to an entry in The Kennel Club's Stud Book.

1912:   The breed's first champion, Noranby Campfire (Culham Copper ex Normanby Beauty) was born. He was bred and owned by Mrs W M Charlesworth. Russian Yellow Retrievers had separate classes at Crufts for the first time following the drawing up of a breed standard and inclusion on The Kennel Club's breed register. Captain H Hardy (Aucheneycheyne) was the first Golden Retriever owner to win in Open competition at a trial with a recognised breed specimen.

1913:   Standard of Points (the original breed standard) was drawn up by breeders. The Kennel Club gave a separate register for Golden Retrievers under the name 'Retrievers Golden, Yellow'. The Golden Retriever Club made application to The Kennel Club for the club's registration. Challenge Certificates were offered for the breed for the first time. The first set of CCs solely offered for the breed was at Manchester Championship Show. They were won by:

Dog CC   Normanby Sandy (born 1910)
           (Sandy of Wavertree ex Yellow Nell)
           Bred by Mr W H Hall, owned by Mrs W M Charlesworth and Lt Col Hendley

Bitch CC   Coquette (born 1910)
           (Sable – unregistered ex Ruby – unregistered)
           Bred by Miss Hardcastle, owned by Mr F W Herbert

One of Colonel Le Poer Trench's St Huberts Retrievers is listed in The Kennel Club Stud Book. Blofield Rufus was the first male Golden Retriever listed in The Kennel Club Stud Book who was awarded a Certificate of Merit at the Eastern

Counties Retriever Society's Trial. His breeding was Ingestre Dred ex Folda. Mrs Charlesworth first exhibited her Goldens at Crufts. One set of CCs was offered jointly for Retrievers Golden, Yellow and Retrievers Russian Yellow at Crufts.

1914: Vixie, owned by Captain Hardy (Aucheneycheyne), was the first female Golden Retriever to win in a trial. She was placed second in the Gamekeepers National Association Trial. Field trials stopped during the First World War and only resumed in 1920. Breeding was only permissible during 1914–1918 under Kennel Club licence.

1915: Retrievers Golden, Yellow and Retrievers Russian Yellow had CCs for each breed. Gosmore Kestrel, originally registered Normanby Birdie (Klip ex Gosmore Birdie, born 1913), owned by Miss Crawshaw, was the first Golden to win three CCs. He was not credited with the Champion title as he did not have a working qualification and Show Champion titles were only permitted by The Kennel Club from 1958 onwards.

1917: Last entry in The Kennel Club's Stud Book for a Retriever (Russian Yellow) of the St Huberts affix.

1918 First Golden Retriever kennel in North America was formed (Canada) but the Gilnockie name was not registered until 1922 by Burt Armstrong.

1919: The Guisachan estate was put up for auction but remained unsold for 16 years. From the late 1930s it remained unused and now stands in ruin. The breed's

Ch Noranby Dutiful, the first Golden Retriever to win an all-breed competition.
Photo: Ralph Robinson of Redhill

Ch Noranby Diane, dam of Dutiful and Deidre. Photo: Ralph Robinson of Redhill

	first Dual Champion was born – Balcombe Boy (Culham Tip ex Culham Amber II). He was bred by Lord Harcourt and owned by Mr R Hermon.
1920:	The term 'Yellow' was dropped and the current designation of Retrievers (Golden) was adopted by The Kennel Club. The breed's first bitch champion was born – Bess of Kentford (Rufus of Kentford ex Snettisham Lady). She was bred by Mr A Meek and owned by the Honourable Mrs E D Grigg (Kentford). Colonel Le Poer Trench died.
1921:	The Golden Retriever Club ran its first Field Trial Stake. Noranby Campfire made his Field Trial début aged 9 years (see 1912) and was the breed's first champion.
1922:	The breed's first Field Trial Champion (excluding Balcombe Boy who achieved Dual Champion Title) was born – Eredine Rufus (Wonham Peter ex Wonham Dinah) bred by Lady Norton Griffith. Originally he was owned by a Mr H Scott and afterwards by the Honourable Mrs E D Grigg. Balcombe Boy won both his bench and field titles to become the breed's first Dual Champion.
1923:	The Golden Retriever Club produced its first year book.
1924:	Eredine Rufus won his Field Trial Champion title (see 1922).
1925:	First Irish KC breed registrations were recorded.
1927:	Golden Retrievers were first recognised as a breed by the Canadian KC at about this time, although there is evidence to suggest that breed specimens existed in the country much earlier.
1928:	The Kennel Club included a rule to permit a dog to run for a qualifier at a

recognised Field Trial to obtain its Champion Title if it had won a minimum of one CC and had not managed a Certificate of Merit or more at a trial. Foxbury Peter became the first Canadian Champion.

1932: Mrs Charlesworth's Book of the Golden Retriever was published. Golden Retrievers were first recognised as a breed by the American KC at about this time.

1933: Goldens were first shown in Holland. Speedwell Pluto (UK import) became the first Golden Retriever to gain his bench title in the USA and did the same in 1934 in Canada.

1934: Guide Dogs for the Blind Association was founded.

1935: Ch Noranby Dutiful (Ch Heydown Grip ex Noranby Diane), owned and bred by Mrs Charlesworth, was the first Golden Retriever to win an all-breed competition by going Best Gundog at the South Durham show in June.

1936: The breed standard was amended twice to include ideal weights and heights of males and females. This followed enquiries made several years earlier by Mrs Armstrong (Gilnockie) in America to Mrs Charlesworth for advice about their standard.

1937: The first Field Trial was held in the USA. FT Ch Haulstone Larry (born 1934, Haulstone Lark ex Haulstone Gipsy), owned and bred by Mr J Eccles, was the first Golden ever to win the IGL Retriever Championships. He was only three generations on from an interbred litter sired by a yellow Labrador, FT Ch Haylers Defender.

1938: Kennel Club Junior Warrant (JW) was introduced on 1 January for dogs aged 6–18 months of age obtaining 25 points in breed classes. Championship shows first prize = 3 points. Open shows first prize = 1 point (and Championship show first prizes where CCs were not on offer). Had to be applied for, as today.

1939: Dorcas Bruin, born 25.3.37 (Ch Davie of Yelme ex Sally of Perrott), bred and owned by Mrs E Stonex, was the first Golden Retriever and gundog (excluding Cocker Spaniels) to win a Kennel Club Junior Warrant. GRC of America was incorporated

1940: GRC of America held its first licensed trial.

1940–45: No title holders in the bench or field were created during these years as Championship shows and Field Trials were not permitted following the outbreak of the Second World War. Only sanction shows with a 25-mile entry catchment radius were allowed.

1946: The Golden Retriever Club of Scotland, the Northern Golden Retriever Association and the United Retriever Club were founded. Championship Breed Club shows were permitted following the end of the Second World War.

1947: General Championship shows and Field Trials were resumed after the end of the Second World War. The first post-war Champion bitch was Noranby Destiny (b. 1943, Bristle of Tone ex Noranby Dumpling) who was bred and owned by Mrs Charlesworth. She went on later to gain her Dual Champion title. Ch Torrdale Happy Lad, born in 1945 (Torrdale Sandy Boy ex Ch Dukeries Dancing Lady), became the first post-war Champion dog. In the same year at Peterborough he also became the first Golden Retriever to achieve a Best In

Show award at a general Championship show. He was bred and owned by Mrs I M Parsons. The Northern GRA held its first Field Trial.

1948: The first post-war Field Trial Champion was Stubblesdown Golden Lass born in 1944 (Stubbings Golden Garry ex Stubbings Golden Olympia), bred by Mr F D Jessamy and owned by Mr W E Hickmott. The GRC of Scotland held its first Field Trial.

1949: FT Ch Stubblesdown Golden Lass became the first post-war Dual Champion. The URC held its first Field Trial at 'Ingestre', the estate of the Earl of Shrewsbury and Waterford where his keeper, Mr MacDonald, bred the Ingestre Goldens.

1952: Retrievers (Golden) were officially recognised by The Kennel Club as a British breed. The Northern GRA held its first Championship Show. Mrs Charlesworth's new book about Golden Retrievers was published. FT Ch Treunair Cala, born in 1948 (Treunair Ciabhach or Treunair Lunga ex Gay Vandra), became the first unquestionably pure-bred Golden to win the IGL Retriever Championship. He gained his title in five days. He was bred, owned and handled by Miss E J C Train who later became known as Mrs Jean Lumsden.

1953: Mrs Stonex's book *The Golden Retriever* was first published. The All Ireland GRC was founded.

1954: Mrs Charlesworth died. Mrs June Atkinson won the IGL Retriever Championship with her FT Ch Mazurka of Wynford born in 1952 (FT Ch Westhyde Stubblesdown Major ex FT Ch Musicmaker of Yeo), who was also bred and handled by her.

1956: The breed's first Obedience Champion and holder of Working Trial qualifications, Castelnau Pizzicato CDex UDex WDex, was born (Ch Camrose Fantango ex Castelnau Concerto). He was bred by Miss M Baker and owned and trained by Mrs K Needs. He obtained his title in about 1960 and distinguished himself by winning the Crufts Obedience Championship (Dogs). GRC of Nederlands was formed.

1957: The All Ireland GRC was disbanded.

1958: Show Champion title introduced in the United Kingdom for certain breeds including the Golden Retriever. The Golden Retriever of America Club abandoned the British breed standard for one of its own formulation.

1959: In the USA, the true facts and origins of the breed as presented by Mrs Stonex and the 6th Lord Ilchester (Lord Tweedmouth's nephew) were officially recognised by their Kennel Club. The first Canadian breed club, GRC of Ontario, was formed.

1960: In Britain the true facts and origins of the breed as presented by Mrs Stonex and the sixth Lord Ilchester were officially recognised by The Kennel Club. GRC of Ontario ran its first trials.

1961: Sh Ch Danespark Angela, born 1956 (Danespark Gorse ex Danespark Linda), was the first Golden to be placed runner-up in the Gundog Group at Crufts. She was bred and owned by Mr F Dadd.

1962: The All Ireland GRC was re-established.

1963:   The GRC celebrated its 50th Anniversary. The URC held its first Championship show.

1964:   The first Obedience Champion bitch was born – Nana of Bournemouth (Sh Ch Anbria Tantalus ex Duchess of Wykeham). She was bred by Dr I Hadfield and owned and handled by Mr R J Knight. She was line bred to Ch Camrose Fantango, as was the first male Obedience Champion. She obtained her title in about 1970. The first Golden Retriever Club was founded in Australia – the GRC of New South Wales.

1965:   Sh Ch Gainspa Florette of Shiremoor, born in 1961 (Drofserla Chancery ex Gainspa Glamour), became the first Golden Retriever and only bitch in the breed to win the Gundog Group at Crufts. She was bred by Mrs E Metcalfe and owned by Mr J Raymond.

1966:   The All Ireland GRC held its first Championship show in conjunction with the Athy All Breed Championship show.

1967:   The Crufts qualification was introduced by The Kennel Club. Previously, entry had been open to all. The qualification has been amended several times to date.

1968:   The GRC of Wales was founded.

1969:   The Ulster GRC was founded. HM Queen Elizabeth II visited the Golden Retriever ring at Crufts.

1970:   The breed became officially recognised by The Kennel Club as a Scottish breed.

1971:   The Ulster GRC held its first Field Trial. The Welsh GRC held its first Championship show.

1973:   The South West GRC was founded. Initially membership was restricted to those living in their designated counties. This was rescinded later and application for membership made open to all. Breeding of Dogs Act.

1976:   The Midland GRC was founded.

1977:   The Ulster GRC held its first Championship show.

1978:   The Eastern Counties GRC, the GRC of Northumbria, the Southern GRS and the Berkshire Downs and Chilterns GRC were founded. The Midland GRC and the South West GRC held their first Championship shows.

1979:   Ch Brensham Audacity, born in 1976 (Ch Stolford Happy Lad ex Moonswell Dora of Brensham), bred and owned by Mrs M Wood, became the second Golden Retriever and first dog to win the Gundog Group at Crufts to date. He did not have his title at the time. The first Interclub Working Test took place.

1980:   The Eastern, Northumbrian and Southern breed clubs all held their first Championship shows. The first Golden Retriever Breed Clubs' Conference took place.

1981:   The Berkshire Downs and Chilterns GRC held its first Championship show. Eastern Counties GRC held its first Field Trial. Ch Styal Stefanie of Camrose, born 1973, became the breed record holder after winning her 27th CC. Her sire, Ch Camrose Cabus Christopher, was also a breed record holder with 41 CCs until 1986. Her dam was Ch Styal Sibella. Breeder: Mrs H Hinks, owners: Mrs J Tudor and Miss R Wilcock.

1982:	Mr Robert Atkinson, son of June, won the IGL Retriever Championship with his FT Ch Little Marston Chorus of Holway, born in 1978 (FT Ch Holway Chanter ex Belway Dove). She was bred by Mr M Dare but owned and handled by Robert Atkinson. The North West GRC was founded.
1985:	The GRC of Northumbria held its first Field Trial.
1986:	Ch Styal Scott of Glengilde, born 1978 (Ch Nortonwood Faunus ex Styal Susila – sister to the bitch breed record holder) became the current breed record holder after winning his 42nd CC. North West GRC held its Championship show. The Breed Standard was reviewed in 1985 and revised and standardised by The Kennel Club in this year.
1987:	The Yorkshire GRC was founded.
1989:	The South West GRC held its first Field Trial.
1990:	The Kennel Club revised the age range that a JW could be won from 6–18 months to 12–18 months.
1991:	The Golden Retriever Breed Clubs' Conference was disbanded.
1992:	The Yorkshire GRC held its first Championship show. The GRC was de-registered by the Kennel Club.
1993:	The Ulster GRC celebrated its 25th anniversary. The Golden Retriever Breed Council was approved and registered by The Kennel Club.
1994:	Another full revision of the Breed Standards was undertaken by The Kennel Club.
1995:	The GRC was re-registered by The Kennel Club and granted licences to hold Field Trials and Open shows but not a Championship show.
1996:	The GRC of Scotland, Northern GRA and URC all celebrated their 50th anniversaries. Belgium GRC was formed.
1996–7:	The GRC of Northumbria and Yorkshire GRC had their Championship status removed by The Kennel Club, following a CC-reduction for the breed for two years, but regained the status from 1998. 1997: The Kennel Club revised the age range (back to 6-18 months) and criteria for JWs for the second time (see Chapter 8).
1998:	Berkshire Downs and Chilterns GRC and the North West GRC had their Championship status removed by The Kennel Club following its decision to allow a maximum of 40 sets per breed, but regained the status from 1999. The SWGRC celebrated its 25th anniversary.
1999:	Eastern Counties GRC had their Championship status removed by The Kennel Club for one year only, for the reasons given above. The removal only affected one club as The Kennel Club increased the sets of CCs available to a maximum of 41 for our breed. The Southern GRC held their first field trial.
2000:	The GRC had their Championship status reinstated by The Kennel Club and all other Golden Retriever breed clubs were granted a set of CCs but the NWGRC subsequently had theirs withdrawn. A Pet Passport Pilot Scheme was launched. Breeding and Sale of Dogs (Welfare) Act of 1999 came into force.
2001:	NWGRC had their CCs reinstated.

CHAPTER FOURTEEN

Statistics of the Breed

(From information and records available)

United Kingdom Breed Registrations

Year	No. of registrations	
1912	18	First year KC has registration data for the breed.
1913	73	
1914	58)	
1915	36)	
1916	32)	First World War.
1917	14)	
1918	2)	
1920	58	
1921	120	
1925	375	
1930	563	
1935	961	
1938	1073	
1939	704)	
1940	178)	
1941	170)	
1942	278)	Second World War.
1943	562)	
1944	890)	
1945	1,385)	
1947	2,652	
1950	2,414)	1952–1954 and in 1956 registrations were under 2,000.
1955	2,090)	
1960	2,551	
1965	3,323	
1970	5,189	
1975	5,950	
1980	10,274	
1985	11,451	Fourth largest breed registered.
1990	15,983	Sixth largest breed registered.
1995	15,925	Third largest breed registered. 314 exports to 35 different countries, mainly Belgium, Denmark, France, Germany, Italy, Holland, Spain and the United States.

Litter Analysis 1987

Puppies recorded: 18,586
Litters recorded: 2,824
Average size: 6.6
Puppies registered: 9,842 (53%)
The reason why the number of puppies recorded and registered differs is because it was unnecessary for breeders to register all puppies in a litter individually under The Kennel Club's registration's procedure in operation at the time. Breeders only had to register a litter, and then individual puppies as required. This procedure was subsequently revised.

Crufts Golden Retriever Breed Class Entries

(excludes Gamekeeper's Association Classes)

Year	No. of entries	
1908	8	Entry open to all. Golden Retrievers were entered under the Flat Coated Retriever breed but defined by colour.
1909	8	One class for the breed was scheduled under the Any Varieties.
1910	10	One Breed class was scheduled: Open Dog/Bitch.
1911	9	
1912	11	Russian Yellow Retriever entry = 15. Also included three of the Golden Retrievers! This was the first year they had a separate classification.
1913	50 (5 classes)	Russian Yellow Retriever entry = 15. One set of CCs was available between the Russian Yellow Retrievers and Retrievers, Golden Yellow. They were won by Col Le Poer Trench's Russian Yellow Retrievers.
1914	78 (6 classes)	Russian Yellow Retriever entry = 9. All belonged to Col Le Poer Trench except one dog, Farnborough Duke, that was from his St Huberts breeding. The CC arrangements were the same as for 1913 but on this occasion they were won by Retrievers, Golden Yellow.
		Dog CC disqualified; not awarded as Noranby Cadmium had been entered incorrectly as Normanby Cadmium by his owner Mr Hordern.
		Bitch CC, Top Twig owned by Mr D MacDonald and bred by Mr H Hall (would have become a Show Champion under current Kennel Club Rules).
1915	70	Russian Yellow Retriever entry = 15. Separate CCs were offered for both the Retriever, Golden Yellow and the Russian Yellow Retriever. No further classes were scheduled for the Russian Yellow Retriever from 1915 onwards.
1916	44	
1917	26	

1918–1920		No shows held.
1921	45	
1925	231	
1927	263	Highest pre-Second World War entry.
1930	232	
1935	215	
1939	251	
1940–1947		No shows held.
1948 (Oct)	259	
1950	448	The show was cancelled in 1954 due to industrial action. Previously only the LKA in 1926 had to be abandoned in the year of the General Strike.
1955	349	My figure based on class numbers (Crufts catalogue index states 356).
1960	435	My figure based on class numbers (Crufts catalogue index states 437).
1965	492	My figure based on class numbers (Crufts catalogue index states 479).
1966	496	Last year entry was open to all.
1967	325	Entry by qualification only began.
1970	396	
1975	265	
1980	271	
1985	238	
1990	321	
1991	642	Crufts Centenary Year – record entry.
1995	535	
2000	633	In 1997 qualifications were extended to certain additional Championship award winners, and again in 1999 for the first time to include BIS and BPIS winners from general all breed open shows. RBIS winners were included from 2000.
	(22 classes)	

Crufts Group Winners

Two out of a possible 44 since group judging was introduced in 1957, none prior to this.

1965   Sh Ch Gainspa Florette Of Shiremoor. Born 30.1.61
            (Drofserla Chancery ex Gainspa Glamour)
            Bred by Mrs E J Metcalfe
            Owned by Mr J Raymond

1979   Ch Brensham Audacity. Born 16.3.76 *
            (Ch Stolford Happy Lad ex Moonswell Dora of Brensham)
            Bred and owned by Mrs M Wood
            *This was his first CC win; his title was gained later that year at WELKS.

Ch Brensham Audacity, winner of the Gundog Group in 1979.
Photo: Diane Pearce

Ch Coombstock Disco Dancer, runner up in the Gundog Group 1988.

Sh Ch Tulliallan Bradley, Group 4 winner in 1997.
Photo: Kipps

Crufts Reserve Group Winners (Group 2)

1961   Sh Ch Danespark Angela. Born 20.11.56
(Danespark Gorse ex Danespark Linda)
Bred and owned by Mr F Dadd

1974   Sh Ch Gainspa Fanfare. Born 31.12.68
(Ch Cabus Boltby Combine ex Sh Ch Gainspa Oonah)
Bred by Mrs E J Metcalfe
Owned by Mrs E Anderson

1988   Ch Coombstock Disco Dancer. Born 29.3.83
(Ch Okus Buccaneer ex Coombstock Fashion)
Bred and owned by Mrs J Newton

Group 4 Winner (Group 3 and 4 places were introduced in 1995)

1997   Sh Ch Tulliallan Bradley. Born 3.3.93
(Linavon Inxs ex Tulliallan Amber Rose)
Bred and owned by Mr and Mrs B Wilkinson
This was his first CC win. He gained his title later that year at the SKC (May).

Miss Joan Gill pictured with her Ch Simon of Westley, aged 9½ years. Five times winner of the Gold Challenge Trophy.

Other Crufts Records
Bench Section
First Golden and bitch to win three CCs in 1922, 1924 and 1925
Ch Noranby Daydawn. Born 12.6.21
(Dual Ch Balcombe Boy ex Noranby Daybreak)
Bred and owned by Mrs W M Charlesworth

First dog to win three CCs in 1929, 1931 and 1933
Ch Michael Of Moreton. Born 10.2.25
(Rory of Bentley ex Aurora)
Bred by Mr H Jenner
Owner Mr R Kirk

First Golden to win more than one CC in consecutive years, in 1916 and 1917
Ch Noranby Campfire. Born 24.7.12
(Culham Copper ex Normanby Beauty)
Bred and owned by Mrs W M Charlesworth

Gold Challenge Trophy Winner (five times)
(for best dog or bitch having an award at a field trial held under Kennel Club Rules)
Ch Simon Of Westley. Born 23.4.53
(Ch Camrose Fantango ex Westley Frolic of Yelme)
Bred and owned by Miss Joan Gill
(Miss Gill has won the trophy 11 times in all. Her other winners were: Ch Susan of Westley, Ch Camrose Nicholas of Westley, Ch Pippa of Westley, Ch Westley Jacquetta.)

Crufts Obedience Championships
See Obedience Section on page 273.

Table of United Kingdom Breed Champion Title Holders

	1913–1939	1946–1985	1986–1999	Totals
Champions	70	194	55	319
Sh Champions	14*	153#	150	317
FT Champions	9	46‡	23 ‡	78
Ob Champions	0	5	4	9
Dual Champions	2	3	0	5
Totals	**95**	**401**	**232**	**728**

633 post-Second World War

* All won their CCs before the title was introduced in 1958

\# Twenty won their CCs before 1958

‡ There has been an average of just over one FT Champion made up per year since the Second World War, despite an increase in trials. This is due mainly to an increase in runners trying to obtain a place in trials.

United Kingdom Dual Champions from 1900

1st   Balcombe Boy   Dog born 8.3.1919
            (Culham Tip ex Culham Amber II)
            Bred by Lord Harcourt (Culham)
            Owned by Captain R Herman

2nd   Anningsley Stingo   Dog born 30.6.33
            (Ch Heydown Grip ex Anningsley Ann)
            Bred and owned by Mr H Venables-Kyrke

3rd   Stubblesdown Golden Lass   Bitch born 24.12.44
            (Stubbings Golden Garry ex Stubbings Golden Olympia)
            Bred by Mr F D Jessamy (Braconlea)
            Owned by Mr W E Hickmott

4th   Noranby Destiny   Bitch born 19.11.43
            (Bristle of Tone ex Noranby Dumpling)
            Bred and owned by Mrs W M Charlesworth
            (Grand-daughter of Anningsley Stingo and great-great-granddaughter of Balcombe Boy)

5th   David Of Westley   Dog born 6.6.51
            (Also became an Irish Dual Champion and known as an International Dual Champion)
            (Ch Dorcas Glorious of Slat ex Ch Susan of Westley)
            Bred by Miss J Gill
            Owned by Miss L Ross
            (Great-grandson of Anningsley Stingo)

IGL (International Gundog League) Retriever Championship Winners

1937   FT Ch Haulstone Larry   Dog born 15.9.34
            (Haulstone Lark ex Haulstone Gipsy)
            Bred and owned by Mr J Eccles

1952   FT Ch Treunair Cala   Bitch born 11.12.48
            (Treunair Ciabhach or Treunair Lunga ex Gay Vandra)
            Bred and owned by Miss E J C Train (later Lumsden)

1954   FT Ch Mazurka Of Wynford   Dog born 29.4.52
            (FT Ch Westhyde Stubblesdown Major ex FT Ch Musicmaker of Yeo)
            Bred and owned by Mrs J Atkinson

1982   FT Ch Little Marston Chorus Of Holway   Dog born 9.8.78
(FT Ch Holway Chanter ex Belway Dove)
Bred by Mr M Dare
Owned by Mr R Atkinson

United Kingdom Dual Purpose Kennels and Winners

To be included in this table, the kennel and/or owner has bred or owned Champions in both the show and working spectrums. I have defined working to include Obedience as well as field trials. It does not include what might be classified as the more modern aspects of competitive work, such as agility and flyball which do not yet have championship status.

Affix	Name	Title Holder Categories
Amirene*	Mrs M I Woods	Dual Ch (France/Int), Sh Ch
Anningsley	Mr and Mrs H Venables-Kyrke	Dual Ch and Ch
Balcombe	Captain R O Herman	Dual Ch and Ch
Braconlea	Mr F D Jessamy	Dual Ch and Ch
Buidhe	Miss L Ross	Dual Ch and Ch
Castelnau	Miss M Baker	Ob Ch and Ch
Catcombe*	Mr and Mrs D Andrews	FT Ch and Ch
Haulstone	Mr J Eccles	FT Ch and Ch
Holway*	Mrs J Atkinson	FT Ch and Ch (Belgium)

FT Ch Holway Quilla (Mrs J Atkinson) – the last Holway champion to be made up (see page 269).

Kentford	Hon. Mrs R M Grigg	FT Ch, Ch and Dual Ch (India)
Melfricka*	Mr F L and Mrs M E Hathaway	Ob Ch and Sh Ch
Noranby	Mrs W M Charlesworth	Dual Ch and Ch
Standerwick*	Mrs D Philpott and Miss J Gill	FT Ch and Ch
Stubblesdown	Mr W E Hickmott	Dual Ch, FT Ch and Ch
Trewater	Miss J Clark	Ch and FT Ch (Finland)
Westhyde	Mr and Mrs P Fraser	FT Ch and Ch
Westley*	Miss J Gill and Mr and Mrs M Philpott	Dual Ch, FT Ch, Ch and Sh Ch
Wilderness	Captain Sir G Bowyer	FT Ch and Ch
Yeo*	Mrs L Sawtell	FT Ch, Ch and Sh Ch
No Affix (1920s)	Messrs Collins and Cowell	Dual Ch (India) and Ch

*Kennels which have had a title holder made up since 1986. This table does not imply that these are the only kennels that have worked and shown their Goldens. Many other kennels throughout the 20th century have had dual-purpose Goldens but have not quite managed the highest accolade of champion in a particular aspect.

United Kingdom Breed Record Holders
Working – Field Trials
Top kennel/breeder
Holway, Mrs J and Mr R Atkinson and Mrs J Mann (photo on opposite page)
Record held since 1959 with 28 UK title holders (+3 overseas)

Fastest winner of title in 4 days (19.10.96 and 21-22.10.96)
FT Ch Tillwood Theseus Of Holywear
Dog born 13.6.89
(Willowric Andy ex Monkcastle Tessa)
Bred by Mrs Calder
Owned by Mr and Mrs G Hay

Youngest title holder (in about 27 months)
FT Ch Westhyde Stubblesdown Major
Dog born 1.5.50
(Stubblesdown Riot ex FT Ch/Ch Stubblesdown Golden Lass)
Bred by Mr W Hickmott
Owned by Mrs J M Fraser

FT Ch Tillwood Theseus of Holywear.

3 generations of champions.
(l-r) Ch Westley Jacquetta; her daughter Ch Westley Victoria; Victoria's daughters, Ch Westley Martha (sitting) and Ch Westley Mabella (laying down). Photo: Bart van Maren

Showing
Top kennel/breeder
Westley/Standerwick, Miss J Gill, Mr M Philpott and the late Mrs D Philpott with 37 title holders (Westley = 31, Standerwick =6)

Styal, Mrs Hinks' kennel has also bred both dog and bitch CC record holders (see below)

Top Sire
Ch Camrose Cabus Christopher
Born 17.9.68
(Ch Camrose Tallyrand of Anbria ex Cabus Boltby Charmer)
Bred by Mrs Z Morgan (formerly Moriarty)
Owned by Mrs J Tudor
Former record holder with 41 CCs

Top Dam
Ch Westley Victora
Born 24.7.73
(Ch Sansue Camrose Phoenix ex
Ch Westley Jacquetta)
Bred by Miss J Gill and Mrs D
Philpott
Owned by Mr M Philpott

Top Dog and breed CC Winner
Ch Styal Scott Of Glengilde
Born 28.11.78
(Ch Nortonwood Faunus ex Ch
Styal Susila)
Bred by Mrs H Hinks
Owned by Mr and Mrs R Scholes
Held 42 CCs in 1986

Ch Camrose Cabus Christopher, top sire and former
breed record holder.

Ch Styal Scott Of Glengilde. Photo: David Dalton

Top Bitch CC Winner
Ch Styal Stefanie Of Camrose
Born 6.7.73
(Ch Camrose Cabus Christopher ex Ch Styal Sibella)
Bred by Mrs H Hinks
Owned by Mrs J Tudor and Miss R Wilcock
Held 27 CCs in 1981

Fastest Bench Title Holder (in 8 days)
Sh Ch Weirston Witop Class Of Carastene
Dog born 19.6.91
(Amirene Jamie of Carastene ex Loopy Lucy of Weirston)
Bred by Mrs S Hay
Owned by Mrs I MacKenzie

Ch Styal Stefanie Of Camrose. Photo: Diane Pearce

Youngest Show Champion Bench Title Holder (at 16 months)
Ch Alresford Advertiser
Dog born 15.4.51
(Ch Alexander of Elsiville ex Ch Alresford Mall)
Bred and owned by Mrs L Pilkington
Gained his full Champion title later

Youngest Full Champion Bench Title Holder (at 2 years, 2 months, 2 days)
Ch Okus Buccanneer
Dog born 22.4.80
(Ch Moorquest Mugwump ex Saffron Dawn of Okus)
Bred and owned by Mrs C A Gilbert

Sh Ch Weirston Witop Class of Carastene.

Fastest Junior Warrant Winner (in under 2 days at two consecutive Championship shows in 1993) and youngest Junior Warrant Winner (second system) at 1 year and 22 days)
Ch Millgreen Magnum
Dog born 20.11.92
(Sh Ch Tokeida Starstealer ex Catcombe Cher at Millgreen)
Bred by Mr and Mrs D Barnes
Owned by Mr and Mrs R Rains

Ch Alresford Advertiser.

Youngest Junior Warrant Winner (at 7.5 months, first system)
Sh Ch Lacons Enterprise
Dog born 26.1.74
(Ch Camrose Cabus Christopher ex Lacons Annaliesa)
Bred and owned by Mr J W Simister

Ch Millgreen Magnum.

Obedience

The breed has only had nine UK Obedience Champions, so there are fewer achievements to determine breed record holders in this field of work. All nine have been bred and owned by different people and from different stock. The only common factor to link them are that four of the stud dogs were related, three being descendants of Ch Camrose Fantango, and two of the stud dogs were bred by Mrs Barron (Anbria).

First male Golden to win Crufts Dog Obedience Championships, in 1959
Ob Ch Castelnau Pizzicato CDex UDex WDex
Born 23.1.56
(Ch Camrose Fantango ex Castelnau Concerto)
Bred by Miss M Baker
Owned by Mrs K Needs

Only other winner of the Crufts Obedience Championships (Dog), in 1973
Ob Ch Golden Gift CDex
Dog born 6.5.64
(Ch Camrose Tallyrand of Anbria ex Linsun Sharon)
Bred by Mr and Mrs Booth
Owned by Mr John W Burdett

Fastest and First Bitch Title Holder (in about 20 months)
Ob Ch Nana Of Bournemouth. Born 1.7.64
(Sh Ch Anbria Tantalus ex Duchess of Wykeham [Fantango daughter])
Bred by Dr I Hadfield
Owned by Mr Robert Knight

Ob Ch Golden Gift CDex.
Photographer unknown.

Youngest, First Dog, First Breed Title Holder and First with Working Trial Qualifications (3 years 15 days)
Ob Ch Castelnau Pizzicato CDex UDex WDex
See above for further details

Top Obedience CC winner (5 CCs)
Ob Ch Kingsey Golden Lass
Bitch born 9.9.81
(Temevale Foxtrot of Empshott ex Empshott Birthday Maid)
Bred by Mrs J Benham-Crosswell
Owned by Mrs Viv White

Obedience Champion Kingsey Golden Lass.

Working Trials

A number of Goldens have competed in this field of work and have been awarded Working Trial qualifications but only ten have qualified TDex. However none of these have won the required two Firsts in the TD stake at Championship Working Trials so, to date, the breed has no Working Trial Champions.

First Obedience Champion to achieve Working Trial Qualifications
Ob Ch Castelnau Pizzicato CDex UDex WDex. Dog born 23.1.56
(Ch Camrose Fantango ex Castelnau Concerto)
Bred by Miss M Baker
Owned by Mrs K Needs

The only Obedience CC winner believed to hold a TDex qualification
Ob Ch Melnola Bramble CDex UDex WDex TDex. Dog born 13.6.89
(FT Ch Holway Corbiere ex Marshflight Curlew of Melnola)
Bred by Mr and Mrs J Parkinson
Owned by Mr Patrick Holden

Top Kennel/Breeder
Melnola, Mr J and Mrs P A Parkinson
Having bred three and owned one more of only ten Goldens ever to have qualified TDex:-
Melnola Bramble (see above)
Melnola Wild Rose (litter sister to Bramble). Bred and owned by Mr and Mrs J Parkinson.
Melnola Sweet Briar (1st bitch to gain TDex)
Taragindi Solitaire of Melnola

Holway, Mrs J Atkinson, Mr R Atkinson and Mrs J Manns
Bred one TDex winner, Holway Suspect (sired by a Holway bred dog), and bred and owned the sire of two others. (Suspect was brother to FT Ch Holway Corbiere and FT Ch Holway Crosa.)

Top Sire
FT Ch Holway Corbiere. Born 30.3.85
(FT Ch Holway Denier ex FT Ch Little Marston Chorus of Holway)
Bred by Mr R Atkinson
Owned by Mrs J Atkinson

Top Dam
Marshflight Curlew Of Melnola. Born 22.3.86
(Taragindi Solitaire of Melnola ex Lowgate Heather)
Bred by Mr K Morton
Owned by Mr and Mrs J Parkinson

Breed Record and Top Bitch TDex Holder (qualified on 10 occasions)
Melnola Wild Rose CDex UDex WDex TDex. Details as before.

Top Dog TDex Holder (qualified on six occasions)
Courtenay Trudeau CDex UDex WDex TDex
(Rebas Andronicas ex Colbar Jasmine at Courtenaye)
Bred by F Spence
Owned by Mrs D Thompson

Agility
Champion status is not yet awarded in this working activity which makes it difficult to provide information on top record holders, but Goldens do compete. One very special agility Golden male who was a big winner was:
Charles Harvest Sun. Born 21.6.84
(Noravon Troilus of Camrose ex Tanashlie Moonbeam)
Bred by Daphne Rogers
Owned by Mr Barrie Harvey

Charlie appeared in the Pedigree Chum Olympia Finals in 1987, 1989 and 1991; the Barbour Pairs Finals for two years; and in the Crufts winning agility team (Barking) in 1991, 1992 and again in 1993 when the team came second. He was a 'golden flyer' and achieved the best round time against the collies on several occasions. He was the first Golden ever to qualify for the finals in 1987.

**International Dual Ch David of Westley, winner of 24 FT awards, 4 CCs and 8 Green Stars.
From a picture by Louisa Nally painted before he won his titles.**

APPENDIX 1 - USEFUL ADDRESSES

The Kennel Club
1–5 Clarges Street
Piccadilly
London W1Y 8AB
Tel: 08706 066 750

The Scottish Kennel Club
3 Brunswick Place
Edinburgh EH7 5HP
Tel: 0131 665 3920

American Kennel Club
51 Madison Avenue
New York
NY10010
Tel: 212/696 8200
Fax: 212 696 8329

Fédération Cynologique Internationale
13 Place Albert I
B-6530
Thuin
Belgium
Tel: 0032 503 262 11820
Fax: 0032 503 262 2560

Pro-Dogs (Charity)
Rocky Bank
4 New Road
Ditton
Maidstone
Kent ME20 6AD
Tel: 01732 848499
(PAT Dogs, tel 01732 848 499)

Canine Concern
Smocks
Wellington
Somerset TA21 9PW

Blue Cross (Registered Charity)
Room 582
Shilton Road
Burford
Oxon OX18 4BR
Tel: 01993 822 651

Wood Green Animal Shelter (Charity)
London Road
Godmanchester
Huntingdon
Cambs PE29 2NH
Tel: 01480 830 014

Royal Society for the Prevention of Cruelty to Animals (RSPCA)
Causeway
Horsham
West Sussex RH12 1HG
Tel: 01403 264 181

National Canine Defence League (NCDL) (Charity)
Headquarters:
17 Wakley Street
London EC1V 7LT
Tel: 0207 837 0006
Fax: 0207 833 2701

Guide Dogs for the Blind Association
206 High Street
Bromley
Kent BR1 1PW
Tel: 0208 464 1433

Dogs for the Disabled (Charity)
The Old Vicarage
London Road
Ryton on Dunsmore
Coventry CV8 3ER
Tel: 01203 302 050

The Battersea Dogs Home
4 Battersea Park Road
Battersea
London SW8 4AA
Tel: 0207 627 9292

Hearing Dogs for the Deaf
London Road
Lewknor
Oxon OX9 5RY
Tel: 01844 353 898

National Dog Tattoo Register
PO Box 3389
Manningtree
Essex CO11 2LN
Tel: 01206 397 510

**Association of Private Pet
Cemetries & Crematoria**
Nun Close
Armathwaite
Carlisle
Cumbria
Tel: 01697 472 272

National Dog Warden Association
18 Poplar Grove
Southbank
Middlesborough TS6 6SY

**Ministry of Agriculture, Fisheries & Food
(MAFF) - Pet Travel Scheme**
Room 222
10 Whitehall Place
London SW1A 2HH
Tel: 0207 270 8095

British Small Animal Veterinary Association
Woodrow House
1 Telford Way
Waterwells Business Park
Quedgeley
Glos GL2 4AB
Tel: 01452 726 700

British Veterinary Association
7 Mansfield Street
London W1M OAT
Tel: 0207 636 6541
Fax: 0207 436 2970

Canine Epilepsy Support Group
Contact: Peter White
Tel: 01302 370 920

Royal College of Veterinary Surgeons
62-64 Horseferry Road
London SW1P 2AF
Tel: 0207 222 2001

**British Association of Homeopathic
Veterinary Surgeons**
Alternative Veterinary Medical Centre
Chinham House
Stanford in the Vale
Faringdon
Oxon SN7 8NQ
Tel: 01367 710 324
Fax: 01367 718 243

British Homeopathic Association
27A Devonshire Street
London W1N 1RJ
Tel: 0207 935 2163

Dog World Publications
Somerfield House
Wotton Road
Ashford
Kent TN23 6LW
Tel: 01233 621877
Fax: 01233 645 669

Our Dogs
5 Oxford Road
Station Approach
Manchester M60 1SX
Tel: 0161 236 5534
Fax: 0161 236 0892

APPENDIX 2 - CLUBS

UNITED KINGDOM

Berkshire Downs and Chilterns
Mr B Wicklow
Corton Kennels
Quakers Lane
Goatacre
Calne
Wilts SN11 9JG
Tel: 01249 760128

Eastern Counties Golden Retriever Club
Mrs B Webb
116 Cambridge Road
Great Shelford
Cambs CB2 5JJ
Tel: 01223 842358

Golden Retriever Breed Council
Mrs B Mills
Millwater
Laddingford
Maidstone
Kent ME18 6BX
Tel: 01622 871699

Golden Retriever Club
Gp Cpt R B Bridges
Durridge House
Kerswell Green
Kempsey
Worcs WR5 3EP
Tel: 01905 371315

Golden Retriever Club of Northumbria
Mrs A Byrne
16 Parklands
Hamsterley Mill
Rowlands Gill
Tyne and Wear NE39 1HH
Tel: 01207 544367

Midland Golden Retriever Club
Mrs F Stewart
Oakapple Cottage
Leigh
Nr Worcester WR6 5LE
Tel: 01886 832275

North West Golden Retriever Club
Mrs S Baldwin
Lofty Top
Werneth Low Road
Hyde
Cheshire SK14 3AA
Tel: 0161 3680310

Northern Golden Retriever Association
Mr S Spratt
Delmar
Lincoln Road
Boothby Graffoe
Lincoln LN5 0LB
Tel: 01522 811556

South Western Golden Retriever Club
Miss F Coward
Green Acres
Ibsley Drove
Ibsley
Hants BH24 3NP
Tel: 01425 653146

Southern Golden Retreiever Society
Mrs A Stephenson
Timberdown
33 Guildford Road
Lightwater
Surrey GU18 5RZ
Tel: 01276 473320

Yorkshire Golden Retriever Club
Mrs C Playle
79 Sands Lane
Holme upon Spalding Moor
York YO43 4HJ
Tel/fax: 01430 861994

Golden Retriever Club of Scotland
Mrs M Murray
Castle House
Ballinshoe
Kirriemuir DD8 5QF

Ulster Golden Retriever Club
Miss E Fearon
2 Cloverhill Glen
Bangor, Co. Down BT19 6XX
Northern Ireland
Tel: 02891 455513

All Ireland Golden Retriever Club
Mrs M Gaffney
Tyrol
Kenley Drive
Model Farm Road
Cork, Eire
Tel/fax: 021 4385101

Golden Retriever Club of Wales
Mrs J Morgan
19 Little Wind Street
Aberdare
Mid Glamorgan CF44 7EY
Tel: 01685 872044

OVERSEAS

Australia
The GRC of New South Wales Inc.
Hon Sec Russell Britten
60 Sunninghill Circuit
Mt Ousley
2519 New South Wales
Tel/fax: 02 4228 8527

The GRC of Queensland Inc.
Hon Sec Miss Sherry Downs
49 Cloverdale Road
Doolandella 4077
Tel: 07 3879 8941

The GRC of Southern Australia
Hon Sec Wendy Dunlop
9 Bruce Avenue
Mitchell Park
South Australia 5043
Tel: 08 8277 8645

The GRC of Victoria Inc
Hon Sec Carol Stafford
289 Old Warrandyte Road
North Ringwood
Victoria 3134
Tel: 03 9876 1920

The GRC of Western Australia
Hon Sec Mrs Jessica Brown
Lot 41 Passmore Street
Southern River
Western Australia
Tel/fax: 08 9497 1264

The Tasmanian GRC
Hon Sec Mrs D Hinchen
120 Molesworth Road
Molesworth
Tasmania 7140
Tel: 03 6261 1137

Belgium
Golden Retriever Club Belgie
Tel/fax: 052 42 41 42

Canada
The GRC of Canada
Hon Sec Pamela G Martin
PO Box 554
3286 Anne Street
Osgoode
Ontario KOA 2WO
Tel: 613 826 1709

(There are also 8 regional clubs.)

Denmark
Dansk Retriever Klub
Frougdegards Alle 4
5220 Odense 5Ø
Tel: 65 97 34 94

Finland
Kultainen Rengas – Golden Ring R.Y.
Hon Sec Heidi Lautjarvi
Vanhaistent 5 C 36
00420 Helsinki
Tel: 09 535 760

France
Retriever Club de France
8 Rue Jean Mermoz
75008 Paris
Tel: 01 4561 2100

Germany
Golden Retriever Club e.V.
Herr Heimut Fischer
Dopmeyer Strasse 19
D-31823 Springe
Tel: 05041 640 640

Deutscher Retriever Club e.V.
Frau Margitta Becker
Dornhagener Strasse 13
D-34302 Guxhagen
Tel: 05665 2774

Holland
Golden Retriever Club Nederland
Hon Sec Mrs M M G te Riele-Telling
Lijster 6
1713 S H Obdam
Tel: 0226 450 605

Italy
Retriever Club
Via San Fermo 4
27100 Pavia 1
Tel: 382 21255/377 69800

New Zealand
Golden Retriever Club
Hon Sec Glenys Barton
PO Box 35676
Browns Bay
Auckland 1310
Tel: 09 473 6610

Southern Golden Retriever Club
Hon Sec Linda Goffin
227 Lowes Road
Rolleston
Christchurch 8004
Tel: 03 347 8985

Central Golden Retriever Club
Hon Sec Mrs C Stevens
22 Rumgay Street
Lower Hutt 6009
Tel: 04 567 0891

Norway
Norsk Retriever Klubb
Hon Sec Nina Grundetjern
Postboks 3123
4392 Sandnes
Tel: 51 66 4092

South Africa
Golden Retriever Club of TVL
Hon Sec Mrs S Becker
PO Box 3992
Cramerview 2060
Tel: 011 463 8008

Spain
Club Espanal de Retrievers
c/o Simón Garcia 59-1°H
30003 Murcia
Tel: 968 309 887
Fax: 968 309 931

Sweden
Swedish Golden Retriever Club
Hon Sec Ulla Hägglund
Mälby
740 50 Alunda

Switzerland
Retriever Club Schweiz
Hon Sec Mrs Monique Rimensberger
Egetswilerstr 96
8302 Kloten
Tel: 1 803 1065

United States of America
Golden Retriever Club of America
Hon Sec Dianne F Barnes
PO Box 932
Bonner
MT 59823 0932

Club Relations Department: fax 212 696 8309

There are 45 other breed clubs in the various states. Details of these can be obtained from the American Kennel Club. (See page 277.)

APPENDIX 3 - BIBLIOGRAPHY

Adam, Linda (1998), *Old Wives and Dogs Tales*, Broadcast Books

Anderson, Lyn (1991), *Golden Retrievers,* Crowood Press

Bargh, Bernard (1993), *The Golden Retriever*, Ringpress Books

Bloomfield, Betty (1994), *Nursing & Handrearing Newborn Puppies*, Able Publishing

Cartledge, Joe and Liz, *The Dog Directory*, 5th ed., Angela Cavill

Charlesworth, Mrs W M (1952), *Golden Retriever*, Williams & Norgate Ltd

Fischer, Gertrude (1986), *The New Complete Golden Retriever*, 2nd ed., Howell Book House

Fogle, Dr Bruce (1996), *Golden Retrievers*, Dorling Kindersley Ltd

Foss, Valerie (1986), *The Golden Retriever Book of Champions*, Bernard Kayma

Foss, Valerie (1991), *The Golden Retriever Second Book of Champions*, Bernard Kayma

Foss, Valerie (1996), *The Golden Retriever Third Book of Champions*, Bernard Kayma

Foss, Valerie (1999), *The Golden Retriever Fourth Book of Champions*, Bernard Kayma

Gill, Joan (1965, reprinted 1978), *Golden Retrievers*, W & G Foyle Ltd

Hunter, Francis, DVM (1984), *Homoeopathic - First Aid Treatment for Pets*, Thorsons

Hutchinson, General W N (1928), *Dog Breaking*, John Murray

Lee, Laura and Martin (1992), *Absent Friends*, Henston

Macleod, George, MRCVS DVSM (1985), *Homoeopathy for Pets*, 3rd ed., Eagle Press

Miller, Mrs Hugh (1876), *Stories of the Dog and his Cousins*, T. Nelson & Sons

Morris, Desmond (1986), *Dog Watching*, Alden Press Ltd

O' Farrell, Valerie (1989), *Problem Dog*, Methuen

Sawtell, Lucille (revised 1978), *All about the Golden Retriever*, Pelham Books

Stonex, Elma (Reprinted 1987), *The Golden Retriever*, Golden Retriever Club (England)

Timson, Marigold (1989), *Golden Retrievers*, Salamander Books

Titterington, Albert (1987), *The Golden Retriever in Ireland*, Irish Hunting, Shooting, Fishing Magazine

Tudor, Joan (1968), *The Golden Retriever*, 2nd ed., Popular Dogs Publication

Walsh, J E (1994), *Golden Retrievers,*TFH Publications Inc

Wayre, Philip (1969), *A Guide to the Pheasants of the World*, Hamlyn Publishing

Book of the Bitch (1996), Henston Limited

Doglopaedia (1985), Henston Limited

Hutchinson's Dog Encyclopaedia (1930) Hutchinson & Co.

The Ageing Dog (1995), Henston Limited

The TV Vet Dog Book (1983), Farming Press Limited, 1983

APPENDIX 4 - GLOSSARY

Antibiotic	Used to prevent the further growth of or destroy bacteria.
Antihistamine	Used to combat the effect of histamine.
Antiseptic	Used to prevent the further growth of or destroy micro-organisms.
Atrophy	Reduction in the size of cells, fibres or tissues.
Back	Topline of the dog between the croup and withers.
Benign	Term used to describe non-cancerous tumours.
Brisket	The part of the dog's body between the forelegs and below the chest.
Brood bitch	Female with breeding potential.
Callous	Hardened piece of skin from which hair growth ceases.
Congenital	Condition which is present at birth.
Coupling	The length of the dog between the last rib and the pelvis.
Croup	Topline of the dog's body between the front of the pelvis and the tail joint.
Dew claw	Extra claw located near the carpus (wrist on foreleg) or below the hock.
ECG	A record produced of the heart's performance by an electro-cardiograph.
E-Coli	Bacterium present in the intestines.
Elbow	The joint between the forearm and the upper arm.
Epididymus	Duct that stores sperm from testicles until a dog is mated.
Feathering	Term used to describe the long hair on the back of the forearm, upper hindleg (above the hock) tail and beneath the brisket and tuck up.
Forearm	The foreleg bone between the elbow and the wrist.
Gun-shy	A dog that shows fear of guns and gunfire.
Haemorrhage	Escape of blood from blood vessels.
Hard mouth	Too firm a hold, resulting in damage to the game retrieved by the dog.
Hock	The tarsus joint between the bottom of the second thigh and the pastern.
Idiopathic	Of unknown cause.
Infectious	Micro-organisms producing diseases, not always contagious.
Malignant	Term used to describe cancerous growths (acute, capable of spreading and life threatening).
Occiput	Upper back point of skull.
Oestrus	There are 4 stages for a bitch: Pro-oestrus: about nine days of a bitch's season. Oestrus: roughly the next 9 days of a bitch's season when she will allow a dog to mate her. Ovulation occurs 2–3 days after the start of oestrus. Metoestrus: about 13 weeks. Occurs in the unmated bitch. Some bitches may show symptoms of a phantom pregnancy at the end of this stage.

	Anoestrus: period between metoestrus and the start of the bitch's next season. This stage can vary depending on the regularity of a bitch's season.
Pastern	The area between wrist and paw on the dog's foreleg and the area between the hock joint and paw on the hindleg.
Picking up	The retrieval of shot game by dogs and handlers hired for the purpose (not the guns and their dogs).
Point of shoulder	This is the point where the bottom of the dog's shoulder blade (scapular) and top of the upper arm (humerus) meet.
Prolapse	Outward displacement of an internal organ.
Second thigh	The lower thigh on the dog's hind leg, situated between the hock joint and stifle.
Short coupled	Term used in the Breed Standard to describe the correct length of the coupling.
Shoulder	The forequarter's blade. The top part lies just behind the neck and the lower section meets the top of the upperarm.
Shoulder layback	Refers to the set of the shoulder blades. 'Well laid' is used to describe the correct distance between the top of the two blades. 'Good layback' is used to describe the correct distance of the withers behind the neck. 'Upright' is used to describe either or both the incorrect distance of the blades, that is, too close to the head due to lack of blade length, or where the upper arm is too short, not allowing the forelegs to stand well under the body.
Soft mouth	Correct mouth hold of game, which has been retrieved without damage by the dog.
Stenosis	Narrowing of a canal such as an artery.
Stifle	Point where the dog's thigh and second thigh meet on the hindquarters (knee joint).
Stop	The point where the nasal bone and skull meet in between the dog's eyes.
Thigh	The area of the dog's hindquarters from the hip joint to the stifle.
Tuck up	The section of the underpart of the dog's body that curves upwards from the end of the ribs to the loin.
Tumour	Growth.
Ulcer	Breakage in organ's surface.
Upperarm	The humerus which runs between the shoulder base to the dog's elbow joint.
Withers	The highest point of the body immediately behind the neck, from which the dog's height is measured.
Wrist	The area between the forearm's base and that above the front pastern.

INDEX